THE FAMILY, THE MARKET, AND THE STATE IN AGEING SOCIETIES

The International Union for the Scientific Study of Population Problems was set up in 1928, with Dr Raymond Pearl as President. At that time the Union's main purpose was to promote international scientific co-operation to study the various aspects of population problems, through national committees and through its members themselves. In 1947 the International Union for the Scientific Study of Population (IUSSP) was reconstituted into its present form. It expanded its activities to:

- stimulate research on population
- develop interest in demographic matters among governments, national and international organizations, scientific bodies, and the general public
- foster relations between people involved in population studies
- disseminate scientific knowledge on population.

The principal ways through which the IUSSP currently achieves its aims are:

- organization of worldwide or regional conferences and operations of Scientific Committees under the responsibility of the Council
- organization of training courses
- publication of conference proceedings and committee reports.

Demography can be defined by its field of study and its analytical methods. Accordingly, it can be regarded as the scientific study of human populations primarily with respect to their size, their structure, and their development. For reasons which are related to the history of the discipline, the demographic method is essentially inductive: progress in the knowledge results from the improvement of observation, the sophistication of measurement methods, the search for regularities and stable factors leading to the formulation of explanatory models. In conclusion, the three objectives of demographic analysis are to describe, measure, and analyse.

International Studies in Demography is the outcome of an agreement concluded by the IUSSP and the Oxford University Press. This joint series is expected to reflect the broad range of the Union's activities and, in the first instance, will be based on the seminars organized by the Union. The Editorial Board of the series is comprised of:

The Family, the Market and the State in Ageing Societies

EDITORS:

JOHN ERMISCH
NAOHIRO OGAWA

Clarendon Press · Oxford

1994

Oxford University Press, Walton Street, Oxford OX2 6DP

Oxford New York Toronto
Delhi Bombay Calcutta Madras Karachi
Kuala Lumpur Singapore Hong Kong Tokyo
Nairobi Dar es Salaam Cape Town
Melbourne Auckland Madrid
and associated companies in
Berlin Ibadan

Oxford is a trade mark of Oxford University Press

Published in the United States
by Oxford University Press Inc., New York

© IUSSP 1994

British Library Cataloguing in Publication Data
Data available

Library of Congress Cataloging in Publication Data
The family, the market, and the state in ageing societies / editors,
John Ermisch, Naohiro Ogawa.
p. cm. — (International studies in demography)
Includes bibliographical references.
1. Family demography—Cross-cultural studies. I. Ermisch, John.
II. Ogawa, Naohiro, 1944– . III. Series.
HQ759.98.F38 1994 306.85—dc20 93–32724
ISBN 0–19–828818–2

1 3 5 7 9 10 8 6 4 2

Typeset by Graphicraft Typesetters Ltd., Hong Kong

Printed in Great Britain
on acid-free paper by
Biddles Ltd.,
Guildford & King's Lynn

Preface

The chapters in this volume arose from papers presented at a seminar organized by the Committee on Economic Consequences of Alternative Demographic Patterns of the International Union for the Scientific Study of Population. The seminar took place in Sendai, Japan, from 19 to 21 September 1988. It brought together more than 20 economists studying economic aspects of changes in family patterns in industrialized countries. We are grateful for the financial support of the Government of Sendai City and the Japan Aging Research Center.

J. E.
N. O.

Contents

List of Figures   viii
List of Tables   xi
List of Contributors   xiii
Introduction   1

Part I: Market and State Influences on Family Formation

1. Innovation in Family Formation: Evidence on Cohabitation in the United States ROBERT J. WILLIS and ROBERT T. MICHAEL   9

2. The Effects of Cohort Size on Marriage-Markets in Twentieth-Century Sweden THEODORE BERGSTROM and DAVID LAM   46

3. Economic Considerations in the Timing of Births: Theory and Evidence ALESSANDRO CIGNO   64

4. The Demographic Impact of Family Benefits: Evidence from a Micro-Model and from Macro-Data DIDIER BLANCHET and OLIVIA EKERT-JAFFÉ   79

5. Patrilocality, Childbearing, and the Labour Supply and Earning Power of Married Japanese Women NAOHIRO OGAWA and ROBERT WILLIAM HODGE   105

Part II: Intergenerational Transfers in Theory and Practice

6. Fertility, Mortality, and Intergenerational Transfers: Comparisons across Steady States RONALD LEE   135

7. The Intergenerational Distribution of Resources and Income in Japan ANDREW MASON, YOKE-YUN TEH, NAOHIRO OGAWA, and TAKEHIRO FUKUI   158

8. Public Intergenerational Transfers as an Old-Age Pension System: A Historical Interlude? TOMMY BENGTSSON and GUNNAR FRIDLIZIUS   198

9. Private and Public Intergenerational Transfers: Evidence and a Simple Model HELMUTH CREMER, DENIS KESSLER, and PIERRE PESTIEAU   216

Name Index   233
Subject Index   235

List of Figures

1.1 Tree-Diagram of First and Second Partnership, White Males   14

1.2 Tree-Diagram of First and Second Partnership, White Females   15

1.3 Tree-Diagram of First and Second Partnership, Black Males   16

1.4 Tree-Diagram of First and Second Partnership, Black Females   17

1.5 Duration of Time to First Partnership, by Gender or by Race   19

1.6 Stability of First Partnership, by Selected Characteristics   20

1.7 Stability of Second Partnership, by Selected Characteristics   21

1.8 Stability of Cohabitation with First Partner   23

1.9 The Competing Risks of Cohabitation: Formal Marriage and Dissolution of First Partnership   23

1.10 Distribution of Predicted Probabilities of Cohabitation in First Union   38

1.11 Predicted Probabilities of COHAB1 by Date of Beginning of Partnership   39

2.1 Fluctuations in the Size of Cohorts in Sweden, 1883–1942   47

2.2 Male–Female Sex-Ratios in Sweden, 1883–1942   48

2.3 Mean Age at Marriage for Males and Females in Sweden, 1883–1942   49

2.4 Proportions of Males and Females Marrying by Age 40 in Sweden, 1883–1942   49

2.5 Sex-Ratio and Husband–Wife Age-Differences in Sweden, 1883–1942   51

2.6 Sex-Ratio and Relative Proportions of Males and Females Marrying in Sweden, 1883–1942   52

2.7 Scatter-Plot of Sex-Ratio and Husband–Wife Age-Differences in Sweden, 1883–1942   54

2.8 Scatter-Plot of Sex-Ratio and Relative Proportions of Males and Females Marrying in Sweden, 1883–1942   55

2.9 Pay-off Matrix for Swedish Marriage Assignments   59

2.10 Husband–Wife Age-Differences in Sweden, 1895–1945   60

3.1 Birth-Rate by Marriage Duration and Years of Work
Experience at Marriage   73

3.2 Birth-Rate by Marriage Duration and Occupation in Last
Job before First Birth   74

3.3 Birth-Rate by Marriage Duration and Years of
Post-Compulsory Education   74

4.1 Estimating W_{res} and α from the Intercept and Slope of a
Simple Regression   84

4.2 Evolution of the Parameters since 1961   85

4.3 The Impact of Various Measures of an Allocation of FF 1000
at Parities One to Three   87

4.4 A Comparison of Benefits per Child by Parity in OECD and
COMECON Countries   90

6.1 The Effect on the Population Growth-Rate of a One-Year
Gain in Life Expectancy at Birth   147

6.2 The Age Distribution of Gains in Person-Years Lived   148

6.3 The Percentage Distribution by Broad Age-Group of Gains
in Person-Years Lived when e_0 Rises   149

6.4 The Proportional Increase in Person-Years Lived in Broad
Age-Groups when e_0 Rises by One Year   150

7.1 Flowchart of the Model to Examine Changes in the
Intergenerational Distribution of Income in Japan   161

7.2 Number of Households by Age of Household Marker   179

7.3 Members of Households in Various Age-Groups   181

7.4 Effective Labour per Household   183

7.5 Wealth per Household   184

7.6 National Income per Household   186

7.7 Disposable Income per Household   187

7.8 Disposable Income per Capita   188

7.9 Bequests and Inheritances by Age of Head of Household   190

7.10 Inheritances as a Proportion of Disposable Income   191

8.1 Main Groups of Workers in the Agricultural Sector in
Sweden, 1751–1870   201

8.2 Ageing in the Countryside and Towns of Sweden and in
Stockholm, 1760–1980   203

8.3 Employment in Different Economic Sectors in Sweden,
1870–1985   207

8.4 Percentage of the Population Aged 65 and over in Selected
Countries, 1987–2050   210

9.1 Bequests as a Proportion of GDP in France, 1826–1976   221

9.2   Public Debt as a Proportion of GDP in France, 1820–1980   222

9.3   Public Expenditure on Education as a Proportion of GDP
       in France, 1870–1980   223

9.4   Alternative Solutions to the Bequests-for-Attention Exchange   229

List of Tables

1.1	Descriptive Statistics for Selected Variables by Race and Sex	25
1.2	Definitions of Selected Variables	26
1.3	Determinants of Cohabitation, Basic Probit Equation	29
1.4	Determinants of Cohabitation, Expanded Probit Equation	33
1.5	Actual and Predicted Probabilities of Cohabitation by Race, Education, and Year Union Began	36
2.1	Ordinary Least-Squares Regression Age-Difference between Husband and Wife by Male–Female Sex-Ratio in Sweden, 1883–1942	53
2.2	Ordinary Least-Squares Regression Ratio of Proportion of Males and Females Marrying by Male–Female Sex-Ratio in Sweden, 1883–1942	54
4.1	Proportion of Women Having n Children and Labour-Force Participation after the Birth of this nth Child	82
4.2	Estimated Values of Standardized Parameters	83
4.3	Monthly Wage Rates for Men and Women in 1981 FF	83
4.4	Data for Some EC and Nordic Countries	95
4.5	Multiple Regression Results with the Total Fertility Rate as the Dependent Variable	98
4.6	Multiple Regression Results Including Time-Dummies	100
5.1	Distribution of Earnings of Wives and Husbands, by Labour-Force Status of Women: Married Japanese Women of Childbearing Age, 1988	108
5.2	Probit Analysis of Wife's Labour-Force Participation as a Paid Employee for Married Japanese Women of Childbearing Age, 1988	116
5.3	Estimated Probabilities of Working as Full-Time Paid Employees	117
5.4	Multinomial Logit Regression Coefficients for Labour-Force Participation of Married Japanese Women among Alternative Types of Employment	120
5.5	Computed Probabilities of Being in Alternative Employment Statuses by Type of Household	123

5.6   Reasons for Working by Current Work Status: Married
        Japanese Women of Childbearing Age in the Labour-Force,
        1988   124

5.A1   Means and Standard Deviations of Explanatory Variables
        of Wife's Labour-Force Participation as a Paid Employee
        for Married Japanese Women of Childbearing Age, 1988   130

5.A2   Means and Standard Deviations of Explanatory Variables of
        Labour-Force Participation of Married Japanese Women
        among Alternative Types of Employment   131

7.1   Statistical Estimates for Labour-Share Equation   166

7.2   Age- and Sex-Specific Labour-Force Participation Rates   167

7.3   Statistical Estimates of Age–Earnings Profile   170

7.4   Estimated Age–Wealth Profile, 1980   172

7.5   Real Wealth Estimates   173

7.6   Results of Government Redistribution Survey   174

7.7   Tax- and Benefit-Rates for Government Sector   175

7.8   Key Demographic Variables   176

7.9   Headship Rates Using Data from the 1984 FIES and 1985
        Census   177

7.10   National Income Aggregates, 1985–2025   182

7.11   Factors of Production and their Share   182

7.12   National Income by Source   183

7.13   Variance in Log of Per-Household Income   187

7.14   Variance in Log of Per Capita Income   188

7.15   Trends in Bequests and Wealth   189

8.1   People Aged 65 Years and Above Relative to Persons in the
        Labour-Force Aged 20–64 in the Year 2025, Based on the
        1989 Official Population Estimate   211

8.2   Percentage of Workers' Income Transferred to the Retired,
        According to Different Assumptions, under the Same Pension
        Rules as Today   212

9.1   An Illustration of the Various Intergenerational Transfers   218

List of Contributors

TOMMY BENGTSSON   Department of Economic History, University of Lund, Lund, Sweden

THEODORE BERGSTROM   Department of Economics, University of Michigan, Ann Arbor, Michigan, USA

DIDIER BLANCHET   Institut National d'Études Démographiques (INED), Paris, France

ALESSANDRO CIGNO   Facoltà di Scienze Politiche, Università di Pisa, Pisa, Italy

HELMUTH CREMER   Department of Economics, Virginia Polytechnic Institute and State University, Blackburg, Virginia, USA

OLIVIA EKERT-JAFFÉ   Institut National d'Études Démographiques (INED), Paris, France

GUNNAR FRIDLIZIUS   Department of Economic History, University of Lund, Lund, Sweden

TAKEHIRO FUKUI   Statistics Bureau, Management and Co-ordination Agency, Tokyo, Japan

ROBERT HODGE*   University of Southern California, Los Angeles, California, USA

DENIS KESSLER   École des Hautes Études en Sciences Sociales, Paris, France

DAVID LAM   Department of Economics, University of Michigan, Ann Arbor, Michigan, USA

RONALD LEE   Department of Demography, University of California, Berkeley, California, USA

ANDREW MASON   Population Institute, East–West Center, Honolulu, Hawaii, USA

ROBERT MICHAEL   The Irving B. Harris Graduate School of Public Policy Studies, University of Chicago, Chicago, Illinois, USA

NAOHIRO OGAWA   Population Research Institute, Nihon University, Tokyo, Japan

PIERRE PESTIEAU   Faculte d'Économie Publique, Université de Liège, Liège, Belgium

YOKE-YUN TEH   Population Institute, East–West Center, Honolulu, Hawaii, USA

xiv   *List of Contributors*

ROBERT WILLIS   Department of Education and The Irving B.
Harris Graduate School of Public Policy Studies,
University of Chicago and Economics Research
Center/NORC, Chicago, Illinois, USA

* deceased

Introduction

Over the past twenty years, there have been dramatic changes in patterns of family formation and dissolution in developed countries. In Western Europe, North America, and Australia people have been marrying later and consensual unions (cohabitation without marriage) have become more common. Women in all developed countries have been changing the timing of childbearing over their lives, and it seems likely that recent generations of mothers will end up having smaller families than those in which they grew up. As the decline in fertility followed prolonged baby booms in most countries, the size of cohorts entering labour- and marriage-markets has changed dramatically. The decline in fertility was accompanied by continuing falls in mortality, which in some countries, like Japan, have been dramatic, and which may have played a role in altering the interaction among family members during their lives as well as producing a more aged population. Divorce has increased dramatically in most developed countries, and patterns of remarriage have altered; in some countries, consensual unions have increased sharply among the previously married population. These changes in the incidence of divorce and the timing and incidence of marriage and remarriage have produced a large increase in families headed by a single parent in many countries.

A major aim of this volume is to explore the economic consequences of these developments in family patterns. These consequences include changes in people's economic behaviour, particularly in the labour-market, and in patterns of consumption and intergenerational transfers of money and care, and changes in economic inequality among families, households, and individuals. Furthermore, there are consequences for state policies, including education, taxation systems, income support, state pensions, and other redistributive policies. For instance, women's labour supply and human capital accumulation appear particularly likely to be affected by these developments in family patterns. Their labour-force participation over the life cycle, lifetime earnings profiles, and pension rights are all likely to be influenced. The growing number of families headed by a mother is likely to affect the degree of inequality of economic resources among families and have implications for child support rules, day-care provision, and state income support policies.

But, of course, the changes in family patterns did not occur in a vacuum: they were influenced by economic developments, like changes in women's earning opportunities, and by state policies. For instance, equal opportunities policies may have changed the timing of childbearing and family size and patterns of union formation and dissolution; state support for children could also affect family size and the timing of childbearing; and income support policies may affect cohabitation and (re)marriage patterns.

Market and State Influences on Family Formation

As noted earlier, cohabitation without marriage has become much more common in recent years in a number of countries, but outside Scandinavia, relatively little is known about this institution. The first chapter of this volume, by Robert Michael and Robert Willis, 'Innovation in Family Formation: Evidence on Cohabitation in the United States', helps remedy this situation. It analyses the choice of whether to cohabit or not in an economic framework. The authors pose two main questions: (1) Why would a couple choose cohabitation rather than legal marriage? and (2) what are the characteristics of those who choose each? Using cohabitational histories among a sample of 32-year-old Americans (the Fifth Follow-up Survey of the National Longitudinal Study of the High School Class of 1972), the authors attempt to answer these questions.

The analysis finds that, in contrast to contemporary Sweden, the average duration of cohabitation in the United States is short, only about one year. This suggests that American cohabitation primarily serves the purpose of a trial marriage. The authors conjecture that the dramatic rise in divorce, which began in the mid-1960s, played an important role in encouraging cohabitation, as a response to increased uncertainty about the stability of a marital partnership. Several findings suggest that the better the economic prospects and circumstances of the male are at the time of the formation of a partnership, the less likely he is to cohabit, but the opposite is the case for women.

This first chapter stresses the institutional response to uncertainty and caution concerning choice of partner. In contrast, the second chapter by Theodore Bergstrom and David Lam, stresses the choice of when to enter a partnership, ignoring who the particular partner is. The authors analyse this issue by applying a theory of 'partner assignments' to marriage-markets in twentieth-century Sweden. In particular, they study the effects of cohort size on age at marriage (rather than partnership). In their model, the age-gap between husbands and wives plays a central role in absorbing the marriage squeeze pressures arising from changing cohort size.

They are able to replicate the rapid fluctuations in age-difference between spouses actually observed in Swedish cohorts born between 1915 and 1925, which was the period of the most dramatic fluctuations in cohort size in recent Swedish history. They are less successful, however, for later cohorts. In addition to other reasons that the authors suggest, the failure for later cohorts may reflect the growing importance of cohabitation without marriage in Sweden, making marriage age a less reliable indicator of 'age at partnering'. As the first chapter indicates, this is increasingly the case in the United States as well. Nevertheless, it is remarkable that a simple model, which ignores factors other than demographic ones, is able to track the age-difference between spouses as well as that presented in Chapter 2 does.

One important source of fluctuations in cohort size is changes in the timing of births, which is the issue addressed in Chapter 3 by Alessandro Cigno. Taking the formation of partnerships as given, he focuses on economic considerations in the timing of births. He tackles the difficult problem of modelling the optimal timing of childbearing, in the context of a woman's employment career. For example, the analysis predicts that women with steeper earnings profiles work more in the early part of their married life, and have children later than women whose earning ability is not much affected by work experience. He uses the theoretical framework to guide two empirical studies of economic influences on the timing of births over a British woman's life. These studies confirm many, but not all, of the predictions of the model.

In Chapter 4 Didier Blanchet and Olivia Ekert-Jaffé take a unique approach to study the interrelationships among fertility, female labour-force participation, and family policy. In particular, they present two very different ways of evaluating the impact of government family allowances on fertility. The first is a simple micro-model of fertility behaviour (e.g. one potentially important simplification is a constant real reservation wage for women). It does, however, take into account the discrete nature of individual fertility decisions, and pays particular attention to the aggregation of these in determining the fertility response to changes in family policy. Parameters of the micro-model are calibrated with synthetic cohort data. The second approach estimates an aggregate econometric model based on the micro one, using pooled time-series, cross-section data on fertility, family benefits, women's real wages, and labour-force participation from OECD countries. Both approaches indicate that higher family benefits can have an important impact on fertility in OECD countries. Recent developments in family policy and fertility in Sweden (Hoem, 1990) and estimates based on very different methods (Ermisch, 1988) support their findings. Other researchers will also find the data collected on family benefits to be very valuable.

In Western society the nuclear household is the norm. In Japan, however, multi-generational households are still fairly common. At present, 30 per cent of Japanese married women of childbearing age live with their own or their husband's parents and/or grandparents. Despite the marked difference in family structure between East and West, there has been a similar rapid rise in the proportion of married Japanese women in paid employment. In Chapter 5, Naohiro Ogawa and Robert Hodge use micro-level data covering married women of childbearing age to study the relationship between women's paid employment, co-residence, and fertility patterns in contemporary Japan. The statistical analysis confirms the finding of most studies conducted in the West that the presence of young children inhibits women's full-time employment. But the authors also find that co-residence strongly encourages wife's participation in the workforce as a full-time paid employee, suggesting that mothers co-residing have a child-care system supported by their parents(-in-law) built into their household structure.

Intergenerational Transfers in Theory and Practice

While the first part of the book concentrates on the interaction between the sexes in marriage, childbearing, and labour-force decisions, resource flows between generations were not ignored. For instance, the model developed in Chapter 3 incorporates decisions concerning bequests and their effect on the cost of children and childbearing, and the analysis in Chapter 5 deals with the influence of interdependence between generations on women's labour-force decisions. Nevertheless, the second part of the book focuses more explicitly on interactions between generations.

In Chapter 6 Ronald Lee makes a major analytical contribution by extending earlier analyses of the impact of the population growth-rate on transfers between generations to consider the effect of mortality change on life-cycle consumption and intergenerational transfers. The analysis includes a framework for modelling mortality change and an assessment of the implications of actual patterns of change. He demonstrates that in both developed and developing countries, mortality decline reduces the present value of life-cycle consumption possibilities by a similar magnitude, but there is a fundamental difference between the two cases. In the latter (i.e. a high mortality setting), mortality decline is expensive because it means the support of a larger number of surviving children. In the former (i.e. low mortality), it is expensive because people live longer, and therefore must reduce their consumption in order to provide for more years of leisure after retirement.

Japan serves as a good example for the low mortality case. The life expectancy of Japanese people is the highest in the world. The rapid growth in the number of elderly over the next few decades may lead to serious conflict over the allocation of resources. Chapter 7, by Andrew Mason, Yoke-Yun Teh, Naohiro Ogawa, and Takehiro Fukui, compares standards of living among different generations, and simulates changes in the distribution of household income and the distribution and level of bequests over the period 1985–2025, on the basis of assumptions about fertility, mortality, the family system, and public policies. A surprising conclusion is the relatively equal distribution of per capita income between elderly and young households. One of the factors behind this outcome is the high level of personal wealth (accumulated through private saving), such that interest income offsets the decline in labour earnings associated with retirement. Another factor is the continued prevalence of extended households in Japan (as noted earlier), which means that many elderly live in households with members of prime working age. Finally, government taxes and transfers also favour households headed by the elderly.

Chapter 8 analyses the roles of private and government transfers in a long-term Swedish context. Tommy Bengtsson and Gunnar Fridlizius study the development of the care of the elderly and money transfers between generations from the mid-eighteenth century to the present day. In particular, they analyse factors behind the historical failure of private transfers in Sweden. They also explore the adjustments that may need to be made in the first half of the next century, when the baby boom generations reach today's retirement age, and suggest that almost sole reliance on public pensions may be a 'historical interlude'.

In the final chapter, Helmuth Cremer, Denis Kessler, and Pierre Pestieau combine nearly 200 years of evidence on major private and public intergenerational transfers in France with theoretical models to examine the interaction between private and public transfers. A taxonomy of the types of transfers provides the basis for studying the nature and determinants of each type of transfer. Their theoretical analysis shows that even in the absence of altruistic behaviour private transfers might occur, and that even though they are not able to restore optimality, public transfers may be necessary.

Clearly the papers in this volume can only cover some aspects of the issues raised at the outset of this introductory chapter. For instance, despite its growing importance, the economic implications of marital instability have not been covered by the papers in this volume. We hope, nevertheless, that this volume provides a stimulus to further research on these issues.

References

Ermisch, J. F. (1988), 'Economic Influences on Birth Rates', *National Institute Economic Review*, 126, 71–81.

Hoem, J. (1990), 'Social Policy and Recent Fertility Change in Sweden', *Population and Development Review*, 16/4, 735–48.

Part I

Market and State Influences on Family Formation

1 Innovation in Family Formation: Evidence on Cohabitation in the United States

ROBERT J. WILLIS AND ROBERT T. MICHAEL

Introduction

Among the many innovations in the structure of family life, cohabitation without marriage is one of the most intriguing. Cohabitation is becoming a more common form of living arrangement in the United States and in Western Europe. The trend towards cohabiting in the United States became noticeable only after the 1960s (see Spanier, 1983; Glick and Spanier, 1980). Its incidence grew dramatically during the 1970s, as illustrated in one county in the state of Oregon where analysis of marriage-licence applications revealed that in 1970 only 13 per cent of couples appeared to be living together at the time of application, but by 1980 that percentage had risen to 53 per cent (see Gwartney-Gibbs, 1986). Recent studies have begun to describe the distribution of cohabitation among the population and to analyse its determinants (see e.g. Bachrach and Horn, 1987; Yamaguchi and Kandel, 1985; Tanfer, 1987).

In Sweden and Norway, cohabitation is a far more widespread phenomenon (see Blanc, 1987; Bernhardt and Hoem, 1985; Hoem and Hoem, 1988; Brunborg, 1979), while the United Kingdom rates appear to be generally similar to those in the USA. For example, Kiernan (1983) reports that about 31 per cent of the first partners in the UK's National Child Development Study data were initially cohabitational. We are unaware of studies of the incidence of cohabitation in most other parts of the world.

As cohabitation is a relatively new focus of study, it has no standard definition. We used the following definition both theoretically and empirically: cohabitation is living with a partner in a marriage-like relationship for a

An earlier version of the paper on which this chapter is based was presented at the Population Association of America meetings in New Orleans in April 1988. Comments by Christine Bachrach are acknowledged, as is the excellent assistance of Karin Hyde over the past two years, as we prepared our data-file for public release and as we have begun the analysis. Michael Brien has also provided fine assistance in recent months, and John Ermisch has provided us with useful comments on an earlier draft. The financial support of NICHD, Grant #HD19373 is also acknowledged. This grant supported the supplemental data collection as well as its analysis; the data reported here are in the public domain.

period of time of one month or more. Such a definition is subject to some interpretation, but we believe that it captures the essence of the phenomenon of interest and is sufficiently unambiguous. Notice that this definition does not specifically rule out same-gender partners or multiple or overlapping partnerships; our data, however, do not report simultaneous multiple partnerships and explicitly rule out same-gender partners.

In this chapter we address the following issues: Why would a couple choose cohabitation instead of marriage? What are the characteristics of those who choose each? What does the descriptive evidence on cohabitational histories among a national sample of 32-year-olds tell us about the institution of cohabitation in the United States today?

Why Choose Cohabitation instead of Marriage?

Our society continually experiments with modifications in family structure, such as the multiple-site dwellings of married couples whose careers necessitate residence in distant cities, extended time-intervals in which one partner is away from home for business reasons (e.g. an overseas job assignment, military duty, or undercover or confidential assignment), or for social reasons (e.g. incarceration). So the institution of marriage itself admits a rather wider range of living arrangements than we usually have in mind when we identify a couple as 'married'. Is cohabitation anything more than one more modification in this range of living arrangements that are generically called marriage?

We think it is. The primary difference, we think, is the level of commitment to the partnership. Consider as illustrative of this difference the act of forming a marriage or a cohabitational partnership. A marriage is a very public act in most societies. In our own, one typically announces the intention to marry some length of time prior to the event; one asks family and friends to attend a public ceremony in which expressions of the long-term commitment between partners are exchanged; the legally binding event is frequently announced to the community at large. The social events surrounding the beginnings of a cohabitation, by contrast, are far less elaborate, less public, and thus are more easily reversed.

Cohabitation is short-duration marriage. The commitment to the partnership is closely related to its expected duration. So the question arises, why would a couple (or one of its two members) prefer a short duration for the partnership? Some reasons involve uncertainty.

There may be uncertainty about whether one wants to have any partner. A short-term testing or trial partnership may be a reasonable way to address that uncertainty about oneself and the institution *per se*. There may be uncertainty about the particular person chosen as a partner. A test period with that partner may appear to be a reasonable strategy for dealing with that uncertainty. There may be uncertainty about some other high-priority event that dictates avoiding a long-term commitment to a partner—a job or training opportunity or another and preferred partner who may become available. With any one of these three uncertainties, the couple may expect, and even prefer, a partnership based initially on an expected short-term duration.

By social custom, religious encouragement, and legal stricture, formal marriage is assumed to be long-term: 'till death do us part'. As the incidence of divorce and separation has grown since the mid-1960s in the United States, it has become increasingly realistic for a couple to consider the likelihood that their marriage might terminate by separation rather than continue to the death of a partner. So there is uncertainty about the duration of the partnership, even if there is no other uncertainty. The realization of a substantial risk of divorce may encourage many couples to hedge their bets somewhat, experimenting with the partnership by cohabitation, at least initially. (The reasons for the rise in the divorce-rate is not our subject here; see Becker *et al.*, 1977; Preston and McDonald, 1979; Michael, 1988.) An intriguing finding reported by Gwartney-Gibbs in her study of marriage licence applicants provides a piece of evidence that cohabitation serves the purpose of a trial marriage, thus intended to reduce the risk of a mismatch. She reports that when the couples applying for marriage licences are partitioned as to prior cohabitation or not, those couples that had cohabited were less homogamous with respect to age, previous marital status, and race. She suggests, and we agree, that this finding implies that 'premarital cohabitation may serve as a means of reducing the risk of unsuccessful marriages among unlike partners' (1986: 429).

Another reason for a short-duration partnership, unrelated to uncertainty, is postponement. There may be a known, preferred opportunity that will become available at a future date, and the current partnership may be formed with certain knowledge that it is to be temporary. Uncertainty or postponement may cause the couple to expect a short duration for the cohabitational partnership, and yet economic, psychological, and social benefits of a marriage or marriage-like relationship may encourage formation of a partnership. These benefits derive from the functions of cohabitation and marriage that we suggest are probably similar. They include economic functions (e.g. economies of scale and efficiencies of division of labour), psychological functions (e.g. the support, companionship, and sexual relationship of a partner), and social functions (e.g. the raising of children and conforming to social expectations about the adult role of spouse or partner). But just as the benefits of a partnership encourage its formation despite the uncertainties, there are powerful incentives for forming long-duration unions, and these, we think, discourage couples from permitting the institution of cohabitation to become a long-term substitute for marriage.

One of the more subtle but important decisions made by couples is the extent to which they will specialize in developing skills which complement and substitute for each other. As a simple example, one partner may develop skills in financial management while the other develops skills in house or car maintenance. These skills reflect tasks for which partners can substitute for each other; that specialization is efficient, but only if the couple expects to remain together. If the couple specializes and then splits up, neither partner is endowed with an appropriate bundle of skills to carry out needed functions. Each is then faced with either acquiring new skills, while depreciating some of the expertise previously acquired, or seeking another partner who happens to have developed the same bundle of skills as the former partner. If the couple expected the partnership to be of short duration, it would be better not to invest heavily in acquiring co-ordinated skills. But the efficiency gains from that co-ordination are foregone, and that encourages a longer commitment to the partnership.

The same principle holds for complementary skills. Another simple example makes this point: if one's partner enjoys tennis, it may be an attractive investment strategy for the other partner to acquire tennis skills too. There the complementarity between partners is expanded as are the benefits realized from the partnership. If the expected duration of the partnership is short, however, the incentives to make these efforts for the sake of complementarity with this partner will be weakened. In turn, the less effort made to develop skills, interests, and experiences that are optimal in this particular partnership, the less successful the partnership will be and the less costly will be its dissolution, and thus the more likely it will be to dissolve. So the expectations about the duration of the partnership affect the efforts made by partners to deepen their commitment to each other. These initial expectations affect incentives to invest in partner-specific human capital and thus induce divergent probabilities of divorce across couples, reinforcing initial differences in expectations. While couples have incentives to form cohabitational partnerships because of uncertainties, they also have incentives to convert these partnerships into long-run commitments to obtain the benefits of specialization. Bachrach and Horn (1987: 14) suggest the dichotomy of a cohabitation as either a prelude to marriage or a substitute for marriage, and we contend that it is the former—a short-run, trial marriage, not a long-run alternative to marriage. We suggest that the expected duration of the partnership is the primary determinant of the initial choice between a formal marriage and a cohabitation and that there are powerful incentives that force cohabitational partnerships to be converted into more formal, longer duration unions or into separation.

Before turning to empirical evidence on cohabitation, we note that there is another dichotomy regarding cohabitation suggested in several studies (e.g. Macklin, 1978; Bennett et al., 1988). It distinguishes cohabitation as a trial marriage from cohabitors as a 'select group of people for whom relationships in general . . . are characterized by a lack of commitment and stability' (Bennett et al., 1988: 128). This distinction has implications about the predicted, subsequent behaviour of cohabitors, but it too associates cohabitation, as compared to marriage, with less commitment to the partner. We will return to this notion that cohabitors are different in their attitudes and behaviour generally in a subsequent section of this paper.

Evidence from the NLS/72 1986 Follow-Up Survey

The evidence on cohabitation presented in this chapter is drawn from a questionnaire module designed by the authors in the Fifth Follow-up Survey of the National Longitudinal Study of the High School Class of 1972. The NLS/72 is a national sample of individuals who were high-school seniors in 1972, first interviewed in the spring of that year and resurveyed in 1973, 1974, 1976, and 1979. A sub-sample of 14,489 individuals was selected for reinterview in the Fifth Follow-up Survey conducted by the National Opinion Research Center in 1986. Of these, 12,841 (88.6 per cent) provided completed cases. All five waves of data are available as a public-use tape in the 'NICHD-edition' of the NLS/72.

The 1986 survey obtained retrospective, event-history data on cohabitations and marriages (the appendix to this chapter contains this segment of the questionnaire). Most previous data used in the study of cohabitation in the United States had information only about current status or on cohabitations censored by current marital status. (For an exception, see Thornton, 1988.) In this section, we use these uncensored event-histories on this national sample of 32-year-olds, all of whom reached the senior year of high school, to describe the frequency, duration, and outcome of cohabitational partnerships.

Figs. 1.1 to 1.4 show the patterns of cohabitation and marriage behaviour reported in this survey in the form of tree-diagrams. Fig. 1.1 reports on the white men: at the top we see that of the 4,907 white men in the sample, 85 per cent (or 4,138 of them) report having a marital or cohabitation partner, while 15 per cent (740 of them) report never having had a partner. Of those who had a partner, 72 per cent (2,959 of them) reported that they were married at the start of their partnership, while 28 per cent (1,142 men) reported that they began their partnership living with but not married to their partner. Of those 1,142, 74 per cent (856 men) reported that they subsequently did marry that partner, and of those 74 per cent (633 men) were still living with her at the time of the 1986 interview. The remaining 26 per cent (222 men) had left that first partner, and of those 63 per cent (140 men) reported that they had had a second partner.

In the diagram there are three routes to ending the first partnership: 751 men married initially and then separated; 222 cohabited initially and then married and subsequently separated; and, finally, 212 of the cohabiting men never married their partner and separated subsequently. About 67 per cent of each of these three groups of men who separated from their first partners (1,185 men in total) reported having a second partner (791 men). This last

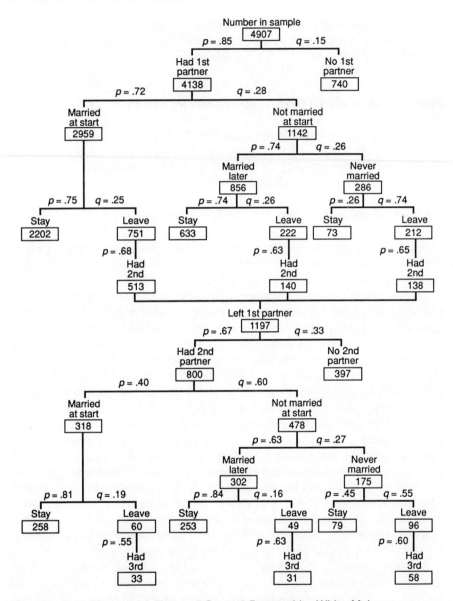

Fig. 1.1 Tree-Diagram of First and Second Partnership, White Males

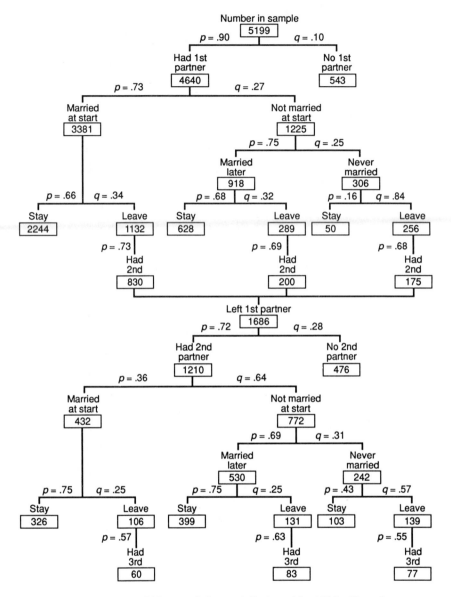

Fig. 1.2 Tree-Diagram of First and Second Partnership, White Females

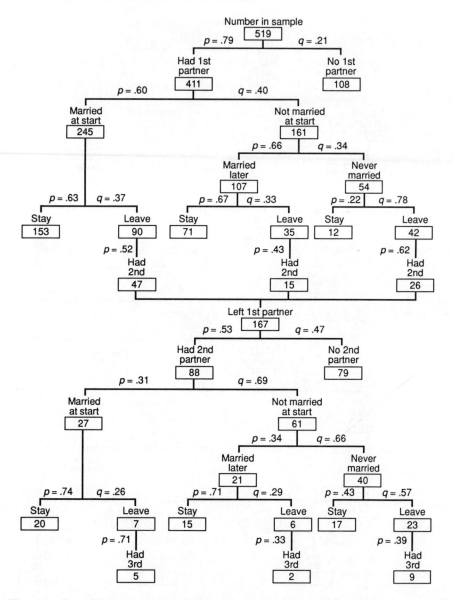

Fig. 1.3   Tree-Diagram of First and Second Partnership, Black Males

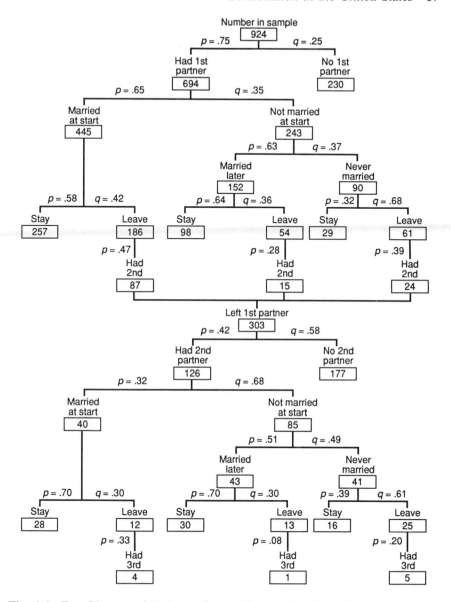

Fig. 1.4 Tree-Diagram of First and Second Partnership, Black Females

fact is displayed again, with small differences in the sample sizes, in the bottom half of the tree. There the numbers are reported as 1,197 men, of whom 800 had had a second partner. Of these, 40 per cent reported that they were married to that partner when they began living with her, while 60 per cent reported that they were not married to the partner at the beginning.

Figs. 1.2, 1.3, and 1.4 show the reported behaviour of white females, black males, and black females, respectively. The four tree-diagrams contain several interesting descriptive findings about these 32-year-old adults:

1. A very large majority of adults take partners: 9 of every 10 white females and 3 of every 4 black females, with the men's percentages lying between these extremes.

2. A large fraction of these partnerships began as cohabitations instead of formal marriages: about 1 in 4 of the whites and more than 1 in 3 of the blacks. In the second partnership more than 60 per cent began as a cohabitation, not as a marriage. Note that this rate of cohabitation is much higher than that reported in a cross-sectional sample of current marital status or living arrangement (see e.g. Glick and Norton, 1977; Bachrach and Horn, 1987). Here we see the incidence at the start of the partnership, not the current status.

3. Most cohabitations are converted to marriages. Of those whose first partnership began as a cohabitation, two-thirds to three-quarters subsequently married that partner. In the second partnership, whites married the partner very frequently, but for blacks that rate is much lower.

4. The stability of the formal marriages is in the range of 60 to 75 per cent by the time of the 1986 survey. There is no great apparent difference in the stability of the marriage dependent on whether it was preceded by a cohabitation. The cohabitations that were not converted to marriages exhibit much less stability.

5. Most who end a first partnership soon form another. Of those whose first partnership ended, two-thirds of the white and about half of the black men, and 40 per cent of the black women formed a second partnership.

These tree-diagrams are static, capturing lifetime behaviour patterns up to the 1986 survey when respondents were aged about 32. We turn next to descriptive graphs that introduce a dynamic element in the data. Fig. 1.5 shows, by a Kaplan–Meier plot, the time-pattern of entry into a marriage or cohabitational partnership. Here we disregard whether the event began as a marriage or as a cohabitation. The starting-point for these graphs in Fig. 5.1, the time-point '0' on the horizontal time-line, is the date of the 1972 survey. At that time 100 per cent of each group had not yet entered a partnership (either a marriage or a cohabitation). Panel A partitions the sample by gender, the lower curve depicting the pattern for women: it shows that by the fifth year, i.e. by 1977, approximately 50 per cent of these women had begun a marital or cohabitation partnership; for men, about 35 per cent had begun a partnership by that date. The graph indicates that by the date of the recent

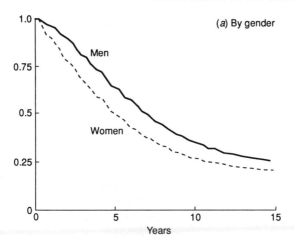

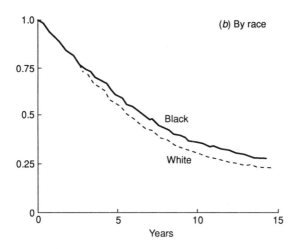

Panel *A*: By Gender
Panel *B*: By Race
Timing begins in 1972 as high-school seniors
Fig. 1.5   Duration of Time to First Partnership, by Gender or by Race

survey, 1986, nearly 15 years after high school, almost 80 per cent of the women and 70 per cent of the men had entered their first partnership. Those final percentages are the proportions reflected in the static tree-diagrams above (Figs. 1.1–1.4), except for some difference of coverage in the sub-samples used to construct the trees and the graphs. Substantively, Panel *A* of Fig. 1.5 reflects the common demographic finding that women enter into marriage at earlier ages than men; it suggests that this holds true when co-habitation as well as formal marriage is considered. Panel *B* partitions the same

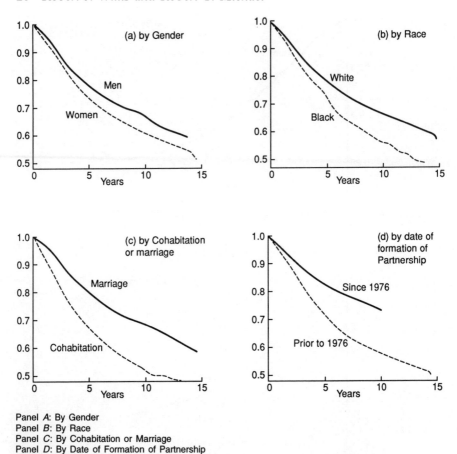

Panel *A*: By Gender
Panel *B*: By Race
Panel *C*: By Cohabitation or Marriage
Panel *D*: By Date of Formation of Partnership

Fig. 1.6   Stability of First Partnership, by Selected Characteristics

data by race and indicates that whites enter these partnerships slightly earlier than blacks. A large majority of all four groups have entered a partnership by the date of the 1986 survey.

Fig. 1.6 shows the dynamic pattern of a very different event—the termination of the first partnership. Here the starting-point in time, time-point '0' on the horizontal scale, is the date of the beginning of that partnership, including both marriages and cohabitations. The figure tracks the pattern of separation. Panel *A* shows that pattern separately by gender, revealing a faster rate of separation for the women. (This may seem intuitively implausible, since each partnership has both a man and a woman in it. But it should be emphasized that these samples of men and women are not reporting on the same partnerships and the composition of the samples of men and women may be quite different.) Notice that the vertical scale in Fig. 1.6 is not the same as in Fig. 1.5.

Panel *A* indicates that at the ten-year anniversary of the start of the

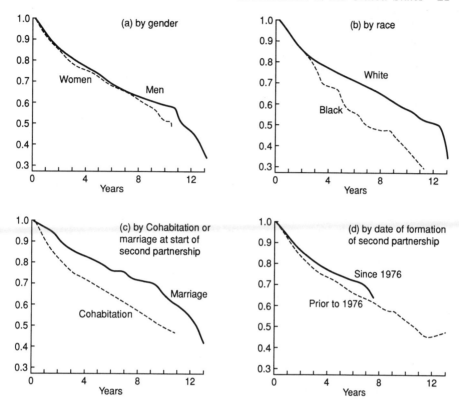

Panel *A*: By Gender
Panel *B*: By Race
Panel *C*: By Cohabitation or Marriage at Start of Second Partnership
Panel *D*: By Date of Formation of Second Partnership

Fig. 1.7   Stability of Second Partnership, by Selected Characteristics

partnership, about 35 per cent have ended in separation. There is a slightly higher rate of separation for women than men (Panel *A*) and a slightly higher rate for blacks than whites (Panel *B*), substantially higher rates for those in cohabitation partnerships than for those formally married at the outset (Panel *C*), and very much higher rates for those who formed the partnership by 1976 (i.e. within four years of high school completion) than for those who formed it after that date. (We note that we have not shown confidence bands on these graphs and that the sample sizes are not particularly large, so some of the smaller vertical differences in these graphs do not reflect statistically significant differences in behaviour.)

Fig. 1.7 shows the stability of the second partnership. This figure is analytically similar to Fig. 1.6, the earlier one showing the timing to termination of the first partnership. Of course, there are many fewer observations on the second partnership, so the curves in Fig. 1.7 are less precisely estimated. We caution that the scales of both axes are different in Fig. 1.7 from those in Fig. 1.6. Substantively, however, the findings from Fig. 1.6 regarding differences by race (panel *B*) and by cohabitation or marriage at the start of the partnership (panel *C*) are replicated in Fig. 1.7. Differences in the stability of first partnerships by gender and by date of formation of the union disappear for second unions, however, although note that the gender differential for first unions is not very large. The large differential by date of union for first unions and its disappearance for second unions is more interesting. A possible explanation is as follows. The instability of early first unions reflects unmeasured characteristics such as 'lack of commitment' which lead individuals to form unions quickly, without much search, because they do not feel that they will be locked into the relationship if things do not work out. In contrast, given that all individuals in the sample were high school graduates in the same year, the date of the second relationship is less closely correlated with the length of search and, hence, less correlated with unmeasured characteristics such as degree of commitment. In addition, it is possible (but not logically necessary) that the sample of individuals at risk of a second union is more homogeneous in terms of unmeasured characteristics because those with the strongest sense of commitment are not in this risk set.

The final two figures contain one of our most important findings: they show that cohabitational partnerships are extremely short-lived. In Figs. 1.6 and 1.7 we looked at separation of the partnership and noted in panel *C* whether the union had begun as a formal marriage or as a cohabitation; there we defined the end of the partnership to be the separation of the partners. In Figs. 1.8 and 1.9 we define the end of the cohabitation to take place either when the partners separate or when the partners formally marry. So in Figs. 1.8 and 1.9 we are defining cohabitation to be a status distinct from formal marriage. Fig. 1.8 shows that by the end of one year, about 45 per cent of cohabitations have ended either in marriage or dissolution—the half-life of a cohabitation is about one year! By the end of the second year, about 70 per cent of the cohabitations have ended; and by the end of five years, 90 per cent have ended. Cohabitational partnerships are not of long duration.

Fig. 1.9 shows us whether these cohabitations turn into formal marriages or into dissolution of the partnership. We see that a vast majority become formal marriages. (Note that this graph is structured differently from the previous ones, essentially flipped upside-down.) The upper curve in Fig. 1.9 shows the percentage of the cohabitations that have ended in the formation of a formal marriage. We see that by the end of the first year about 37 per cent of the cohabitations have ended by becoming marriages; by the end of the fifth year, about 65 per cent of the cohabitations have become marriages. The lower graph shows the percentage of cohabitations that have ended by dissolution of the partnership. By the end of the first year about 8 per cent of the cohabitations have ended by dissolution; by the fifth year, about 20 per cent have ended thus. So if we add these two routes of exit from cohabitation,

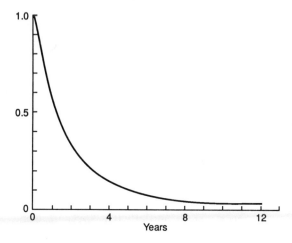

Fig. 1.8 Stability of Cohabitation with First Partner

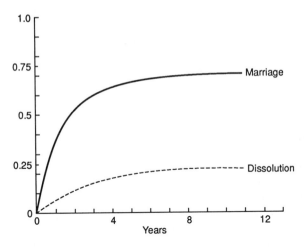

Fig. 1.9 The Competing Risks of Cohabitation: Formal Marriage and Dissolution of First Partnership

we see that by the end of the first year about 45 per cent of cohabitations have ended.

Thornton (1988:14) uses event-histories collected in 1985 on a sample of men and women about a decade younger than our sample. He finds generally the same phenomenon: about two-thirds of cohabitations end within two years. For his younger cohort, however, most of the men end their cohabitations by dissolution not marriage, while the preponderance of the women report their cohabitations ending in marriage.

We think the pattern of behaviour shown in Figs. 1.8 and 1.9 is important: it implies answers to some of the questions raised in the previous section of the paper. The function of cohabitation appears to be a trial marriage, a decision to avoid the long-term, public commitment—at least for a time—that marriage implies. Within a short time of living together, however, cohabiting couples appear to make a decision about the partnership and either dissolve it or convert it into a formal marriage. This decision is made rather quickly. Most couples go from cohabitation into marriage. By the fourth anniversary of the beginning of the cohabitation, two-thirds have married, one-sixth have dissolved the partnership, and only one-sixth are still together as cohabiting partners.

If we are correct in suggesting that cohabitational partnerships and formal marriages differ in the degree of commitment between partners—in terms of investing in complementary skills and efficient specialization—then it is not a long-standing difference. Quite quickly the couple decides either to make the commitment more permanent by formally marrying, or to dissolve the partnership. Thus, cohabitation seems to be an institution used to search intensively for a marital partner and not an institution that is in some more fundamental way a replacement for marriage. Of course, these descriptive graphs cannot confirm our interpretation, but our speculation here seems consistent with the dynamic pattern of behaviour observed in this data.

Who Chooses to Marry and Who Chooses to Cohabit?

We focus on the choice a couple makes between a formal marriage and a cohabitation at the beginning of their partnership. Much of the related existing literature studies determinants of the age at which a marriage or partnership is formed, and while we hold the age at the formation of the partnership constant in our inquiry, our focus is on a different decision. In addition, in the growing literature on cohabitation, most studies use data that only have information on current cohabitations or on the number of cohabitations, and thus they look at characteristics of currently cohabiting couples. But that focus masks much of the dynamic relationship of interest here. We distinguish three sets of determining variables: (1) static family background factors; (2) time-varying attributes of the respondent; and (3) characteristics of the spouse. All are listed by race and gender and with summary information in Tables 1.1 and 1.2.

We use nine static family background variables. INTACT is a dummy variable indicating that the respondent's parents were stably married during the respondent's youth. That background factor is frequently found to be an important determinant of the age of marriage, the onset of sexual intercourse, and other related phenomena. EDFATHER and EDMOTHER are the reported schooling levels of the respondent's parents. They, like PARINC (the family of

	White Males (N = 4091)		White Females (N = 4599)		Black Males (N = 401)		Black Females (N = 674)	
	mean	std. dev.	mean	std. dev.	mean	std. dev.	mean	std. dev.
COHAB1	0.273	0.45	0.249	0.43	0.356	0.48	0.336	0.47
EDFATHER	12.685	2.43	12.593	2.42	11.545	1.91	11.108	1.80
EDMOTHER	12.434	2.00	12.276	2.02	11.592	1.94	11.449	1.79
PARINC	12,399	4,952	11,641	4,885	7,099	4,442	6,394	4,194
INTACT	0.749	0.43	0.718	0.45	0.414	0.49	0.457	0.50
LSIZE	2.647	1.30	2.587	1.23	2.740	1.32	2.964	1.29
PROTST	0.385	0.49	0.447	0.50	0.434	0.50	0.340	0.47
CATHOLIC	0.292	0.45	0.279	0.45	0.049	0.22	0.069	0.25
JEW	0.017	0.13	0.018	0.13	—	—	—	—
NORELIG	0.064	0.24	0.030	0.17	0.065	0.25	0.034	0.18
OLD	0.957	2.08	1.303	2.80	1.010	2.32	2.112	4.36
YNG	1.008	1.47	1.296	1.61	1.170	1.47	1.473	1.73
OLDSQ	5.233	28.00	9.511	41.54	6.380	28.79	23.462	72.40
YNGSQ	3.163	7.40	4.277	10.46	3.514	7.31	5.153	9.80
AGEA*	75.320	1.09	74.752	1.40	75.207	1.15	74.822	1.46
AGEB*	77.681	1.70	77.007	1.50	77.702	1.76	77.429	1.72
AGEC*	80.568	1.30	80.300	1.01	80.612	1.33	80.517	1.26
BA*	0.217	0.41	0.185	0.38	0.112	0.31	0.163	0.37
Y85*	10.018	0.29	9.389	0.29	9.686	0.29	9.826	0.41
FY*	8.890	2.40	7.910	2.66	8.596	2.46	7.288	3.21
ACU*	0.704	1.11	0.465	0.85	0.774	1.20	0.808	1.15
ACX*	3.101	2.61	1.981	2.24	2.804	2.72	1.951	2.38
ACS*	1.802	2.10	1.450	1.83	1.276	1.71	1.522	1.79
WRK*	0.759	0.39	0.551	0.45	0.758	0.38	0.562	0.46
SCH*	0.131	0.32	0.081	0.25	0.104	0.26	0.124	0.31
UNP*	0.155	0.30	0.141	0.30	0.132	0.30	0.178	0.33
WGE*	2.155	0.56	1.817	0.63	1.996	0.66	1.774	0.75

Table 1.2.   Definitions of Selected Variables

Label	Variable Definitions
COHAB1	Dummy equal to one if union is cohabitation
EDFATHER	Education of father
EDMOTHER	Education of mother
PARINC	R's Parents' income in 1972
INTACT	R's mother and father lived together in 1972
LSIZE	Size of place where R lived in 1972
PROTST	Dummy equal to one if R is Protestant
CATHOLIC	Dummy equal to one if R is Catholic
JEW	Dummy equal to one if R is Jewish
NORELIG	Dummy equal to one if R has no religion
OLD	Partner's age minus R's age or zero
YNG	R's age minus partner's age or zero
OLDSQ	OLD squared
YNGSQ	YNG squared
AGEA*	Age at union: spline: 18–22
AGEB*	Age at union: spline: 23–26
AGEC*	Age at union: spline: 26–32
BA*	Dummy equals 1 if has BA degree at time of union
Y85*	Predicted log earnings at age 32 based on information at time of union
FY*	Log current earnings at time of union
ACU*	Accumulated unemployment at time of union
ACX*	Accumulated work experience at time of union
ACS*	Accumulated school since H.S. graduation at time of union
WRK*	Dummy equal to one if working at time of union
SCH*	Dummy equal to one if in school at time of union
UNP*	Dummy equal to one if unemployed at time of union
WGE*	Log current wage at time of union

origin's income level reported by the respondent in 1972), reflect the socio-economic status of the respondent's family, and these factors are expected to influence the aspirations, values, and lifetime plans as well as resources and opportunities available to the respondent. LSIZE reflects size of the town in which the respondent lived as a high-school senior, and may also affect both expectations and opportunities. CATHOLIC, PROTST, JEW, and NORELIG are dummies defined as 1.0 if respondent's religious affiliation was Catholic, Protestant, Jewish, or if he or she reported no religious affiliation, respectively. The omitted category includes non-response, Eastern religions, and a large number who reported themselves as 'Other Christian' instead of 'Protestant'. So its distinction from the Protestant dummy variable is unclear. Other studies have found these static family background variables to be important determinants of the onset of various adult roles such as parent or spouse; we investigate if they also influence whether the first partnership is a cohabitational union or a formal marriage.

The time-varying respondent attributes are measured at the time of the formation of the partnership. They include age and aspects of the respondent's education and labour-market status. These date-specific measures are designated by an asterisk (*) as a suffix in their name, e.g. BA* is a dummy variable with the value 1 if the respondent had a BA degree at the time the partnership was formed. We use a spline function for age, with AGEA*, AGEB*, and AGEC* measuring the respondent's age at the formation of the partnership if it occurred between 1972 and 1976 (for A), between 1976 and 1980 (for B), or between 1980 and the survey date in 1986 (for C); thus these kinks in the spline function occur at approximately ages 22 and 26.

FY* is the respondent's annual earnings, in natural logs; WGE* is the respondent's hourly wage-rate, in natural logs. (For respondents with no observed earnings, potential wage-rates were computed and used as the value of WGE*.) The variable Y85* is a more complex variable based on work underway and reported in Willis and Weiss (1988); it is an estimate of the respondent's 1985 earnings based on an equation using information known at the time of the formation of the partnership. In particular, Y85* uses information on schooling level, degree attainment, unemployment, employment, and the prior earnings history of the respondent. As time passes and the respondent accumulates a longer earnings history and gets closer to 1985, the estimate of Y85 becomes more accurate. So, for a respondent who marries very soon after completing high school, that Y85 value is a less accurate estimate of the realized earnings in 1985 than for a respondent who married several years later, having established for himself or herself and having revealed to the partner (and to our estimation equation) much more about his/ her track-record at earning a wage. This increased precision in estimating future earnings may be one of the important benefits of delaying marriage.

We have also included in some of our analyses ACU*, ACX*, and ACS*. These measure the accumulation as of the date of the start of the partnership of the respondent's unemployment experience (U), employment experience (X), and years of schooling experience beyond high school (S). These three variables are based on dummy variables reflecting the respondent's activities in October of each year. For example, the ACX variable is defined as the sum of the annual dummy variables indicating employment in October for all years prior to the date of the start of the partnership. (For the final year before the formation of the marriage or cohabitation, the two dummies for the October before and after the formation are prorated.)

The spouse characteristics used in this analysis are limited to the spouse's age relative to the respondent's age, with OLD (or OLDH for the women respondents) indicating the number of years the spouse is older than the respondent, and YNG (or YNGH for the women respondents) indicating the number of years the spouse is younger that the respondent. (In both cases the age-difference is normalized on the typical age-difference for spouses at the age at which respondents formed the partnerships in this sample.) The suffix SQ on the OLD or YNG variable indicates it is a squared term to permit a non-linearity to the estimated relationships.

We use as our statistical model a probit relationship of the form:

$$P = F(z) = (1/\sqrt{2\pi}) \int_{-\infty}^{XB} \exp(-e/2)de$$

where P is the probability that the couple chooses a cohabitation not a marriage, F is the cumulative normal probability function, z is a threshold index, X is the vector of explanatory variables and B is its vector of coefficients, and e is an error term that is assumed to be normally distributed in the index function:

$$z = XB + e.$$

P reflects the probability that the couple chooses a cohabitational partnership instead of a formal marriage, and is based on the dummy variable COHAB1 defined as 1 if the partnership was a cohabitation not a marriage at the outset. The interpretation of the coefficient (when adjusted for the mean proportion cohabiting) is the influence of a unit change in that variable on the probability that the couple choose cohabitation instead of marriage, evaluated at the mean. We report two probit equations, each estimated separately for white men, white women, black men, and black women. (Each has been run weighted by the respondent's expansion weight to provide more appropriate estimates of the national behaviour of the populations from which these samples are drawn.)

Consider the substantive findings in these tables. For whites, the likelihood of cohabiting is substantially lower—about 7 percentage points lower—for those who grew up in intact families. For blacks, however, that background factor has no relationship to the choice between cohabiting or marrying, according to Table 1.3, panels C and D. In general, in this paper (as frequently reported elsewhere as well, see e.g. Michael and Tuma, 1985), we find that many of the factors that help to explain behaviour among young white adults have much less influence for young blacks.

Parents' education and income also play a role for the whites but not for the blacks. For white men and women, father's education is positively related to the choice of a cohabitation. It is not a big effect—1 or 1.3 percentage points per additional year of schooling—but it is statistically significant. Mother's education has no influence here for any of the four groups. For white men but not women, parents' income also has a positive relationship. It may be that the higher education and income reflect a more liberal social attitude toward cohabiting. It may instead reflect a financial capacity to set

Table 1.3. Determinants of Cohabitation, Basic Probit Equation

	White Males		White Females		Black Males		Black Females	
	coeff.	t-value	coeff.	t-value	coeff.	t-value	coeff.	t-value
EDFATHER	0.022	1.92	0.037	3.38	0.020	0.45	0.063	1.79
EDMOTHER	0.008	0.63	0.014	1.09	-0.045	-0.95	-0.053	-1.37
PARINC*1000	0.016	2.91	-0.001	-0.10	-0.010	-0.57	-0.004	0.24
INTACT	-0.195	-3.83	-0.197	-4.07	0.022	0.15	-0.156	-1.35
LSIZE	0.095	5.16	0.051	2.78	0.052	0.94	0.151	3.22
PROTST	0.026	0.43	0.069	1.24	-0.197	-1.30	-0.001	-0.01
CATHOLIC	0.017	0.28	-0.011	-0.18	-0.535	-1.54	0.330	1.60
JEW	0.470	2.84	0.492	3.22	—	—	—	—
NORELIG	0.621	6.63	0.505	4.15	0.129	0.48	0.515	1.83
NJOBS	0.074	6.07	0.103	8.58	0.108	2.47	0.006	0.13
OLD	0.120	6.18	0.115	7.05	0.211	2.28	0.092	1.99
YNG	-0.070	-1.73	-0.011	-0.36	-0.112	-0.86	0.028	0.35
OLDSQ	-0.003	-2.51	-0.004	-3.69	-0.013	-1.42	-0.000	-0.08
YNGSQ	0.014	1.90	0.006	1.60	0.023	0.99	0.007	0.58
AGEA*	0.062	2.21	0.112	5.28	0.026	0.33	0.062	1.25
AGEB*	0.099	4.89	0.104	5.02	0.023	0.38	-0.074	-1.42
AGEC*	0.008	0.42	-0.009	-0.37	-0.136	-1.97	0.117	2.13
BA*	-0.220	-3.33	-0.241	-3.71	0.292	1.24	-0.327	-1.91
Y85*	-0.081	-0.74	0.112	1.25	-0.299	-1.06	-0.371	-2.08
CONSTANT	-13.877	-5.62	-18.381	-9.10	-9.588	1.39	-5.869	-1.29
No. obs.	4,091		4,599		401		674	
chi sq. (19)	469.74		510.79		46.80		90.07	
Log-Likelihood	-2,161.52		-2,323.78		-237.80		-385.12	

up a joint household as a cohabiting couple somewhat earlier than the couple may wish to make its decision about a formal marriage.

For three of these four groups, living in larger cities tends to raise the likelihood that one cohabits. Only black men reveal no such relationship. Whether it is opportunity, necessity, anonymity, or something else that promotes this tendency among whites and black women remains a subject for further inquiry.

Several parallel findings are reported in the literature. For example, Clayton and Voss (1977) report a positive effect of father's education on the incidence of cohabitation among young men in their sample; intactness of family of origin has been found to be related to delay in the onset of sexual activity, which in turn is correlated with incidence of cohabitation. Several studies have found, as we do, that living in larger cities is associated with a higher likelihood of cohabitation.

Religion matters here for whites but, again, not for blacks: Jews and those who report no religion have a much higher likelihood of cohabitation. The omitted religion category in these probit equations is the 'other' category, but the findings tell us that Catholics, Protestants, and 'others' behave similarly. It is the 'no religion' and Jewish groups who have substantially higher rates of cohabitation.

The age or date of entry into the first partnership has an effect on the choice between marriage and cohabiting for whites but not for blacks. White men and women who enter their partnership at a relatively later age are more likely to cohabit—for men, for example, the likelihood of cohabiting rises with each year of age at a rate of 1.9 percentage points in the interval 1972 to 1976 (ages about 18 to 22), and at the rate 3.1 percentage points in the interval 1976 to 1980 (ages 22 to 26). The relationship is stronger for white women than for white men. For whites, teens who form partnerships tend to marry, while at a slightly higher age, they are more likely to begin with a less formal cohabitation. We think this finding reflects the dramatic trend towards cohabitation in the USA during the period 1972–86 in which this cohort were aged from 18 to 32. Those who formed their partnership in the later years were more prone to cohabit, reflecting the national trend towards that pattern. With this one cohort we cannot distinguish the effect of the life-cycle from the known trend.

One of the more revealing findings in the literature pertaining to this point is found in Gwartney-Gibbs (1986). She points out that in her 1970 cross-sectional data, most of the cohabiting couples who applied for marriage licences were young, but that by 1980 'the age distribution of premarital cohabitants had spread considerably into the next older age group' (age 25–34) (1986: 427). If cohabitation is a means of intensive marital search, one might expect a higher incidence at younger ages of formation of the partnership. We think this relationship may be swamped in our data by the strong time-trend. Data on the life-histories of several cohorts will be required to sort this out. This trend is even more pronounced in Sweden, where Hoem and Hoem (1988: 402) report that in 1965 41 per cent of new first unions were formal marriages, but that by 1977 that percentage had fallen to only 4 per cent.

While we have emphasized here the confluence of social trend towards cohabitation and the ageing of the cohort we study, one might also offer a quite different interpretation of the tendency for those who form their first partnership at a relatively older age to begin with a cohabitation. If risk aversion is an unmeasured characteristic in our sample, it may be correlated both with the tendency to delay the start of a partnership, and with the tendency to form a more tentative cohabitational union. We have not undertaken the econometric re-specification that this interpretation would call for, but mention it in passing.

Our results suggest that over the period 1972–86, the percentage of cohabiting whites and blacks converge as they age—a higher percentage of blacks form cohabiting unions at a young age and there is little age-gradient exhibited, so that as the two groups age, the rates of cohabitation converge at the higher rate of blacks.

The variable OLD has a very consistent but, we think, perplexing effect: for all four groups, both men and women, if the partner is older than the respondent (relative to the norm), the couple is more likely to cohabit than to marry. Having a younger partner seems to have no influence on the choice and the squared terms are not important, but there is a strong statistical relationship between the older age of the partner and the report of a cohabitation. Were it of opposite signs for the genders, we could understand that, but it is not. Could it be that the younger partner consistently treats the relationship as a more official partnership, and therefore reports an affair as a cohabitation, while the older partner just does not report that relationship so readily until later when a formal marriage takes place? Surely the specific date of the beginning of a cohabitation is not as clear-cut as the date of the beginning of a formal marriage. Another possibility is that partnerships with greatly differing ages cohabit at the start, and since our sample is relatively young, all the couples in our sample with large age-differences have the respondent as the younger partner.

Those with a BA degree at the date the partnerships are formed behave differently than those without the BA, but the relationship is different for whites and for blacks. For whites, a BA is associated with a lower likelihood of cohabitation—almost 4 percentage points lower for men and about 6 percentage points lower for women. For black men, those with a BA were far more likely to cohabit at the start of their partnership. For black women, as for whites, the estimated effect is negative, but for blacks it is not statistically significant. The final variable in the equation is Y85*, the estimate of the respondent's 1985 earnings based on information available to the respondent and partner when the partnership began. Here, the pattern of results is intriguing. For white men this effect is very large and very strong: higher expected earnings is associated with lower likelihood of cohabiting. The men with better earnings prospects marry at the beginning of the partnership. So do the black men and likewise the black women. Only the white women exhibit no such tendency. Their earnings prospects seem irrelevant to the choice between cohabitation and marriage.

Table 1.4 shows an expanded version of the equation in Table 1.3. In this longer equation, eight additional time-varying variables and one additional personal attribute are added. These additional variables have little effect on the coefficients of the static background factors for either white men or white women, but do reduce the influence of the dynamic variables—time of formation, BA, and Y85—for the men. (As we add more detail about the respondent, the overall explanatory power increases but our capacity to sort out separate effects diminishes.)

The new variables added in Table 1.4 include the respondent's earnings (FY) and actual or potential hourly wage rate (WGE) at the time the partnership is formed, and several measures of accumulated experience in employment, unemployment, and schooling as well as the current status of each at the time of the formation of the partnership. For white men, a rise in the hourly wage rate appears to be associated with a lower likelihood of cohabiting, and accumulated unemployment raises the likelihood of cohabiting. We have probably engaged in 'overkill' here: we have too many variables measuring subtly different phenomena. What Tables 1.3 and 1.4 seem to tell us is that white men with better labour-market prospects and job-market experience at the time of the formation of the partnership tend to marry rather than to cohabit.

For white women, the story is different. We see here a tendency to cohabit if a woman has greater labour-market opportunities, as reflected in her annual income (FY) or her current employment (WRK) or her current participation in schooling (SCH). For these white women, as well, a history of accumulated unemployment promotes cohabitation instead of formal marriage. So for whites, one can see reflections of the traditional gender roles in marriage: the better he is doing or the better his prospects in the labour-market, the more likely they are to marry at the start; the better she is doing currently (or the more involved she is in the labour-market), the less likely they are to marry at the start.

For black men the results are much weaker, but one sees here the strong tendency to cohabit, not to marry, if a man is currently unemployed. Black women are more likely to cohabit, not marry, if they have substantial job-market experience, accumulated unemployment, or if they are still in school. This is quite similar to the pattern observed for white women.

One other variable is included in the two tables reported here: NJOBS, the total number of jobs held by the respondent over the seven-year interval

Table 1.4. Determinants of Cohabitation, Expanded Probit Equation

	White Males		White Females		Black Males		Black Females	
	coeff.	t-value	coeff.	t-value	coeff.	t-value	coeff.	t-value
EDFATHER	0.024	2.05	0.036	3.24	0.034	0.70	0.042	1.18
EDMOTHER	0.017	1.29	0.012	0.99	-0.061	-1.27	-0.042	-1.08
PARINC*1000	0.016	3.04	-0.001	-0.19	-0.013	-0.71	0.004	0.23
INTACT	-0.188	-3.66	-0.208	-4.25	-0.065	-0.41	-0.129	-1.10
LSIZE	0.098	5.34	0.052	2.85	0.074	1.23	0.115	2.53
PROTST	0.017	0.28	0.080	1.42	-0.085	-0.52	-0.045	-0.36
CATHOLIC	-0.005	-0.07	-0.016	-0.25	-0.581	-1.63	-0.369	-1.76
JEW	0.460	2.74	0.507	3.29	—	—	—	—
NORELIG	0.611	6.45	0.445	3.62	0.025	0.09	0.454	1.61
NJOBS	0.071	6.75	0.093	8.18	0.082	1.83	0.034	0.81
OLD	0.133	6.78	0.114	6.96	0.213	2.66	0.098	2.11
YNG	-0.043	-1.05	-0.011	-0.37	-0.086	-0.64	-0.003	-0.03
OLDSQ	-0.004	-2.72	-0.004	-3.63	-0.010	-1.44	-0.001	-0.35
YNGSQ	0.010	1.34	0.007	1.68	0.025	1.03	0.011	0.84
AGEA*	0.037	1.22	0.092	3.74	0.080	-0.90	0.052	0.93

Table 1.4. (Cont.)

	White Males		White Females		Black Males		Black Females	
	coeff.	t-value	coeff.	t-value	coeff.	t-value	coeff.	t-value
AGEB*	0.031	1.22	0.063	2.24	-0.092	-1.23	-0.121	-1.88
AGEC*	-0.032	-1.31	-0.031	-1.01	-0.121	-1.42	0.094	1.47
BA*	-0.112	-1.36	-0.235	-2.80	-0.254	-0.79	-0.094	-0.45
FY*	-0.012	-1.05	0.021	2.15	-.061	-1.85	0.005	0.22
ACU*	0.178	7.30	0.132	4.30	0.164	2.00	0.126	2.20
ACX*	0.031	2.00	0.002	0.08	0.021	0.45	0.067	1.75
ACS*	-0.014	-0.73	0.002	0.11	0.157	2.26	-0.089	-1.72
WRK*	-0.099	-1.28	0.150	2.47	0.294	1.21	0.060	0.39
SCH*	0.142	1.80	0.523	6.07	0.719	2.32	0.642	3.31
UNP*	0.117	1.52	0.130	1.79	1.133	4.23	0.249	1.43
WGE*	-0.100	-2.42	-0.002	-0.07	0.165	1.39	-0.082	-1.02
CONSTANT	-4.279	-1.21	-11.280	-2.78	21.808	2.19	-3.324	-0.45
No. obs.	4,091		4,599		401		674	
chi sq. (19)	551.07		581.50		98.62		111.32	
Log-likelihood	-2,120.85		-2,288.43		-211.89		-374.50	

from 1979 to the survey in 1986. We consider this variable to be an indicator of a personal characteristic, not a measure of job-market behaviour *per se*. We suggest that people with a high number for NJOBS behave differently—they are less stable in relationships generally. For whites, this variable is very consistently associated with a higher likelihood of cohabiting, but not so for blacks. It is also associated with lower earnings. Bennett, Blanc, and Bloom (1988) suggest, as mentioned above, that some cohabitors may be a select group for whom relationships in general lack stability. The strong performance of the variable NJOBS, a fixed-effect measure, seems to offer substantial support for this notion.

How Well does the Probit Equation Perform?

To explore how well or how poorly these probit equations perform in predicting the choice about cohabiting or marrying, Table 1.5 shows the actual and the predicted proportions who cohabit, arrayed by gender, race, date of formation of partnership (in three categories: before 1976, 1976–80, and since 1980), and by whether the respondent had a BA degree at the date of the formation of the partnership. In panel *A* (white males) we see that overall 27 per cent cohabit and that this percentage rises dramatically by date: only 19 per cent of those who formed their partnership by 1976, 28 per cent of those who formed their partnership between 1976 and 1980, and 39 per cent of those who formed their partnership since 1980 cohabited. The interaction of date of formation and the holding a BA degree shows a similar age-pattern for both those with and without the BA degree.

Now compare these percentages on the top row (the actual percentages) with those on the second row (the predicted percentages). They are extremely similar, i.e. the equation did a very good job of partitioning accurately the proportions of these white men who did cohabit and the proportion that did not for the groups defined by date of formation and holding a BA. For white women (panel *C*), the large differences by both date and presence of a BA can be seen; both are quite well replicated in the predictions based on Table 1.3*B*. Panel *B* reports on the fewer black men: here we see the absence of a pattern by date, but again the probit equation does quite well at replicating the actual patterns. For black women (panel *D*), the reverse effect of BA is seen, and here the predicted values are less accurate reflections of the actual pattern. In general, and in similar tables (not shown), the array of the data by other characteristics shows a good conformity between the actual and predicted values, indicating that the probit equations do perform well in partitioning the observations on the choice between cohabitation and marriage.

As another use of the estimated equations in Table 1.3, we show plots of the predicted distributions of the probability of cohabiting. Fig. 1.10 shows

Table 1.5. Actual and Predicted Probabilities of Cohabitation by Race, Education, and Year Union Began (based on probit model in Table 1.4)

	A. White Males				B. Black Males			
	<1976	1976–80	>1980	TOTAL	<1976	1976–80	>1980	TOTAL
No BA								
actual	0.19	0.30	0.41	0.26	0.38	0.44	0.20	0.35
predicted	0.19	0.28	0.42	0.26	0.37	0.39	0.28	0.35
no. obs.	1467	881	435	2783	163	96	60	319
BA								
actual	0.27	0.25	0.37	0.30	0.53	0.33	0.50	0.40
predicted	0.20	0.26	0.36	0.30	0.38	0.44	0.34	0.40
no. obs.	52	699	557	1308	2	49	31	82
TOTAL								
actual	0.19	0.28	0.39	0.27	0.38	0.42	0.25	0.36
predicted	0.19	0.28	0.40	0.27	0.37	0.40	0.29	0.36
no. obs.	1519	1580	992	4091	165	145	91	401

C. White Females

	<1976	1976–80	>1980	TOTAL
No BA				
actual	0.18	0.30	0.47	0.23
predicted	0.18	0.31	0.46	0.23
no. obs.	2379	705	278	3362
BA				
actual	0.21	0.32	0.35	0.32
predicted	0.20	0.29	0.40	0.32
no. obs.	93	744	400	1237
TOTAL				
actual	0.18	0.31	0.41	0.25
predicted	0.18	0.31	0.43	0.25
no. obs.	2472	1449	678	4599

D. Black Females

	<1976	1976–80	>1980	TOTAL
No BA				
actual	0.31	0.39	0.48	0.36
predicted	0.31	0.36	0.49	0.35
no. obs.	314	129	87	530
BA				
actual	0.17	0.29	0.19	0.24
predicted	0.24	0.20	0.30	0.25
no. obs.	11	84	49	144
TOTAL				
actual	0.30	0.36	0.38	0.34
predicted	0.31	0.31	0.43	0.34
no. obs.	325	213	136	674

(a) White men

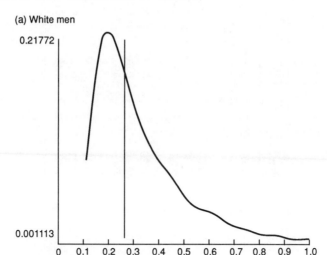

(b) White women

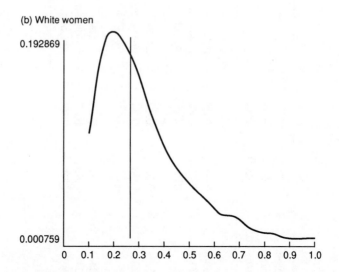

Panel *A*: White Men
Panel *B*: White Women
Fig. 1.10   Distribution of Predicted Probabilities of Cohabitation in First Union

these distributions for white men (panel *A*) and white women (panel *B*). One sees here that while the mean is about .27 for both groups, the distribution has a large positive skew. Fig. 1.11 shows these distributions by the date of the formation of the partnership. Here again we see that those who formed their partnership before 1976 had a lower probability of cohabiting, while those who formed that first partnership after 1980 had a much higher probability of cohabiting.

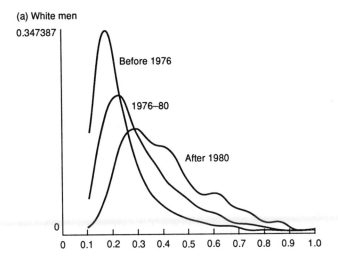

(a) White men

0.347387

Before 1976

1976–80

After 1980

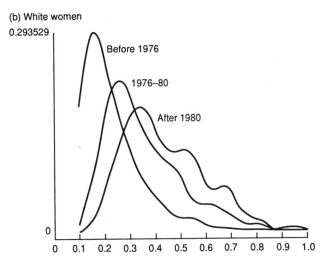

(b) White women

0.293529

Before 1976

1976–80

After 1980

Panel *A*: White Men
Panel *B*: White Women

Fig. 1.11 Predicted Probabilities of COHAB1 by Date of Beginning of Partnership

Summary

The descriptive evidence on cohabitation among this cohort of the baby-boom generation tells us that about one-quarter of the whites and one-third of the blacks began their first partnership as a cohabitation, and nearly two-thirds of second partnerships began as cohabitations. These cohabitations were not of long duration, however. The half-life of the first cohabitation is only about one year, and a large majority of them end in formal marriage to that partner.

These facts suggest to us that in the United States, cohabitation among this cohort serves the purpose of a trial marriage, an opportunity for intensive search in the marriage-market. A subsequent decision informed by the early experience of the cohabitation is made rather quickly about converting that partnership into a formal marriage or dissolving it. It seems a reasonable conjecture that the dramatic rise in divorce rates that began in the mid-1960s played an important role in encouraging cohabitation as an institution for responding to the increased uncertainty about the stability of a marital partnership. Without committing publicly or permanently to the prospective partner, cohabitation permits the couple to test out the relationship before stronger, legally sanctioned, commitments are made.

We emphasize that our conclusion applies only to the USA and only to the cohort we have studied. Hoem and Hoem have shown how much more widespread and how much more stable cohabitational unions have become in Sweden in recent years. Whereas they report that half of consensual unions in Sweden in the mid-1960s ended in marriage within a year's time—as we report here for this cohort of 32-year-olds in the USA in 1986—by the mid-1970s that percentage in Sweden had fallen to less than 5 per cent married during the first year of the union (Hoem and Hoem, 1988: 403). Whether the United States will follow this Swedish pattern remains to be seen. Other inquiries spanning the whole age spectrum (e.g. the new National Survey of Households and Families), or focusing on younger cohorts (e.g. the Thornton data referred to above) need to be used to address that question.

Our probit equations investigate correlates of the choice between marrying or cohabiting at the beginning of the first partnership. Family background factors are found to be associated with that choice for whites but not for blacks. Whites who were raised in intact families are less likely to cohabit, and father's education and income seem to raise the likelihood of choosing cohabitation.

In our data the older the person is (up to about age 25 or to 1980) when the partnership is formed, the more likely the partnership is to have begun as a cohabitation. We think this reflects the trend towards cohabitation more than life-cycle effects, but we cannot distinguish between the two in this single cohort; it may also result from heterogeneity in risk-taking, for which we have not adjusted.

We have several findings that suggest that the poorer the economic prospects and circumstances of the male at the time of the formation of the partnership, the more likely he is to cohabit. This is consistent with less commitment to the partnership among couples where the economic gains from marriage are less. The distinctive pattern for white women regarding labour-market variables reinforces this interpretation: men with better job-market prospects tend not to cohabit, but women with better job-market prospects do, being less inclined to make long-term commitments to that partner.

References

Bachrach, C. A. and Horn, M. J. (1987), 'Married and Unmarried Couples, United States, 1982', *Vital and Health Statistics*, 23/15.

Becker, G. S., Landes, E. M., and Michael, R. T. (1977), 'An Economic Analysis of Marital Instability', *Journal of Political Economy*, 85/6 (Dec.), 1141–87.

Bennett, N. G., Blanc, A. K., and Bloom, D. E. (1988), 'Commitment and the Modern Union: Assessing the Link between Premarital Cohabitation and Subsequent Marital Stability', *American Sociological Review*, 53, 127–38.

Bernhardt, E. and Hoem, B. (1985), 'Cohabitation and Social Background: Trends Observed for Swedish Women Born between 1936 and 1960', *European Journal of Population*, 1, 375–95.

Blanc, A. K. (1987), 'The Formation and Dissolution of Second Unions: Marriage and Cohabitation in Sweden and Norway', *Journal of Marriage and the Family*, 49 (May), 391–400.

Brunborg, H. (1979), 'Cohabitation without Marriage in Norway', Article 116, Central Bureau of Statistics, Oslo, Norway.

Clayton, R. R. and Voss, H. L. (1977), 'Shacking up: Cohabitation in the 1970s', *Journal of Marriage and the Family*, 39, 273–83.

Glick, P. C. and Norton, A. J. (1977), 'Marrying, Divorcing, and Living Together in the U.S. Today', *Population Bulletin*, 32 (Oct.), 1–39.

Glick, P. C. and Spanier, G. (1980), 'Married and Unmarried Cohabitation in the United States,' *Journal of Marriage and the Family*, 42, 19–30.

Gwartney-Gibbs, P. A. (1986), 'Institutionalization of Premarital Cohabitation', *Journal of Marriage and the Family*, 48, 423–34.

Hoem, B. and Hoem, J. (1988), 'The Swedish Family: Aspects of Contemporary Developments', *Journal of Family Issues*, 9/3 (Sept.), 397–424.

Kiernan, K. E. (1983), 'The Structure of Families Today: Continuity or Change?' in *The Family*, British Society for Population Studies, OPCS Occasional Paper no. 31, 17–36.

Macklin, E. D. (1978), 'Nonmarital Heterosexual Cohabitation', *Marriage and Family Review*, 1 (Mar./Apr.), 1–12.

Michael, R. T. (1988), 'Why has the U.S. Divorce Rate Doubled within the Decade?' in T. P. Schultz (ed.), *Research and Population Economics*, Greenwich, Conn.: JAI Press, 367–99.

Michael, R. T. and Tuma, N. B. (1985), 'Entry into Marriage and Parenthood by Young Men and Women: The Influence of Family Background', *Demography*, 22/4 (Nov.), 515–44.

Preston, S. H. and McDonald, J. (1979), 'The Incidence of Divorce within Cohorts of American Marriages Contracted since the Civil War', *Demography*, 16/1, 1–25.

Spanier, G. (1983), 'Married and Unmarried Cohabitation in the United States: 1980', *Journal of Marriage and the Family*, 45, 277–88.

Tanfer, K. (1987), 'Patterns of Premarital Cohabitation among Never-Married Women in the United States', *Journal of Marriage and the Family*, 49 (Aug.), 483–97.

Thornton, A. (1988), 'Cohabitation and Marriage in the 1980s', *Demography*, 25/4, 497–508.

Willis, R. J. and Weiss, Y. (1988), 'Divorce Settlements and the Distribution of Welfare between Husbands and Wives', paper presented to IUSSP Committee on Economic Consequences of Alternative Demographic Patterns, Sendai City, Japan, 19–21 September 1988.

Yamaguchi, K. and Kandel, D. B. (1985), 'Dynamic Relationships between Premarital Cohabitation and Illicit Drug Use: An Event-History Analysis of Role Selection and Role Socialization', *American Sociological Review*, 50 (Aug.), 530–46.

Appendix: Extract from Questionnaire used in Fifth Follow-up Survey

39. Now we would like some information about any marriages or marriage-like relationships you have had. Have you ever been married or involved in a marriage-like relationship?

    1. Yes (GO TO Q.40)
    2. No (SKIP TO Q.77)

*40. Please start with the first time that you got married or lived in an intimate relationship with an unrelated adult of the opposite sex. Do not count any living arrangements which lasted LESS THAN ONE MONTH.

    ANSWER THESE QUESTIONS FOR YOUR FIRST PARTNER

    A. When did you begin living with this person?
    §   ☐☐ ☐☐
                                         MONTH YEAR

    B. Were you married to this person when you started living together? (CIRCLE ONE)
    §
    1. Yes (SKIP TO D)
    2. No (GO TO C)

    C. Did you ever marry this person? (CIRCLE ONE)
    §
    1. Yes →☐☐ ☐☐
            MONTH YEAR
    2. No

    D. How old was your partner when you began living together?
       (IF UNSURE, GIVE YOUR BEST ESTIMATE)

       AGE OF PARTNER ☐☐

    E. How many children were produced from this relationship? (ENTER NUMBER. IF NONE, WRITE IN 'O'.)

       NUMBER OF CHILDREN ☐☐

    F. Are you still living with this person? (CIRCLE ONE)
    §
    1. Yes (SKIP TO Q.43)
    2. No (ENTER MONTH AND YEAR YOU
       PARTED)→☐☐ ☐☐(GO TO G)
              MONTH YEAR

    G. How did this relationship end? (CIRCLE ONE AND GIVE DATE)
    §
    Separation.................................... 1 ⎤
    Divorce or annulment............................ 2 ⎬→☐☐ ☐☐
    Death of partner..................................... 3 ⎦ MONTH YEAR

H. Did you have any other marriages or marriage-like relationships? (CIRCLE ONE)

1. Yes (GO TO Q.41)
2. No   (SKIP TO Q.43)

*41. ANSWER THESE QUESTIONS FOR YOUR SECOND PARTNER

A. When did you begin living with this person?
§   (WRITE IN MONTH AND YEAR)
□□ □□
MONTH YEAR

B. Were you married to this person when you started
§   living together? (CIRCLE ONE)

1. Yes (SKIP TO D)
2. No   (GO TO C)

C. Did you ever marry this person?
§   (CIRCLE ONE)

1. Yes →□□ □□
        MONTH YEAR
2. No

D. How old was your partner when you began living together?

AGE OF PARTNER □□

E. How many children were produced from this relationship? (ENTER NUMBER. IF NONE, WRITE IN 'O')

NUMBER OF CHILDREN □□

F. Are you still living with this person?
§   (CIRCLE ONE)

1. Yes (SKIP TO Q.43)
2. No   (ENTER MONTH AND YEAR YOU
        PARTED)→□□ □□ (GO TO G)
            MONTH YEAR

G. How did this relationship end?
§   (CIRCLE ONE AND GIVE DATE)

Separation.. 1⎤
Divorce or annulment............................ 2 ⎮→□□ □□
Death of partner..................................... 3 ⎦ MONTH YEAR

H. Did you have any other marriages or marriage-like relationships? (CIRCLE ONE)

1. Yes (GO TO Q.42)
2. No   (SKIP TO Q.43)

*42. ANSWER THESE QUESTIONS FOR YOUR THIRD PARTNER

A. When did you begin living with this person?
§   (WRITE IN MONTH AND YEAR)
□□ □□
MONTH YEAR

B. Were you married to this person when you started
§   living together? (CIRCLE ONE)

1. Yes (SKIP TO D)
2. No   (GO TO C)

C. Did you ever marry this person?
§   (CIRCLE ONE)

1. Yes → ☐☐   ☐☐
          MONTH YEAR

2. No

D. How old was your partner when you began living together?

    AGE OF PARTNER ☐☐

E. How many children were produced from this relationship? (ENTER NUMBER. IF NONE, WRITE IN 'O')

    NUMBER OF CHILDREN ☐☐

F. Are you still living with this person?
§   (CIRCLE ONE)

1. Yes (SKIP TO Q.43)
2. No   (ENTER MONTH AND YEAR YOU
    PARTED)→ ☐☐   ☐☐ (GO TO G)
            MONTH YEAR

G. How did this relationship end?
§   (CIRCLE ONE AND GIVE DATE)

Separation.. 1⎤
Divorce or annulment............................. 2⎢→ ☐☐   ☐☐
Death of partner....................................... 3⎦   MONTH YEAR

H. Did you have any other marriages or marriage-like relationships? (CIRCLE ONE)

1. Yes   How many more→ ☐☐
2. No

2 The Effects of Cohort Size on Marriage-Markets in Twentieth-Century Sweden

THEODORE BERGSTROM AND DAVID LAM

Large, short-run fluctuations in the birth-rate have been an important demographic feature of industrialized, low-fertility populations in the twentieth century. Since females normally marry men who are two or three years older than themselves, these fluctuations result in large imbalances between the size of male and female cohorts who would normally marry each other. These imbalances must somehow be resolved, either by a change in traditional patterns of age at marriage or by changes in the proportions of the population of one sex or the other who never marry.

Following a suggestion by Becker (1973; 1974; 1981), we have developed an implementable general equilibrium model of marriage assignments, which can be used to predict the way in which marriage patterns adjust to change in the numbers of males and females in each cohort. This model poses equilibrium in the marriage-market as an application of the linear programming assignment problem, which was introduced to economics by Koopmans and Beckman (1957). For the purposes of this paper, we suppose that persons of the same sex differ only by the year in which they were born. Each individual has a preferred age of marriage. Any two people who marry each other must, of course, marry at the same time. Therefore, the total pay-off to a marriage between any male and female is a function of the age-difference between them. The more their age-difference diverges from the difference between their preferred ages at marriage, the greater must be the loss of utility to one or both from marrying at an age that is not ideal. If we posit a particular pay-off structure to marriages as a function of the age of marriage of each partner, then given the size of each cohort, we can compute the optimal assignment of marriage partners by cohort. The fit of the predicted assignments from our model can then be compared with actual marriage patterns.

Swedish marriage patterns during the twentieth century are ideal for testing our assignment model. Excellent data exist on marriages and cohort size for single years of age and single calendar years going back to the 1890s. Dramatic fluctuations in fertility in Sweden have created large differences

Financial support was provided by the National Institute for Child Health and Development, Grant No. R01-HD19624. Helpful comments were provided by Warren Sanderson and Tommy Bengtsson.

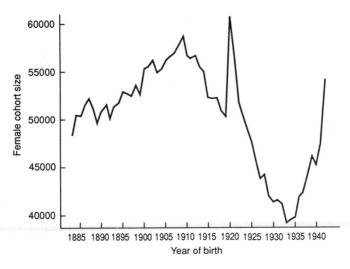

Size of female cohort born in year *t*, evaluated at age 15.

Figure 2.1 Fluctuations in the Size of Cohorts in Sweden, 1883–1942

between the size of male and female cohorts who would normally marry each other. Nevertheless, the median age-difference between husbands and wives has remained in the range of two or three years. We hope to use our assignment model to shed some light on the way that the marriage-market absorbed these cohort size changes. As we will show, the simple form of the assignment model that we present in this chapter is partially, but not entirely, successful in this endeavour.

The first section of the chapter presents descriptive statistics of marriage patterns in twentieth-century Sweden. We follow this with an outline of our equilibrium theory of marriage assignment. Finally, we compare actual marriage patterns with those predicted by a simple implementation of our model which assumes that the difference between preferred age of marriage for the two sexes did not change over the entire period.

Cohort Size and Age at Marriage in Twentieth-Century Sweden

Sweden has experienced sharp fluctuations in fertility during the twentieth century. This is demonstrated in Fig. 2.1, which shows the fluctuations in the size of Swedish cohorts for the years 1883 to 1942. The figure plots the size of female birth cohorts in Sweden, evaluated when the females are aged 15. As the figure demonstrates, Sweden experienced a sharp peak in fertility in 1920 and a major trough in the early 1930s. This decline was followed by a rapid increase into the 1940s.

The large changes in cohort size in Sweden over this period cause dramatic

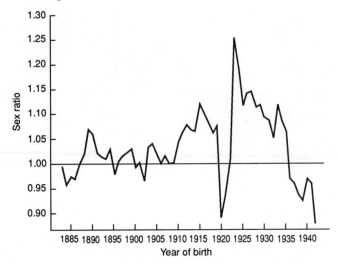

Number of males born in year *t* – 3 divided by number of females born in year *t*; both sexes evaluated at age 15.

Figure 2.2   Male–Female Sex-Ratios in Sweden, 1883–1942

imbalances in the sex-ratios typically used to analyse marriage squeezes. Fig. 2.2 shows the sex-ratio that we will use throughout the paper, the number of potential husbands available to women born in a given year if every woman married a man three years older. Specifically, the sex-ratio shown is the ratio of the number of males born in year *t* – 3 (measured at age 15) to the number of females born in year *t* (also measured at age 15).[1] The figure shows, for example, that if every woman married a man three years older, the 1923 cohort of women would have had more than 1.25 potential husbands for every woman, while the 1942 cohort would have had less than .9 potential husbands for every woman.

Figs. 2.3 and 2.4 demonstrate secular trends in Swedish marriage patterns, trends which are similar to those of many other European populations in the twentieth century. Fig. 2.3 shows the mean age at marriage for male and female birth cohorts, conditional on marriage by age 40.[2] The mean age at marriage fell sharply for both men and women, declining by around three

[1] For example, the point plotted for year of birth 1920 is the size of the 1917 male birth cohort at age 15 (i.e. the number of 15-year-old males in 1932) divided by the size of the 1920 female birth cohort at age 15 (i.e. the number of 15-year-old females in 1935). If all females married men three years older, the graph shows the ratio of eligible females to eligible males for each female birth cohort.

[2] In the results presented here we truncate the cohort marriage histories at age 40 for calculation of both the mean age at marriage and the proportions marrying. We use age 40 in order to maximize the number of cohorts with comparable histories while still including the greatest part of each cohort's marriage experience. We have compared these results with results using age 45 and 50 as the truncation point for those cohorts which permit such comparisons. None of the general patterns we indicate here are sensitive to the use of age 40 as the truncation point.

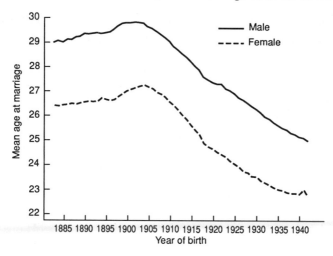

Figure 2.3 Mean Age at Marriage for Males and Females in Sweden, 1883–1942, by Year of Birth, Conditional on Marriage by Age 40

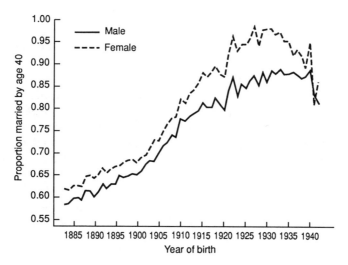

Figure 2.4 Proportions of Males and Females Marrying by Age 40 in Sweden, 1883–1942, by Year of Birth, Conditional on Marriage by Age 40

years for both sexes between the 1900 cohort and the 1940 cohort. In spite of the large changes in the mean age at marriage for both sexes, the difference between these ages remained in the range of two to three years throughout the entire period. This persistent difference in mean age at marriage must imply that husbands are on average older than their wives by two to three years of age throughout this period. The consistency of the gap between the mean age at marriage for males and the mean age at marriage for women is especially striking when confronted with the sharp fluctuations in sex-ratios shown in Fig. 2.2.

Fig. 2.4 shows the cumulative proportions of men and women in each cohort who married before age 40. Over time, these proportions increase sharply for both sexes, with a larger increase for women than for men. The proportion of women married by age 40 (a number only slightly smaller than the proportion of women who eventually marry) rose from slightly over 60 per cent before 1900 to over 95 per cent in the late 1920s. After 1930 there is a decline in the proportion of females who marry, while the proportion of males who marry stays roughly constant.

The fluctuations of cohort size and of sex-ratios documented in Figs. 2.1 and 2.2 could be resolved in the marriage-market in two possible ways. One response is that the fluctuations lead to changes in the proportions of males or females marrying for each cohort. For example, one simple adjustment would be that the number of females who marry is determined entirely by the supply of potential husbands, with the proportion of females marrying absorbing all fluctuations in sex-ratios. A second way of resolving these imbalances is through changes in the age-difference between husbands and wives.

The following analogy may help one to see how the adjustment works. Suppose that men and women are entering a ballroom through separate doors, and we have the task of assigning partners to those that enter. If the males and females file into the room at the same speed then we can simply pair up each man with the woman that enters at the same time. But if the men begin to flow into the room faster than the women, this won't work. We have two options. One is to let the number of matches be determined by the slower flow of entering women. 'Surplus' males might be turned away (or put in storage near the refrigerator). Alternatively, we might try to reach back into the line of women to find partners for every man that enters. Although this could not work as a permanent solution if the men continued to enter faster than the women, it could be a successful strategy if the speeds of the two lines will eventually adjust so that the women enter faster than the men. Thus we might succeed in assigning a partner to each man and woman in spite of the short-run problem caused by the different speeds at which the two groups enter the room.

When husbands tend to be older than their wives, fluctuating cohort sizes create exactly this kind of problem. If cohort sizes are relatively constant then men and women can form marriages with a two- or three-year age-difference between spouses without difficulty. A temporary decrease in fertility, however, will be analogous to women beginning to enter the ballroom at a slower speed, since younger cohorts will be smaller than their predecessors. We would predict then, that the marriage market would have to respond with some combination of a decrease in the proportion of males marrying and an increase in the age-difference between spouses. The increase in the

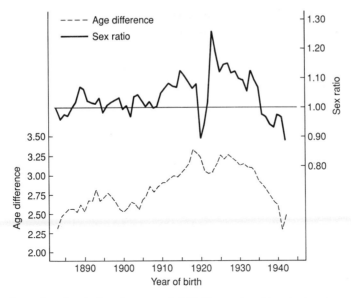

Note: Sex-ratio: number of males born in year *t* – 3 divided by number of females born in year *t*. Age-difference: mean age at marriage of men born in year *t* – 3 minus mean age at marriage of women born in year *t*.

Figure 2.5 Sex-Ratio and Husband–Wife Age-Differences in Sweden, 1883–1942

age-difference corresponds to reaching further down the line of women to find matches for all of the men in the ballroom analogy above. An increase in fertility would have the opposite effect, leading to increases in the relative proportion of males from previous cohorts marrying and a decrease in the age-difference between spouses.

Swedish marriage data make it possible to analyse adjustments in both the age-difference between spouses and in proportions marrying in response to cohort size fluctuations. Fig. 2.5 presents evidence on the potential contribution of changes in the age-difference between spouses in absorbing the large fluctuations in cohort size in Sweden over the period 1883–1942. Published data giving cross-tabulations of age of husband by age of wife in single years of age do not exist. An approximate time-series for the age-difference between husbands and wives can be constructed by comparing the mean age of marriage for women with the mean age of marriage for men born three years earlier, roughly corresponding to the average cohort these women marry into. Fig. 2.5 presents a time-series of the difference between the mean age at marriage of female cohorts and the mean age at marriage of males from the cohort three years older. Fig. 2.5 also shows the sex-ratio (the ratio of males born in year *t* – 3 to females born in year *t*) for comparison.

Fig. 2.6 presents a series that compares the proportion of females married by age 40 in each cohort with the proportion of males married by age 40 in

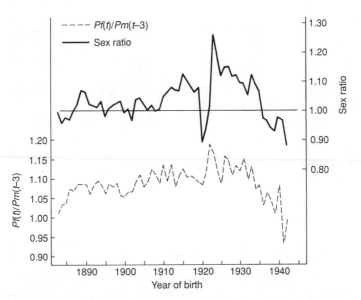

Note: Sex-ratio: number of males born in year *t* − 3 divided by number of females born in year *t*.
Relative proportions marring: proportion married by age 40 of women born in year *t* divided by
proportion married by age 40 of men born in year *t* − 3.

Figure 2.6   Sex-Ratio and Relative Proportions of Males and Females Marrying
in Sweden, 1883–1942

the cohort born three years earlier. Specifically, the graph shows the ratio of
the proportion of women married by age 40 to the proportion of men married
by age 40 in the cohort born three years earlier. The figure also shows the
sex-ratio (the ratio of males born in year *t* − 3 to females born in year *t*) for
comparison.

Figs. 2.5 and 2.6 indicate that both husband–wife age-differences and relative proportions marrying move in directions consistent with the adjustments
implied by long-term and short-term changes in sex-ratios. The male–female
sex-ratio begins to increase above unity beginning in about 1900. At the same
time, the age-gap between spouses begins to rise and the relative proportion
of males marrying begins to decrease. The effects of short-term fluctuations
can be seen in the experience of the unusually large 1920 cohort. The reduced male–female sex-ratios caused by the fertility boom in about 1920 are
associated with a decline in the age-gap between spouses and a decrease in
the relative proportion of females marrying, in comparison to adjacent cohorts.
The decrease in the male–female sex-ratio beginning in the mid 1920s, a
result of the slowdown and eventual reversal of the major fertility decline of
previous decades, also leads to a decline in the age-difference between spouses
and a decrease in the relative proportion of females marrying.

In order to look more closely at the relationship between the sex-ratio and
the age-difference, we present estimates of a regression using the time-series

Table 2.1. Ordinary Least-Squares Regression Age-Difference between Husband and Wife by Male–Female Sex-Ratio in Sweden, 1883–1942

Variable	Coefficient	Standard error	*T*-statistic	Mean	Standard deviation
Age-Difference (*Dependent Variable*)				2.842	0.268
Sex-ratio	2.2608	0.4036	5.601	1.037	0.070
Constant	0.4979	0.4194	1.187		
R^2	.3510				
N	60				

Notes: The dependent variable is the difference between the mean age at marriage of males born in year $t-3$ and the mean age at marriage of females of born in year t. The sex-ratio is the ratio of the number of males born in year $t-3$ (evaluated at age 15) to the number of women born in year t (evaluated at age 15).

of the age-difference between spouses and the male–female sex-ratio. Table 2.1 shows the results of the regression for the set of cohorts born from 1883 to 1942, the cohorts for which our data provide complete marriage histories up to age 40. The results show a statistically significant effect in the predicted direction. Higher sex-ratios (i.e. ratios of males born in year $t-3$ to females born in year t) lead to increases in the age-difference between husbands and wives for that pair of cohorts.[3] Specifically, the results imply that an increase in the sex-ratio by .1 will raise the age-difference between spouses by .23 years. The predicted mean age-difference between husbands and wives when the sex-ratio is 1 is about 2.75 years. The R^2 for the regression indicates that fluctuations in sex-ratios alone can explain 35 per cent of the variance in the age-difference between spouses over this 60-year period.

The relationship between the sex-ratio and the age-difference between spouses can be seen more directly in Fig. 2.7, which shows a scatterplot of the age-difference plotted against the sex-ratio. The figure also shows the ordinary least-squares regression line for the regression of the age-difference on the sex-ratio shown in Table 2.1. The plot shows a clear relationship in the predicted direction, with increases in the relative supply of potential husbands leading to increases in the age-gap between husbands and wives, a result consistent with the demographic constraint on marriage-market equilibrium.

A similar regression demonstrates that proportions marrying also respond to changes in the sex-ratio in Sweden during this period. Table 2.2 presents estimates of an OLS regression in which the dependent variable is the ratio of the proportion of males married in the cohort born in year $t-3$ to the proportion of females married in the cohort born in year t. This is the inverse

---

[3] More precisely, it leads to increases in the difference between the mean age at marriage of men born in year $t-3$ and the mean age at marriage of women born in year t, our proxy for the mean age-difference between husbands and wives for women born in year t.

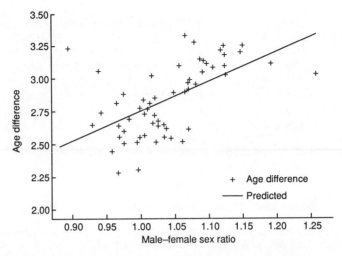

Note: Mean age at marriage of men born in year $t - 3$ minus mean age at marriage of women born in year t, and least-squares regression line.

Figure 2.7   Scatter-Plot of Sex-Ratio and Husband–Wife Age-Differences in Sweden, 1883–1942

Table 2.2.   Ordinary Least-Squares Regression Ratio of Proportion of Males and Females Marrying by Male–Female Sex-Ratio in Sweden, 1883–1942

Variable	Coefficient	Standard error	*T*-statistic	Mean	Standard deviation
$P_m (t - 3)/P_f(t)$ (*Dependent Variable*)				.920	0.038
Sex-ratio	–.3458	0.0536	– 6.447	1.037	0.070
Constant	1.2786	0.0557	22.944		
R^2	.4262				
N	60				

Notes: The dependent variable is the ratio of the proportion married by age 40 for males born in year $t - 3$ to the proportion married by age 40 for females born in year t. The sex-ratio is the ratio of the number of males born in year $t - 3$ (evaluated at age 15) to the number of women born in year t (evaluated at age 15).

of the ratio shown in Fig. 2.6. Once again, the results show a statistically significant effect in the predicted direction. In this case a higher sex-ratio (males born in year $t - 3$ to females born in year t) leads to decrease in the relative proportion of males marrying for that pair of cohorts. The R^2 for the regression indicates that fluctuations in sex-ratios alone can explain 43 per cent of the variance in the relative proportions of males and females marrying over the period 1883–1942.

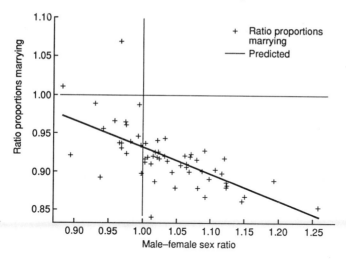

Note: Proportion married by age 40 of men born in year *t* – 3 divided by proportion married by age 40 of women born in year *t*, and least-squares regression line.

Figure 2.8 Scatter-plot of Sex-Ratio and Relative Proportions of Males and Females Marrying in Sweden, 1883–1942

Fig. 2.8 plots the ratio of proportions marrying and the predicted proportions implied by the regression in Table 2.2. The results imply that at a sex-ratio of unity only 93.2 per cent as many men marry as women. This is partly a result of the fact that only marriage histories up to age 40 are used, although the discrepancy between proportions of males and females marrying persists when marriage histories up until age 50 are used. The regression implies that an increase in the sex-ratio from 1 to 1.1 would decrease the relative proportion of men marrying from .932 to .889. If all of the 10 per cent 'surplus' of men were to go unmarried, then the relative proportion of men marrying would decline to $.9 \times .932 = .838$.[4] The change in the proportion marrying, then, accounts for something less than half of the response to the fluctuating sex-ratio, with adjustments in the age-difference between spouses working to absorb the remainder.

Marriage-Markets and the Linear Programming Assignment Algorithm

We believe that the descriptive data presented in the previous section can be better understood as the equilibrium of a marriage-market in which marriage

---

[4] The ratio shown is the ratio $p = \dfrac{M_m/N_m}{M_f/N_f}$, where M_i is the number married from sex i and N_i is the total number eligible for sex i. If we increase N_m by 10 per cent and leave all other values constant, p will decrease to $p/1.1 \approx .9p$.

behaviour must respond to the supply and demand for each sex and each cohort. In such a model, we would expect that persons of the same sex but different ages would be substitutes for each other, albeit imperfect substitutes, with persons being closer substitutes the closer their ages. In contrast to our equilibrium model, earlier, 'one-sex' models of marriage would find historical averages of age-specific marriage rates for one sex (usually female), and apply these rates to later age-distributions in order to project the number of marriages that will take place in subsequent periods. As should be evident from the descriptive statistics that we have just presented, a severe weakness of this approach is that a male one-sex model would predict very different numbers of marriages in any period than a female one-sex model. (One-sex models and their weaknesses are discussed in detail by Keyfitz (1971), McFarland (1972), Mahsam (1974), Das Gupta (1972), Schoen (1981), Sanderson (1983), Pollak (1986; 1987) and Caswell and Weeks (1986).)

Pollak (1986; 1987) has reformulated the 'two-sex problem' by replacing the constant age-specific fertility schedule of the classical theory with more fundamental relationships. These are a 'birth matrix' and a 'mating rule'. The birth matrix postulates an expected number of births per period from a marriage of an age i male to an age j female. The mating rule is a function that determines the number of marriages of type i males to type j females for all i and j as a function of the vector listing the numbers of males and females of each age and sex in the population. Pollak shows that if these relationships remain constant over time and if the mating rule follows certain natural conditions, the dynamic system so defined will converge to a constant equilibrium growth-rate, yielding a constant equilibrium age-structure. Pollak imposes only certain very general conditions on the mating function such as non-negativity, homogeneity, continuity, and that the number of persons of a given sex who marry must not exceed the number of persons of that age and sex in the population.

Pollak's mating rule can be thought of as a 'reduced form' description of the dependence on the outcome of a marriage-market on supplies and demands of the two sexes from various cohorts. Our model looks behind this reduced form by posing an explicit structure of pay-offs to the possible patterns of mating. We can then analyse marriage-market equilibrium under this structure. In particular, we take advantage of an idea proposed by Becker (1981), who suggested that the problem of finding an efficient and stable assignment of marriage partners can be usefully viewed as an application of the linear programming assignment problem.

The assignment problem was originally devised as a model for the efficient assignment of workers to jobs. For each worker, i, in job, j, there is a money value of output a_{ij} which could be produced if worker i is assigned job j. The assignment problem finds the assignment of workers to jobs that maximizes the total value of output subject to the constraint that each worker has only one job and each job is done by only one worker. The solution to the

assignment problem not only reveals an optimal assignment, but it also im-
putes 'shadow prices' to each worker and job in such a way that if each
worker were paid his shadow price as a wage and each job received its shadow
price as a rent, the optimal assignment would be a competitive equilibrium.

It would be reasonable to apply the assignment problem to the case of
marital sorting if the 'value' of a marriage could be measured by a single
number, as money income can. On the face of it, this seems an outrageous
simplification of what marriage is about. In a marriage there are many joint
decisions to be made about many matters that are far removed from money.
There may also be substantial differences in tastes, in skills, and in initial
wealth between potential marriage partners. As it turns out, we have been
able to show that the complexity of interaction in a marriage can be quite
well modelled by the presence of a large number of shared public goods in
the marriage. For a broad and interesting class of preferences over public and
private goods, it happens that there is 'transferable utility'. This means that
although many complex joint decisions must be reached about household
public goods, the efficient amount of public goods in a marriage is determined
independently of the distribution of private goods within the marriage. When
this is true, the assignment problem model of marriage as proposed by Becker
can be applied directly.[5]

We present here a simple model of the marriage-market that is empirically
implementable and yet rich enough to capture much of the character of the
marriage squeeze. Suppose that an individual's utility depends only on his or
her age at marriage and on consumption of private goods. Of course, any two
people who choose to marry each other must marry on the same day. This
effect can be nicely modelled by treating the date of the wedding as a local
public good, entering into both of the potential partners' utility functions.
Each person's wedding date enters their utility function because this date
determines their age of marriage.

Let $\overline{A}_i$ be person i's preferred age at marriage. To enable us to fit our
model empirically, suppose that individual i has a quadratic loss function for
marrying at a less than ideal age. In particular, let C_i be person i's consumption of private goods, let W_i be the year of i's marriage and B_i the year
of person i's birth. Then $A_i = W_i - B_i$ is i's age at marriage. Let $\overline{A}_i$ be i's most
preferred age of marriage. Then let person i's utility be given by

$$U_i(W_i, B_i, C_i) = C_i - [(W_i - B_i) - \overline{A}_i]^2.$$

Suppose now that male i and female j are contemplating marriage. Their utility
functions belong to the class of utility functions for which the optimal choice
of public goods is independent of how the private goods are distributed in the
marriage. As demonstrated in Bergstrom and Lam (1989), the implication of
these special functions is that the optimal time for i and j to marry if they do

---

[5] A detailed description of how this works out can be found in Bergstrom and Cornes (1981;
1983). For an application to the issue of assortative mating see Lam (1988).

marry is exactly half-way between the favourite date of i and the favourite date of j.

Consider, for example, a male i born in 1924 and a female j born in 1926. Suppose that i's preferred age at marriage is 25 and j's preferred age at marriage is 21. Then i would prefer to marry in 1949 and j would prefer to marry in 1947. The efficient time for this couple to marry if they do marry would be in 1948. In this case, each person would be missing his or her favourite age of marriage by one year. Because of the special utility function that we have assumed, the model displays transferable utility. That is, for any two people i and j of opposite sexes, there is a number A_{ij} which is the total utility generated by an optimally timed marriage between i and j. Persons i and j can divide this utility in any way that adds up to A_{ij} by redistributing private goods between them.

Suppose that all males preferred to marry at age $\overline{A}_m$ and that all females preferred to marry at age $\overline{A}_f$. Then, given the assumption of a quadratic loss function, we can find the pay-off matrix which reports the value A_{ij} of a marriage between a cohort i male and a cohort j female. This is the structure we will impose in order to apply our model to Sweden. Since we know from our historical series the number of persons of each cohort and sex, once we impose a pay-off matrix we can solve a linear program to assign the cohorts to each other in an optimal way.

Comparing Predicted to Actual Swedish Marriage Patterns

The equilibrium model that we will compare with the Swedish historical data is one of extreme simplicity. We assume that individuals do not care who they marry, but only care about when they marry, and that the difference between the preferred marriage age of males and the preferred marriage age of females has been constant throughout the entire period and is equal to three years. Specifically, we assume that the matrix of pay-offs to possible pairings of male and female cohorts is that shown in Fig. 2.9. The zeros along the third super-diagonal indicate that marriages of males from a given cohort to females from the cohort born three years later are the 'best' marriages. The negative numbers indicate a utility loss compared to the ideal marriage for all other marriages, with the penalty increasing quadratically away from the diagonal of ideal marriages.

Given this pay-off matrix, we will use a linear programming algorithm to solve for the assignment of partners that maximizes the total pay-off from marriages in the population of men and women born in Sweden between 1895 and 1945. More precisely, these cohorts were measured by the number of persons of each cohort and sex who reached age 15 in Sweden between 1910 and 1960. In this way we avoid statistical problems caused by sex differences in infant mortality. This procedure also allows us to consider only

| | | Female birth cohort *j* | | | | | | | |
	⋯	1920	1921	1922	1923	1924	1925	1926	⋯
	⋮	⋮	⋮	⋮	⋮	⋮	⋮	⋮	⋮
	1920	... −9	−4	−1	0	−1	−4	−9	...
Male	1921	... −16	−9	−4	−1	0	−1	−4	...
birth	1922	... −25	−16	−9	−4	−1	0	−1	...
cohort	1923	... −36	−25	−16	−9	−4	−1	0	...
i	1924	... −49	−36	−25	−16	−9	−4	−1	...
	1925	... −64	−49	−36	−25	−16	−9	−4	...
	1926	... −81	−64	−49	−36	−25	−16	−9	...
	⋮	⋮	⋮	⋮	⋮	⋮	⋮	⋮	⋮

Figure 2.9 Pay-off Matrix for Swedish Marriage Assignments. Total utility from a marriage between male born in year *i* and female born in year *j* given quadratic loss function and three-year difference in ideal age at marriage for males and females.

persons who were in Sweden after 1910, at which time emigration from Sweden had essentially ceased. Given this pay-off matrix, we calculate the optimal assignment of partners, assuming that all males and females who reach the age of 15 are assigned marriage partners. One difficulty that has to be resolved is what to do about people born between 1895 and 1945 who married partners who were born outside this interval. We chose to follow the simple procedure of assuming that all women born in 1895, 1896, and 1897 married men who were born three years earlier than they and to assume that all men born in 1943, 1944, and 1945 married women who were three years younger than themselves. Therefore the population of people actually matched to each other by our assignment algorithm are the set of men born in the years from 1895 to 1942 and the set of women born in the years from 1898 to 1945.

The solution to our assignment problem is a 50 by 50 matrix whose *ij*th element is the number of males born in year *i* who marry females born in year *j*. In fact this assignment matrix is very sparse, with positive numbers of marriages concentrated close to the third super-diagonal, the diagonal corresponding to 'ideal' marriages. Actual demographic data on the distribution of age-differences between marriage partners will be much more dispersed than our predicted optimal assignments. The lack of dispersion predicted by our model comes from the fact that we have assumed that persons of the same age are all identical. If we were to allow a distribution of maturity levels among people of the same chronological level, we would obtain more realistic predictions on this account. But even our very simple model will make interesting predictions about the time-path of the mean age-difference between husbands and wives. For a given cohort of men, for example, we calculate the mean year of birth of the wives assigned to that cohort by our linear program.

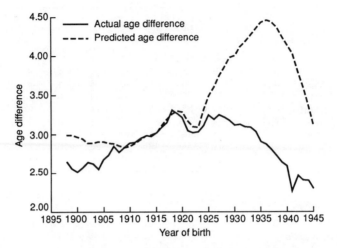

Figure 2.10 Husband–wife Age-Differences in Sweden, 1895–1945. Actual differences and differences predicted by linear program assignment algorithm.

Using this to calculate the mean age-difference between spouses for each cohort, we can compare our results to actual Swedish experience.

Fig. 2.10 shows the mean age-difference for husbands and wives for every female birth cohort resulting from our linear program. The line marked with circles corresponds to our assignments. The line marked with triangles reproduces the actual data for Sweden for the same years, based on the series shown above in Fig. 2.5. The graph has both good news and bad news regarding the ability of our simulated assignments to capture the actual history of age-differences between spouses in Sweden. For the period 1905 to 1923 our assignments track actual experience remarkably well. The most dramatic result is the similarity in the way our assignments deal with the extreme sex-ratio fluctuations between 1915 and 1925. Since these are the largest short-run fluctuations in the age-difference we actually observe in Sweden, our ability to replicate them is encouraging.

As can be seen in Fig. 2.10, our assignments begin to diverge from actual Swedish experience, starting with the cohorts born in the late 1920s. These are the people whose marriages took place in the 1950s and later. Our assignments predicted that the age-difference between husbands and wives would increase during this period, when in fact the actual age-difference declined quite steadily until the end of our period of observation.

Evidently our model is not capturing something that happened during the last part of the period. We can think of at least two important effects that we have left out. One omission is that we fitted our optimal assignments based on the assumption that all members of both sexes choose to marry. This would make no difference to the accuracy of our predictions if the proportions of each sex who marry were constant throughout the period. As Fig. 2.8 indicates, the proportion of members of a given sex and cohort who marry is inversely related to the abundance of its members relative to the size of the sex-cohort group from which it would normally select marriage partners. These effects would tend to moderate the fluctuations in the age-gap between marriage partners that are induced by changes in the relative cohort sizes.

The most suspect of our assumptions is probably the assumption that the optimal age differential for couples remained constant over the entire period. As Fig. 2.3 shows, there was a steady secular decline in the mean age of marriage for the cohorts born after 1905, with a slightly faster decline for males than for females. If the preferred age of marriage for females fell at exactly the same rate as the preferred age of marriage for males, then there would be nothing wrong with our assumption that the optimal age differential remained constant. But, quite possibly, these preferred ages have not fallen at the same rate and the optimal age-difference has therefore diminished. This issue, too, will be addressed in later work.

Conclusions

Swedish cohort size and marriage experience during the twentieth century present intriguing questions. The age-difference between husbands and wives remained in the range of 2.5 to 3.5 years for all birth cohorts born between 1885 and 1940. Yet cohort size fluctuations over this period were so large that if every woman married a man three years older than her, the number of potential husbands per woman would fluctuate dramatically, ranging from .9 to 1.25 in periods as short as five years.

The first part of this paper describes the changes in patterns of age at marriage for each sex. We show that changes in the age-difference between spouses worked in the direction that we predict to respond to changes in sex-ratios. Relative proportions of males and females marrying also move in the direction we predict in response to changing sex-ratios. We discuss a model of marriage-market assignments that can be directly tested against the Swedish experience. In this model, the efficient assignment of marriage partners across birth cohorts can be interpreted as a linear programming assignment problem. We apply a very simple version of our model to the Swedish historical data. This model assumes a pay-off matrix in which the ideal marriages have husbands three years older than their wives, with deviations from this ideal penalized according to a quadratic loss function. The model attempts to assign partners to all men and women born during the period 1895–1945, using only adjustments in the age-difference between spouses to respond to fluctuating cohort sizes. Using the linear program to find the optimal set of marriage assignments between cohorts, we are able to replicate almost perfectly the rapid fluctuations in the age-difference between spouses actually observed in Sweden for the cohorts born between 1915 and 1925. This is the period of the most dramatic fluctuations in cohort size in recent Swedish history. The success of our much simplified model of marriage assignments in replicating actual Swedish marriage patterns during this period indicates that we have captured fundamental features of the way the marriage-market responds to changes in the relative supplies of males and females.

Our model is less successful at tracking the steady decline in the age-difference between spouses beginning with the late 1920s cohorts. We believe that there are two major sources of divergence between the predictions of our model and historical outcomes. First, our implementation of the assignment problem did not allow the proportions marrying to adjust to excess supplies or demands. Second, we assumed that the optimal age-difference between husbands and wives has remained constant over the entire period. Encouraged by our ability to capture some of the major features of Swedish marriage experience using a model in which adjustments occur only in the age-difference between spouses, we will attempt to enrich our model to incorporate non-stationarity and adjustments in proportions marrying.

References

Becker, G. (1973), 'A Theory of Marriage, Part I', *Journal of Political Economy*, 81 (July/Aug.), 813–47.

—— (1974), 'A Theory of Marriage, Part II', *Journal of Political Economy*, 82, S11–S26.

—— (1981), *A Treatise on the Family*, Cambridge, Mass.: Harvard University Press.

Bergstrom, T. and Cornes, R. (1981), 'Gorman and Musgrave are Dual or—An Antipodean Theorem on Public Goods', *Economic Letters*, 371–8.

—— (1983) 'Independence of Allocative Efficiency from Distribution in the Theory of Public Goods', *Econometrica*, 1753–65.

Bergstrom, T. and Lam, D. (1989), 'The Two-Sex Problem and the Marriage Squeeze in an Equilibrium Model of Marriage Markets', paper presented at Annual Meeting of the Population Association of America, Baltimore, Apr.

Caswell, H. and Weeks, D. E. (1986), 'Two-Sex Models: Chaos, Extinction, and Other Dynamic Consequences of Sex', *The American Naturalist*, 128, 707–35.

Das Gupta, P. (1972), 'On Two-Sex Models Leading to Stable Populations', *Theoretical Population Biology*, 3 (Sept.), 358–75.

Keyfitz, N. (1971), 'The Mathematics of Sex and Marriage', *Proceedings of the Sixth Berkeley Symposium on Mathematical Statistics and Probability*, iv, Berkeley: University of California Press.

Koopmans, T. and Beckman, M. (1957) 'Assignment Problems and the Location of Economic Activities', *Econometrica*, 25, 53–76.

Lam, D. (1988), 'Marriage Markets and Assortative Mating with Household Public Goods', *Journal of Human Resources*, 23, 462–87.

McFarland, D. (1972), 'Comparison of Alternative Marriage Models', in T. E. Greville (ed.), *Population Dynamics*, New York: Academic Press, 89–106.

Muhsam, H. (1974), 'The Marriage Squeeze', *Demography*, 11 (May), 291–9.

Pollak, R. A. (1986), 'A Reformulation of the Two-Sex Problem', *Demography* 23, 247–59.

—— (1987), 'The Two-Sex Problem with Persistent Unions: A Generalization of the Birth Matrix-Mating Rule Model, *Theoretical Population Biology* 32, 176–87.

Sanderson, W. (1983), 'A Two-Sex General Equilibrium Marriage Model', in A. C. Kelley, W. C. Sanderson, and J. G. Williamson (eds.), *Modeling Growing Economies in Equilibrium and Disequilibrium*, Durham, NC: Duke University Press.

Schoen, R. (1981), 'The Harmonic Mean as the Basis of Realistic Two-Sex Marriage Model', *Demography* 18, 201–16.

3 Economic Considerations in the Timing of Births: Theory and Evidence

ALESSANDRO CIGNO

Introduction

Two notable features of fertility behaviour in Western Europe and elsewhere in industrialized countries since the end of the Second World War have been a steady decline in completed fertility (the total number of children born to a woman) and fluctuations in the tempo of fertility (the distribution of those births over the mother's fecund period). In Italy, for example, completed fertility has fallen from 2.11 for the cohort of women born in 1939–40, to 2.06 for the one born in 1944–5, to only 1.89 for that of 1949–50. The proportion of that fertility realized before the mother reached age 30 has, however, risen from 68 per cent in the 1939–40 cohort to 74 per cent in the 1944–5 cohort, only to fall to 72 per cent in that of 1949–50. A similar picture emerges for the rest of Western Europe.[1]

As it portends a slow-down in population growth, and an eventual fall in population size, the decline in completed fertility may be thought to be a good or a bad thing depending on how one weighs the advantages of less crowded living conditions against the disadvantages of an ageing population. By contrast, oscillations in the tempo of fertility cannot be regarded as anything other than a costly nuisance, because they cause the period birth-rate to fluctuate, thereby putting strain on the labour-market, on the provision of health and educational services, and on pay-as-you-go pension systems (for a discussion of these issues, see Cigno 1991, chap. 10). Understanding how a couple chooses the dates of birth of its children is, therefore, at least as important as understanding how it decides on the number of children it wishes to have.

There is a further consideration that makes the analysis of birth timing particularly relevant for ageing societies. This is that, in a situation where most women will give birth to zero, one, or two children, over a fertile life-

This paper has benefited from written comments by the discussant, David Lam, and from editorial advice by John Ermisch. Oral comments by Ronald Lee, Robert Willis, and other participants in the Sendai seminar are also gratefully acknowledged. Remaining shortcomings are solely the author's responsibility.

[1] See Höpflinger (1984), Muñoz-Perez (1986).

span of more than thirty years, parents have many degrees of freedom in the choice of the dates of birth of their children. If, as I will show, these timing decisions respond systematically to changes in the economic environment, it is then clear that such changes may trigger very sharp fluctuations in the birth-rate and, consequently, in the age-structure of the population. I would argue, for example, that the rapid decline of the Italian birth-rate over the last two decades or so is to a greater extent the result of a decision to postpone the date of birth of the first (and, for many couples, only) child, than of a desire to further reduce completed fertility. Since there are physiological limits to the extent to which births can be postponed, predictions of future age-structures based on the extrapolation of current fertility trends could be excessively pessimistic.

The Cost of a Child

Let us suppose, along with Becker (1981), that parents derive satisfaction not only from consumption, but also from the quantity and quality of children they put into the world (for alternative views, see Cigno, 1991, chap. 9). The quality of a child—intended here to mean the parents' perception of the quality of life awaiting that child—will increase with the amount of time and commodities expended on the child. Clearly, some minimum amount of specifically maternal time and commodity expenditure is strictly required to put a child into the world and keep him or her alive through childhood. Above those minima—which can be regarded as a kind of set-up cost—commodities, including hired help, and parental time will be substitutable for each other. For simplicity, I shall assume that they are perfectly substitutable. Assuming, further, that the opportunity-cost of a unit of parental time is never less than the cost of hiring an equivalent unit of external help, we can then think of the quality of a child born at a certain date t as an increasing function of the present value at t, I_t, of all non-essential expenditures (including any bequests) incurred by the parents on behalf of that child.

The wage-rate that a person is able to command at any given date may be characterized as the market return to the stock of human capital held by that person at that date.[2] Assume that human capital accumulates at the rate β per unit of time spent in the labour-market. Assume, also, that raising children is, for a woman, the only alternative to paid employment. Setting equal to unity the amount of maternal time required for each child, a woman's labour supply at any date t is $(m - B_t)$, where m denotes her work capacity and B_t the number of children born at t. Thus, the full cost to the parents of having a child at date t is

$$P_t = q + I_t + W_t + \beta\omega\Sigma_{\tau=t+1}^{T}(m - B_\tau)(1 + r)^{t-\tau}, \qquad (1)$$

[2] See Becker (1975).

where q is essential expenditure, W_t the mother's wage rate at t, ω the market rate of return to human capital, r the real interest rate (i.e. the rate of return to other assets) and T the date of the mother's death. It is thus the sum of an actual outlay, an immediate loss of earnings, and a human-capital loss measured by the present value of future wage increments foregone.

Interestingly, a recent analysis of the US National Longitudinal Surveys of Labor Market Experience, Calhoun and Espenshade (1988), finds that, while

... 50 per cent of the impact of each child on foregone lifetime hours of market work occurs within the first five years following the birth of the child ... [the] effect on foregone earnings is more prolonged ... It takes roughly ten years following a birth before 50 per cent of the total impact of each child on foregone market earnings is realised, because potential hourly earnings continue to increase with age as a woman gains additional labour market experience.

In other words, each birth causes a capital loss, as well as an immediate loss of earnings.

The same study finds that the number of working hours lost for each child, while declining in successive cohorts, is insensitive to number of children in the family, and varies much less than expenditure per child across women with different socio-economic characteristics. While the US evidence may not be generally applicable, the assumption of a fixed time-requirement per child appears to be an acceptable simplification as far as women belonging to the same cohort are concerned.[3]

Even with these simplifications, however, the relationship between pattern of childbearing and cost of a child is highly complex. Leaving aside the be-haviour of out-of-pocket expenditure, about which we have nothing to say yet, it is in fact clear from (1) that the opportunity-cost (earnings forgone, plus human-capital loss) of a birth depends not only on its timing, but also on the number and dates of all other births.

For example, the opportunity-cost of a birth will be smaller if the mother has or will have more children, than if she has and will have none, because in the first case either the current wage foregone or the capital loss will be lower. Postponing a birth will raise the current wage loss, but lower the capital loss. The opportunity-cost may thus rise or fall, but it is more likely to fall if the woman already had children and will have no more, than if she has none and will have more, for in the first case the current wage loss is smaller, relative to the capital loss, than in the second.

There is thus no reason to expect that the cost of having a child will always increase or always decrease as, say, the date of birth is postponed. Indeed, no such simple relationship has been established empirically. Consequently, there is no reason to expect that a cost-minimizing birth profile can be determined by a simple rule such as 'have your children as soon as possible' or 'have

[3] Economies of scale would complicate decisions about birth-timing because they create a case for compression of births, whether late or early in the reproductive years.

them as late as possible'. If we want to find answers to our questions, it seems, we have no alternative but to travel the long road of inter-temporal optimization.

Efficient Childbearing Patterns

Following a recent theoretical investigation of inter-temporal family decisions (Cigno, 1989), let us then assume that the parents' lifetime preferences are representable by a weakly separable utility function

$$U = U\left[\sum_{t=a}^{T} u_t(C_t), \sum_{t=a}^{T} v_t(I_t)_t B\right] \tag{2}$$

where a and T denote, respectively, the mother's age at marriage and at death, and C_t is parental consumption at t. The function $U(\cdot)$ is assumed to be strictly quasi-concave, while $u_t(\cdot)$ is strictly concave like $v_t(\cdot)$.

As usual in this type of model, we may interpret $u_t(C_t)$ as the specific satisfaction that the decision-makers, the parents in our case, derive from spending the sum C_t for their own consumption at date t—which may be different (e.g. because the parents in question are impatient to consume) from the satisfaction they would derive from consuming the same amount at a different date. In similar fashion, we may interpret $v_t(I_t)$ as the specific satisfaction that parents derive from spending I_t on a child born at t—which may be different from the satisfaction they would derive from spending the same amount on a child born at a different date. The dependence of v_t on I_t reflects the assumptions made earlier that parents care about the quality of their children's lives and, furthermore, that this quality increases with the amount spent. As for the time-dependence of v_t, this could be purely a reflection of parental time-preference (some couples may be impatient to savour the joys of parenthood, while others might prefer to reserve that for their more mature years), but it could also arise, partly, from parental belief that the quality of the child will vary, holding expenditure constant, with the age of the mother (e.g. because the risk that the child will be born with certain types of handicap increases as the mother approaches the end of her fecund life-span).

In the light of earlier discussion, the budget constraint will be

$$\sum_{t=a}^{T} \left[B_t(q + I_t) + C_t\right](1+r)^{a-t} = A_a + \sum_{t=a}^{T} L_t W_t (1+r)^{a-t}, \tag{3}$$

where

$$L_t = m - B_t \geq 0 \tag{4}$$

denotes the woman's labour supply at t,

$$W_t = \omega(K_a + \beta \sum_{\tau=a}^{t-1} L_\tau) \tag{5}$$

her wage rate at t, K_a her endowment of marketable human capital at marriage, and A_a the couple's assets (defined to include the present value of the husband's lifetime earnings, as well as financial assets), also at marriage.

For an interior solution, a sequence $\{B_t, C_t, I_t, L_t\}$ maximizing (2) subject to (3) will satisfy the dynamic conditions

$$\frac{u_t' - u_{t+1}'}{u_{t+1}'} = r, \tag{6}$$

$$\frac{v_t' - v_{t+1}'}{v_{t+1}'} = r \tag{7}$$

and

$$\frac{(P_{t+1}/v_{t+1}) - (P_t/v_t)}{(P_t/v_t)} = r. \tag{8}$$

The first two of these conditions are easily recognizable as instances of the principle (the Ramsey–Keynes rule) that utility-yielding expenditure must be distributed over time so that its marginal utility will decline at the (real) rate of interest. The third, by contrast, is an inter-temporal arbitrage condition on the normalized 'price' (full cost) of a child: the price per unit of utility at $(t + 1)$, (P_{t+1}/v_{t+1}), must be equal to $(1 + r)$ times the same price at t, (P_t/v_t). If (P_{t+1}/v_{t+1}) were less than $(1 + r)$ (P_t/v_t), it would in fact pay the parents to delay until $(t + 1)$ any birth planned for t, and to lend the sum saved by not having children then at the rate r. Conversely, if (P_{t+1}/v_{t+1}) were more than $(1 + r)$ (P_t/v_t), parents would borrow to anticipate to t any birth planned for $(t + 1)$. Therefore, at an interior optimum, the normalized price of having a child will grow at the rate of interest. All three conditions, it should be noted, descend from the assumption, implicit in (3), that parents-to-be can borrow or lend any amount at the given rate r.

All this ignores the problem that, for any particular couple, the period birth-rate can only be an integer or, if the length of the period is different from nine months, a ratio of integers. If the model were intended to represent the decision process of literally one couple, it might then be impossible to distribute births over time so as to satisfy (8). A way round this is to interpret the solution to the model as the average behaviour of a very large number of couples with similar characteristics, so that it makes sense to approximate the period birth-rate by a continuous variable.

Once we have solved that problem, we must then enquire whether preferences and market conditions are likely to be such that the model will have an interior solution—in particular, whether the optimal birth-rate and labour supply are likely to both be positive for a number of consecutive periods sufficiently large to make (7)–(8) empirically relevant. We have already noted that, on cost considerations alone, parents are unlikely to want to have all their children either as early or as late as possible. This is not likely to be altered by utility considerations. Indeed, given diminishing marginal utilities, utility maximization can be safely expected to spread childbearing out further, rather than concentrate it near any particular date. Indeed there is some evidence that this is what actually happens. If we look at the actual fertility histories of groups of married women with similar personal characteristics, like those shown in Figs. 3.1 to 3.3 (and discussed below) we observe, in fact, that the annual birth-rate never falls to zero for at least the first ten years of married life. We also observe that the birth-rate never reaches a level so high that the mother would have no time left to participate in the labour-market (the highest it gets is less than one birth for every three women in one year). It thus seems worthwhile to investigate the properties of interior solutions.

Next we ask what (7) and (8) tell us, in general, about the characteristics of an optimal distribution of births over time. In other words, are there any 'efficiency' characteristics, common to all optimizing fertility histories irrespective of parental preferences (provided only that those preferences yield an interior solution)? In very general terms, it seems not. However, if v_t is isoelastic with respect to I_t, we have that P_t must grow at the same proportional rate as I_t. Therefore, since q is a constant, the opportunity-cost component (current wage forgone, plus human-capital loss) of the full cost of having a child must also tend to grow, as t becomes larger, at the same proportional rate as I_t. Now, the growth-rate of I_t may be positive or negative, according to whether the real interest rate is greater or smaller than the rate of parental time-preference for children implicit in $v_t(\cdot)$. If the rate of time-preference were greater than r, for example, I_t would decline, i.e. parents would spend less for each successive child. Consequently, the opportunity-cost also would tend to decline. Empirical evidence for the United States reported in Calhoun and Espenshade (1988) suggests that this is indeed the case.

Let us then suppose that the rate of time-preference for children is greater than the real interest rate, so that the opportunity-cost of having a child at t has to decrease as t increases. As pointed out earlier, postponing the birth of a child lowers the opportunity-cost if the consequent fall in the human-capital cost is larger than the rise in the current wage cost. If r were equal to zero, the current wage cost would increase, in moving from t to $(t + 1)$, by $\beta\omega(m - B_t)$, while the capital cost would decrease by $\beta\omega(m - B_{t+1})$. Therefore, if that were the case, a declining opportunity-cost would clearly imply a declining birth-rate. Assuming that r is normally greater than zero, however, the capital cost will fall by a smaller amount, because of discounting, and precisely by $\beta\omega(m - B_{t+1})$ minus the interests on the capital loss of having a child at date t. As the capital loss at t is lower the higher the birth-rate at $(t + 1)$, we may then have fluctuations in the optimal birth-profile.

Cigno (1989) derives explicit solutions for (6)–(7)–(8) under the following parameterization:

$$u_t(C_t) \equiv C_t^\gamma (1 + \delta)^{a-t}, \ 0 < \gamma < 1, \tag{9}$$

and

$$v_t(I_t) \equiv I_t^\alpha (1 + \phi)^{-t}, \ 0 < \alpha < 1. \tag{10}$$

For ϕ (the parameter representing the rate of time-preference for children) greater than r, the solution path of I_t turns out to be downward-sloping all the way, while the solution for B_t turns out to be the sum of two terms, one decreasing all along, the other fluctuating (but tending to disappear as t grows large). For a range of plausible values of r, the birth-profile predicted by the model under this particular parameterization traces the observed profiles rather well. We may then conclude, somewhat tentatively, that parents are more likely to want to have their children early rather than late in married life, and that births may be optimally planned to arrive in batches. For example, using Fig. 3.2 for illustration, as if the charts shown were generated by our model, a married woman in a clerical occupation wanting, say, two children in all is likely to plan those births close together between the fourth and fifth year of marriage. After solving the system of difference equations (6)–(7)–(8) for unspecified initial values of the variables, the solution process is reduced to finding optimal B_a, C_a, and I_a.

The Effects of Personal Characteristics and the Economic Environment

Cigno (1989) shows how the solution sequence is affected[4] by differences in A_a, K_a, and β across women, and by changes in q and ω, under the parameterization shown in (9)–(10).

All the exogenous variables affect the fertility profile via the choice of B_a and I_a. A rise in B_a lifts the whole profile without altering its shape. Other things being equal, a higher B_a is thus associated with higher completed fertility, without any difference in tempo. A rise in I_a, by contrast, lowers the birth-profile, but also makes it decline more steeply, so that fewer children are born, but their dates of birth are more heavily concentrated in the earlier part of marriage. Other things being equal, a higher I_a is thus associated with lower completed fertility, but higher tempo. Additionally, β and ω affect the tempo of fertility in a more direct way as parameters of equations (7) and (8).

---

[4] Moffitt (1984) derives optimal fertility-profiles under very similar assumptions, and comes to conclusions similar to those discussed in the last section about the likely shapes of the profiles. However, the optimal-control format makes that model too complex to yield comparative-dynamics results.

The impacts of A_a, K_a, a, and q on B_a and I_a are generally ambiguous, but some predictions can be made under the usual assumptions that income-effects are dominated by substitution effects, that quality and quantity of children are normal goods, and that the marginal utility of 'children' (the second argument of $U(\cdot)$), does not fall too precipitously. Even so, the effect of initial assets and husband's lifetime earnings on completed fertility remains ambiguous, because both B_a and I_a are increasing functions of A_a, but their effect on tempo is clearly positive. The tempo also rises, but completed fertility falls with any rise in the woman's age at marriage, or in her initial stock of marketable human capital, or in the level of essential expenditure for each child, because B_a is decreasing, and I_a increasing, in a, K_a, and q.

By contrast, the effects of β and ω on B_a and I_a remain ambiguous. Since β and ω directly affect the shape of the birth profile, making it less steep, it is, however, tempting to surmise that their indirect effects (via B_a and I_a) are dominated by the direct effects. Under this further assumption, it can then be concluded that the tempo of fertility is lower for women with steeper career profiles, and will fall if the rate of return to their marketable human capital rises.

In retrospect, none of these comparative-dynamics results is difficult to explain. Since early children have, other things being equal, higher quality than late children, wealthier women have their children earlier, but do not necessarily have more because they also spend more on each child. Women who marry late have fewer children, but have them earlier in married life, because the cost of having a child of any given quality at any given marriage duration is higher for these women than for women who marry early.

A rise in essential expenditure per child, or a higher stock of marketable human capital at marriage, makes it more expensive to increase the quantity of children, but not to increase their quality, which depends only on birth-timing and on non-essential expenditure. Therefore, higher q or K_a will be associated with fewer, but higher-quality, children. Given convexity, this higher quality will be achieved partly by spending more on each child, but partly also by having children earlier. Hence, higher q or K_a will be associated with lower completed fertility and a higher tempo of childbearing.

Other things being equal, the full cost of having a child (P_t) grows more quickly for women whose wage-rate is more directly related to work experience (higher β), than for other women. But the growth-rate of (P_t/v_t) must be the same (equal to r) for all women. Since v_t increases with I_t, the only way of achieving this equality is to let the opportunity-cost element in P_t grow more slowly for high-β than for low-β women. Other things being equal, women with steeper career profiles will then work more in the early part of married life, and have children later than women whose earning ability is not much affected by work experience. The same explanation applies to the effect of the rate of return to marketable human capital, ω.

These results also have policy implications. Taxation of property income and married men's earnings (lower A_a) raises the tempo of fertility, while taxation of married women's earnings (lower ω) has the opposite effect. Reducing wage discrimination against women (both in the sense of equal pay for equal work, and of access to a wider range of careers) reduces the tempo because it raises ω. Child subsidies (lower q) and policies aimed at reducing the age of marriage (lower a) raise completed fertility, but lower the tempo. More education for women reduces completed fertility, but raises the tempo, because it increases K_a.

Uncertainty

All this is on the assumption of perfect birth control and perfect foresight of market conditions. In reality, parents cannot determine the date of birth of a child with any precision. All they are able to determine, through their choice of fertility controls, is the probability that a birth will occur at any given date. Furthermore, parents cannot know, at the date of marriage, how market conditions will evolve over the rest of their life. Consequently, if we want to explain observed behaviour, we should model rational parents as making conditional plans, such that their actions at each date depend on the number of children actually born, and on all market information available, by that date.

Unfortunately, however, modelling birth-timing decisions in a stochastic environment is remarkably difficult. In order to construct tractable models, researchers have thus found it necessary to make drastic simplifications—jettisoning, in effect, much of the economic content. In Newman (1983), for example, income is exogenous, so there is no problem of allocation of the woman's time between income and child-raising. Furthermore, the time and monetary costs of children are fixed, and the only stochastic elements are the dates of births and deaths, with the probability of the former conditional on the level of contraceptive efficiency chosen by the parents. The probability of a birth is conditional on the chosen level of contraceptive efficiency also in Hotz and Miller (1986). The woman's labour supply is endogenous, but her wage rate is a random variable unaffected by work experience. Furthermore, parents are not allowed to borrow or lend, so that the lifetime budget constraint breaks into a sequence of annual budgets.

As a consequence of these simplifications, such models tend to have unrealistic 'bang bang' solutions, with the probability of childbearing piled up either at the start of marriage or at the end of the mother's fecund life-span. In spite of the simplifications, such models have also proved impervious to comparative-dynamics analysis. All we have so far, if we want to explain empirical regularities in fertility behaviour, are thus the predictions of the non-stochastic theory outlined in earlier sections.

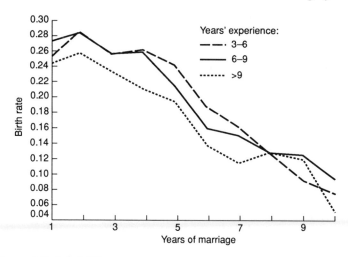

Source: Cigno and Ermisch (1989).
Fig. 3.1 Birth-Rate by Marriage Duration and Years of Work Experience at Marriage

Two Empirical Studies

This section summarizes two recent empirical studies, both of which aim to test the predictions of the theory on data from the Women and Employment Survey. This survey reports the marital, childbearing, and employment histories of a nationally representative sample of British women aged 16–59 in 1980. In order to eliminate complications arising from changes of partner, and to obtain at least approximate measures of completed fertility, women who had not been married to the same man for at least ten years were excluded from the analysis (leaving, none the less, more than 1,600 respondents in the sample).

The data are summarized in Figs. 3.1 to 3.3, which show the average fertility profiles, by duration of marriage, for different categories of women. It is interesting to note how the birth-rate tends to fluctuate around a downward trend in the manner predicted by the theory. Notice, also, how the pattern of childbearing differs for women with different amounts of work experience before marriage, different types of occupation before childbearing, and different levels of education at marriage.

Cigno and Ermisch (1989) estimate an ordered probit model relating the number of children born to a married woman by each year of marriage (up to the tenth) to that woman's observed characteristics at marriage. The procedure accounts for the fact that the number of children born to any particular woman must be a whole number. The estimated model is used in the paper to simulate the average birth-profiles of various groups of women,

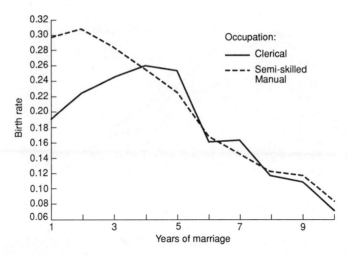

Source: Cigno and Ermisch (1989)
Fig. 3.2 Birth-Rate by Marriage Duration and Occupation in Last Job before First Birth

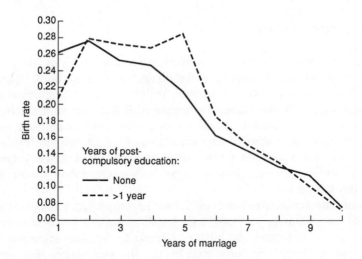

Source: Cigno and Ermisch (1989)
Fig. 3.3 Birth-Rate by Marriage Duration and Years of Post-Compulsory Education

characterized by different combinations of personal characteristics. Differences in these characteristics turn out to be generally associated with differences in both the total number and time-distribution of births desired. As a consequence, it is difficult, in some cases, to distinguish differences of tempo from differences of quantum merely by comparing the birth-profiles associated with different personal characteristics. For this reason, the paper also reports the results of a 'two-limit' tobit analysis of the effects of the same characteristics on two measures of 'early parenthood' (the percentages of completed fertility realized in the first two and the first three years of marriage).

Consistently with the theory, the econometric analysis shows that wealth at marriage (A_a, proxied by the husband's estimated lifetime earnings), wife's age at marriage (a), and wife's endowment of marketable human capital at marriage (K_a, proxied by work experience and number of years of post-compulsory education before marriage) raise the tempo of fertility, while the steepness of the wife's career profile (β, proxied by type of occupation before the birth of the first child) lowers it.

The estimated effect of marriage age on completed fertility (measured by number of children after ten years of marriage) is negative as the theory predicts. The estimated effect of the woman's human capital on completed fertility is negative, as in the theory, if human capital is proxied by work experience, but not if it is proxied by post-compulsory education. This last inconsistency may be taken as an indication that the income-effect of education is not dominated by the substitution-effect as assumed in order to arrive at a firm theoretical prediction. Alternatively, since the estimated effect of wealth on completed fertility is positive, and since wealth is only imperfectly proxied by husband's earnings, the positive effect of education on completed fertility could signify that women who, by birth or marriage, enjoy higher wealth, also tend to have higher education.

The econometric procedure adopted by Cigno and Ermisch does not allow for the fact that the birth of a child alters the mother's characteristics, and may thus alter her behaviour. Furthermore, the procedure does not allow for the accumulation of information about market conditions and the tax-benefit system. In other words, the econometric procedure presupposes, as does the theoretical model with no uncertainty, that parents make unconditional lifetime plans at the date of marriage, and stick to those plans come what may.

An implication of this approach is that it cannot be used to estimate the effects on the behaviour of an individual woman of unanticipated changes in q (e.g. as a result of changes in child-benefit provision) and in ω (e.g. as a result of income-tax changes, or of legislation outlawing sex discrimination in employment) because that would clash with the assumption that parents never change their plans.

A follow-up study of the same data, Barmby and Cigno (1990), recognizes that parents, aware of the imperfect controllability of fertility and of the imperfect predictability of the economic environment, make conditional lifetime plans. According to this view, actions taken at any date can then be expected to depend on all information available by that date. Consequently, the probability that a child is born to a particular woman at a particular date will depend on her fertility history up to then, and on environmental information available at that date, as well as on her characteristics and information available at the time of marriage. Time-series information about wage-rates, taxes, and benefits are used to supplement the survey data for this purpose.

The probability of a child being born to a particular woman in a particular year is modelled there as a logit function of a vector of explanatory variables including—in addition to those figuring in the earlier study—current environmental variables such as the average female and the average male wage-rate, and the benefits payable for a first and for a second child in that year. The dependence of the probability of a birth on the mother's fertility history is captured by allowing the constant term in the exponent of the logit function to shift with the number of children previously born. To the extent that unobserved differences between women (tastes, natural fecundity, etc.) are reflected in the different fertility histories, this simple device has the additional advantage of eliminating a potential source of bias in the estimates.[5]

Despite the difference of econometric procedure, Barmby and Cigno (1990) confirm most of the results of Cigno and Ermisch (1989). Additionally, they find that an increase in the average female wage-rate (holding the male rate constant), causes the probability of a birth to decline more rapidly over the marriage period. The theoretical prediction, untested in the earlier study, that a rise in ω would lower the tempo of fertility is thus supported. By contrast, a rise in the benefit rate payable for the first child, corresponding to a fall in essential expenditure q, is found to raise the tempo of childbearing, rather than lower it as predicted by the theory.

Discussion

It transpires from the two empirical studies summarized in the last section that couples tend to behave, in most respects, as if they were optimizing over time under conditions of certainty. The one significant divergence between the predictions of the deterministic model and observed behaviour concerns the effect of child benefits on the tempo of childbearing: while the theory predicts that such payments tend to reduce the proportion of births occurring in the early part of marriage, it appears from the statistical analysis that the opposite may be true. That, it may be argued, is where uncertainty makes a difference.

According to the deterministic theory outlined in earlier sections, a rise in child-benefit rates makes child quantity cheaper, both in absolute terms and relative to quality. Given the assumption (borne out, where other variables are concerned, by the empirical analysis) that income-effects are dominated by substitution-effects, parents will then want to substitute quantity for quality, and will set out to achieve that partly by spending less on each child, and

---

[5] As pointed out in Heckman and Willis (1975) those unobserved differences generate dependence in the sequence of events described by the fertility profile.

partly by spending later. Consequently, parents will have more children later in life.

Given uncertainty, however, a change in child-benefit rates also affects the relative riskiness of alternative childbearing profiles because, like any other kind of state benefit, child benefits are completely certain in the short term, and less uncertain than income from market sources in the long term. Therefore, a rise in child benefit rates reduces the relative riskiness of plans that involve a greater proportion of income from such a source and, in particular, of plans that involve a greater concentration of benefit receipts in the immediate future (when child-benefit rates are certain to remain at the new, higher level). While reinforcing the positive effect on completed fertility, risk considerations could thus outweigh the negative substitution-effect of child benefits on the tempo of fertility, and encourage early parenthood as the data indicate.

It could also be argued, on the other hand, that the positive effect of child benefits on the tempo of childbirth reflects not uncertainty, but imperfections in the capital markets. If a young couple is unable to borrow against future earnings to finance a birth in the early years of marriage, its choice of birth-profile is then subject to a series of liquidity constraints in addition to a lifetime budget constraint. Under such circumstances, a rise in the child-benefit rate could raise the tempo of childbearing simply by relaxing the liquidity constraints.

Where the effects of other explanatory factors are concerned, however, there is considerable coincidence of theoretical and empirical predictions. Women entering marriage with a large endowment of marketable human capital are likely to have fewer children, but tend to have them earlier. Women intent on climbing steep career ladders are likely to have their children late. A high rate of return to a woman's stock of marketable human capital is likely to be associated with a low tempo of fertility.

These results provide elements for explaining the birth-rate fluctuations that have characterized industrial societies since the Second World War. As pointed out in the introductory section of this chapter, these fluctuations can scarcely be attributed to changes in completed fertility, since the latter has tended to fall steadily from one cohort to the next over the period considered. They have to be explained, therefore, in terms of changes in the tempo of fertility. The baby boom of the 1960s, for example, was the outcome of the rise in the tempo of fertility over the 1950s and 1960s, and subsequent fall at the start of the 1970s. What caused those changes of tempo? Three major changes have taken place, over the period in question, in the factors affecting a woman's participation in the labour-market. One has been the rapid increase in the amount of education received by women (more rapid than the corresponding increase for men, who started from a higher level). This will have had a positive effect on the tempo of fertility through its positive effect on human capital. The other two have been the increase in labour productivity (through technical progress) and the mitigation of sexual discrimination. Both these developments will have tended to raise the rate of return to human capital. The lessening of sexual discrimination, furthermore, has opened up to women career opportunities which it had previously been difficult or impossible for them to enter. Both these developments (corresponding to rises in our β and ω) will have had a negative effect on tempo.

All we have to hypothesize, therefore, in order to explain the fluctuation, is that the positive effect of increasing female education on the tempo of fertility predominated in the two earlier decades, as young women were still catching up with their male counterparts, while the negative effects, particularly that of diminishing discrimination, became predominant at the start of the 1970s (when some countries also passed legislation to that end). Changes in child-benefit and tax regimes may also have a role, particularly in explaining why the fluctuation was sharper in some countries than in others. However, since the phenomenon occurred at more or less the same time in so many different countries, it seems unlikely that local policy changes could actually have been the main cause of the fluctuation.

References

Barmby, T. and Cigno, A. (1990), 'A Sequential Probability Model of Fertility Patterns', *Journal of Population Economics*, 3, 31–51.

Becker, G. S. (1975), *Human Capital*, Chicago: University of Chicago Press.

—— (1981), *A Theory of the Family*, Cambridge, Mass: Harvard University Press.

Calhoun, C. A. and Espenshade, T. J. (1988), 'Childbearing and Wives' Foregone Earnings', *Population Studies*, 42, 5–37.

Cigno, A. (1989), 'The Timing of Births: A Theory of Fertility, Family Expenditures and Labour-Market Participation over Time', in A. Wenig and K. F. Zimmermann (eds.), *Demographic Change and Economic Development*, Berlin: Springer-Verlag.

—— (1991), *Economics of the Family*, Oxford: Clarendon Press.

—— and Ermisch, J. F. (1989), 'A Microeconomic Analysis of the Timing of Births', *European Economic Review*, 33, 737–60.

Heckman, J. J. and Willis, R. J. (1975), 'Estimation of a Stochastic Model of Reproduction', in N. E. Terleckyi (ed.), *Household Production and Consumption*, New York: NBER-Columbia University Press.

Höpflinger, F. (1984), 'Cohort Fertility in Western Europe: Comparing Fertility Trends in Recent Birth Cohorts', *Genus*, 40, 19–46.

Hotz, V. J. and Miller, R. A. (1986), 'The Economics of Family Planning', Pittsburgh: Carnegie-Mellon University.

Moffitt, R. (1984), 'Optimal Life-Cycle Profiles of Fertility and Labor Supply', *Research in Population Economics*, 5, 29–50.

Muñoz-Perez, F. (1986), 'Changements récents de la fecondité en Europe occidentale et nouveaux traits de la formation des familles', *Population*, 41, 447–62.

Newman, J. (1983), *A Stochastic Dynamic Model of Fertility*, New Orleans: Tulane University.

4 The Demographic Impact of Family Benefits: Evidence from a Micro-Model and from Macro-Data

DIDIER BLANCHET AND OLIVIA EKERT-JAFFÉ

This paper presents two ways to evaluate the impact of family allowances on fertility. The first approach consists of an a priori evaluation derived from a small micro-model of fertility behaviour. Inspired by some ideas from the new home economics, and remaining as analytically simple as possible, this model tries to describe a little more realistically, in our view, how people plan the successive births of their children. Taking into account the discrete character of individual fertility decisions, it will pay particular attention to the aggregation of these individual decisions in determining the total level of fertility and its changes in response to changes in family policy.

The second part is empirical and tests the macro-implications of the first model by analysing fertility and family benefits across OECD countries since the early 1970s. This is done by deriving from this first model an aggregate econometric model whose main explanatory variable will be female wages. Then, an index of family benefits is introduced and tested as a complementary variable. It is demonstrated that the empirical relationship between fertility and family allowances which is shown by this second approach agrees with the a priori evaluations of the first part, suggesting a moderate but not insignificant impact of family policy on demographic behaviour.

A Micro-Model of Family Formation

Models derived from the new home economics (NHE) framework can be used to predict the impact of a given level of family benefits on fertility behaviour. Such models imply certain relationships between average family size and various components of child cost, the strength of which can be evaluated with standard econometric methods. These show directly how any reduction of child cost through family allowances will modify fertility. However, some of the assumptions implicit in these models are difficult to accept, and

This study relies on two papers previously published in *Population*, to which the reader can refer for more details about methods and data (Ekert-Jaffé, 1986; Blanchet, 1987).

even though the realism of assumptions is not a necessary condition for good predictions, it may be of some help.

Explicitly, two simplifications of NHE models are problematic when evaluating the impact of family benefits. The first is that they generally assume that fertility decisions are of a marginal nature, while actual decisions are discrete (people choosing to have one more child or not).[1] We wish to understand how family benefits, which are often considered as marginal, can have the non-marginal effect of adding one more child to a family. The second is the assumed homogeneity of people, through the assumption of a representative household. In the real world some people will perhaps choose to have an extra child as a result of family policy, and others will not. We wish to determine what proportion of people belong to the first group, and how this proportion would increase if family benefits were higher. It is our belief that an approach dealing explicitly with these two problems will produce more convincing results than an approach which does not. Quantal choice models are a natural tool for this, and it is such a model that we develop here. In doing so, we will see that we also gain some interesting by-products, like an evaluation of the differential impact of family benefits according to children's parity and according to the labour status of the mother, as well as other insights on distributional aspects of aggregate fertility determination.

The Model

The assumptions of the model are the following:

1. Parents are facing certain costs in raising their families. These costs depend on two things: the number of children, and whether both parents work or not. To represent these costs, we will introduce three series of parameters.

c_n will be the basic cost of raising n children (note that it is a cumulated cost, not the cost of the n_{th} child), 'basic' meaning that it includes all costs which are independent of whether both parents work or not;

$c_{a,n}$ will be the extra cost which arises when both parents are working (childcare being provided from outside the home);

$c_{i,n}$ will be the net extra cost arising when one of the parents does not work. In order to simplify our presentation, we will assume that it will be the mother. This extra cost is mainly an opportunity cost (wages foregone). We mention that it is a 'net' extra cost, since withdrawal from the labour-force may have some positive aspects (e.g. if there is some disutility associated with work).

2. We will then assume that there is a maximum level S of resources that parents are ready to spend for their completed families. Their decision rule

---

[1] This remark does not apply to models using parity-specific fertility rates, where it is the probability of having one more child which is modelled (De Cooman *et al.*, 1987).

will therefore be very simple. They choose the highest number of children which is compatible with the level of S, i.e. the highest n such that:

$$c_n + c_{i,n} < S \text{ or } c_n + c_{a,n} < S \tag{1}$$

which can be rewritten as

$$c_{i,n} < s_n \text{ or } c_{a,n} < s_n \tag{2}$$

introducing the new parameter $s_n = S - c_n$. The mother will be working after the birth of this n_{th} child depending on whether

$$c_{a,n} < c_{i,n} \text{ or } c_{a,n} > c_{i,n} \tag{3}$$

3. Because all people do not have exactly the same number of children, we have to assume that the parameters s_n, $c_{i,n}$, $c_{a,n}$ are not fixed but vary over the population. We must therefore give their distributions. Analytical tractability being our main concern here, we shall make the assumptions which allow us to retrieve the classical situation of the multinomial logit model. These assumptions will be that s_n, $c_{i,n}$, and $c_{a,n}$ can be written as

$$s_n = \bar{s}_n + u \quad c_{i,n} = \bar{c}_{i,n} + u_i \quad c_{a,n} = \bar{c}_{a,n} + u_a \tag{4}$$

with u, u_i and u_a following three centered Gumbel-type distributions, independent from each other and having a common variance of σ^2.

Under these conditions, it can be shown (as reported in the appendix[2]), that, from a given population of potential parents, the proportion b_n who will have n children or more is

$$b_n = \frac{e^{-k\bar{c}_{a,n}} + e^{-k\bar{c}_{i,n}}}{e^{-k\bar{s}_n} + e^{-k\bar{c}_{a,n}} + e^{-k\bar{c}_{i,n}}} \tag{5}$$

and the proportion of mothers working after this n_{th} birth will be:

$$p_n = \frac{e^{-k\bar{c}_{a,n}}}{e^{-k\bar{c}_{a,n}} + e^{-k\bar{c}_{i,n}}} \tag{6}$$

k being equal to σ_0/σ, where σ_0 is the standard deviation of Gumbel's law (which is equal to 1.283).

We will first comment on the adequacy of this model as a model of fertility behaviour, before showing how it can be used to evaluate the impact of family benefits.

Empirical Implementation

Formulas (5) and (6) can be readily interpreted. First, both formulae include the dispersion factor σ. If σ tends to zero for given values of other parameters, then behaviour tends to be more and more homogeneous, in the sense that b_n tends towards zero or one, depending on the average values of s_n, $c_{i,n}$, and

---

[2] See also Blanchet and Blum (1984) for a slightly different version of this model.

Table 4.1. Proportion of Women Having n Children and Labour-Force Participation after the Birth of this n^{th} Child

	b_1	b_2	b_3	p_1	p_2	p_3
1961	0.921	0.694	0.434	0.368	0.212	0.127
1967	0.913	0.659	0.367	0.459	0.258	0.139
1974	0.885	0.563	0.222	0.615	0.380	0.164
1981	0.893	0.668	0.322	0.692	0.536	0.251

$c_{a,n}$.[3] Second, (6) shows that labour-force participation rates (LFPR) at given parities depend positively on the opportunity cost $c_{i,n}$ and negatively on $c_{a,n}$. If we assume that this latter cost increases with parity, while $c_{i,n}$ is relatively independent of the number of children, then we get the natural outcome that the LFPR of mothers decreases with the number of their children.

Lastly, (5) shows that the proportion of parents having n children or more can decline for three reasons:

a decline in $s_n = S - c_n$, which can itself result from a decline in S (decline of the total resources of parents, or change in tastes in a less child-oriented direction, if resources are constant or rising), or from a rise in c_n.

a rise in $c_{a,n}$, i.e. in the cost of combining female labour-force participation and high fertility (as will be the case, for instance, during the transition from a rural society to an urban society where most jobs take place outside the home),

a rise in $c_{i,n}$, i.e. a rise in the opportunity cost corresponding to wages foregone in case of work interruption.

The empirical question concerns which of these explanations dominates in the recent decline of fertility in developed countries. NHE approaches generally favour the latter explanation. This is indeed confirmed, at least for France, by a rough comparison of the model with census and civil registration data. Table 4.1 gives parity progression ratios in 1961, 1967, 1974, and 1981, which can be used to compute period values of the b_ns up to rank 3, and LFPRs for the following years for mothers of young children at each parity. If we combine these last data with the p_ns and if we are more specific about the parametric form of s_n, $c_{i,n}$, and $c_{a,n}$ by assuming:

$$s_n = S - nc, \quad c_{i,n} = c_i, \quad \text{and} \quad c_{a,n} = nc_a \tag{7}$$

then, a simple estimation procedure (Blanchet, 1987) gives the evolutions of S, c, c_i, and c_a (up to the parameter σ), which are reported in Table 4.2.

We see that, at least qualitatively, it is the rise of c_i which is mainly

---

[3] From now on we will omit superscript bars distinguishing between s_n, $c_{a,n}$, and $c_{i,n}$ and their average values, which should not produce any ambiguity.

Table 4.2. Estimated Values of Standardized Parameters

	S/σ	c/σ	c_a/σ	c_i/σ
1961	2.53	0.93	0.54	0.09
1967	2.76	0.94	0.64	0.50
1974	3.02	0.98	0.81	1.20
1981	2.94	0.76	0.74	1.44

Table 4.3. Monthly Wage Rates for Men and Women in 1981 FF

	W_m	W_f
1961	2,971	1,766
1967	3,714	2,400
1974	5,000	3,356
1981	5,776	4,246

responsible for the fertility decline. An interpretation of results in monetary terms is a little more difficult, since the model is not identified (solutions being a mix of the parameters S, c, c_i, c_a and of the dispersion parameter σ). Some auxiliary assumptions are necessary to solve this problem of under-identification.

Among the many possibilities which are available in this respect, we choose to neglect the selection bias of women on the labour-market in order to identify their potential wage with the wage W_f of women actually working, as given in Table 4.3. We also assume that S represents a fixed share α of 'full-work income' of the couple, $W_m + W_f$. Finally, we assume that the reservation wage W_{res}, below which a woman does not work, even without children, is constant. It roughly corresponds to the productivity of homework and to the disutility of work outside the home. In this case we have, at any time:

$$S = \alpha(W_m + W_f) \text{ and } c_i = W_f - W_{res} \tag{8}$$

from which we obtain

$$\alpha \frac{W_m + W_f}{W_f - W_{res}} = \frac{S}{c_i} \tag{9}$$

and

$$W_f = W_{res} + \alpha \frac{W_m + W_f}{S/c_i} \tag{10}$$

Since the ratio S/c_i is known from the results of Table 4.2, this shows that W_{res} and α can be estimated as the intercept and slope of a simple regression of

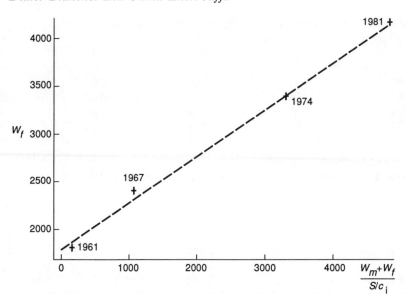

Fig. 4.1 Estimating W_{res} and α from the Intercept and Slope of a Simple Regression

W_f on $(W_m + W_f)/(S/c_i)$. This regression is shown for the four available points in Fig. 4.1. It leads to a value of W_{res} approximately equal to FF1700, and a value of α equal to .5, which is not an implausible value (given the fact that α is the share of total income devoted to children when families are at their peak size and including wages foregone by the mother if she stopped working).

Knowing α, $W_m + W_f$, and S/σ, we are able to compute σ and then to convert all results of Table 4.2 into monetary values. The corresponding solutions are plotted in Figure 4.2. S, by construction, evolves in the same way as $W_m + W_f$. The cost parameters c and c_a also have parallel evolutions. This suggests that these two components of child costs increase roughly in pace with the general improvement in the standard of living, except for c during the last period, which could be precisely the effect of increased child support by the state after 1981. It is c_i which has increased rapidly and which is responsible for the largest part of fertility changes. We note, finally, that there is also an increase in σ, although it is less rapid than that of S: improvements in the standard of living are accompanied by a less than proportional increase in income disparities between people. This corresponds to a progressive decrease of relative inequality, a result which was also to be expected.

The Impact of Various Measures

Having these elements in mind, we are now able to evaluate the impact of various kinds of family policy measures. Analytically, the impact of a reduction

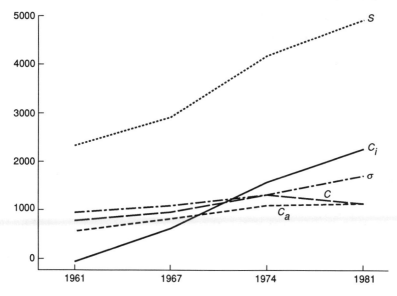

Fig. 4.2   Evolution of the Parameters since 1961

of c_n, of $c_{i,n}$, or of $c_{a,n}$ will be given by minus the derivative of b_n with respect to these three terms.[4] Considering marginal variations, we get:

$$-\frac{db_n}{dc_n} = \frac{\sigma_0}{\sigma}(1 - b_n)b_n \qquad (11)$$

$$-\frac{db_n}{dc_{a,n}} = \frac{\sigma_0}{\sigma}(1 - b_n)b_np_n \qquad (12)$$

$$-\frac{db_n}{dc_{i,n}} = \frac{\sigma_0}{\sigma}(1 - b_n)b_n(1 - p_n) \qquad (13)$$

(11) gives the impact of a global allowance distributed to all parents of children, (12) and (13) respectively give the impact of allowances limited to working mothers (i.e. subsidies for child-care) and to non-working mothers.[5] These results provide a formal expression of a number of simple ideas about the possible impact of family benefits. First, the impact of a given allowance

[4] This assumes that money received by parents from the state is not treated differently from money received from any other source. The impact of benefits will differ from the predictions of the model if this is not the case, but direct estimates of the next part will include this potential difference implicitly (Moffit, 1989). Our formulae also assume that allocations given to families with n children do not affect fertility at higher parities, an assumption which is not fully consistent with the model, but which simplifies computations and leads to more realistic results.

[5] Such a compensation for wages forgone has been reintroduced in the French system in 1984 for mothers of a third child ('allocation parental d'education'), and the opportunity of such a bias in favour of non-working mothers has been the subject of wide debate.

is higher when σ is lower, due to the fact that a marginal measure will affect the behaviour of very few people if individual parameters are very dispersed. Second, the impact varies according to the value of b_n. It is highest for $b_n = 0.5$, which suggests that it is at parities two or three that allowances will have the largest impact. The impact is low if b_n is high because many people already have the n_{th} child, so that allowances only affect a small sub-population. It is also low if b_n is low because most people are very far away from the economic conditions under which they would have their n_{th} child, so that allowances need to be rather high to modify their choices. Last, if we consider allowances specifically directed towards working or non-working mothers, we see that their impact will be proportional to the number of women in these two categories.

The picture is slightly different if we consider what could be called the efficiency of allowances, which is the ratio of their impact divided by their total cost for the community. In the three cases above, these costs are (since allowances are supposed to modify only marginally the values of b_n and p_n):

$$C_n = b_n dc_n \tag{14}$$

$$C_{a,n} = b_n p_n dc_{a,n} \tag{15}$$

$$C_{i,n} = b_n(1 - p_n)dc_{i,n} \tag{16}$$

so that, in any case, the efficiency will be:

$$E_n = \frac{\sigma_0}{\sigma}(1 - b_n) \tag{17}$$

which only depends on parity.

This means that, if we only consider demographic efficiency, i.e. the number of additional births for a given level of overall help, then there is no reason for demographic policy to subsidize preferentially working or non-working mothers. On the other hand, it will be more efficient to help parents at high parities where b_n is very low. This is due to a phenomenon which is well known to policy designers, for which any policy covers two sub-populations: the sub-population of people who would have had the n_{th} child even if there were no allowance; and the sub-population of people who will only have the n_{th} child because of allowances. From the point of view of pure efficiency, we have to minimize the share of the first group, which will be done at parities where b_n is very low: for a given amount of total expenditure, it is more efficient to give high allowances for high-order children, than to give low allowances to children at all parities.

On the other hand, it is possible that, at very high parities, we are in fact addressing very particular sub-groups whose behaviour may be different from that of the rest of the population. Moreover, concentrating help on very high parities may conflict strongly with equity objectives. This raises the problem of the difference between family policy, whose aim is to equalize the standard

Benefits

——— All mothers   —·—· Working mothers   —— — — Non-working mothers

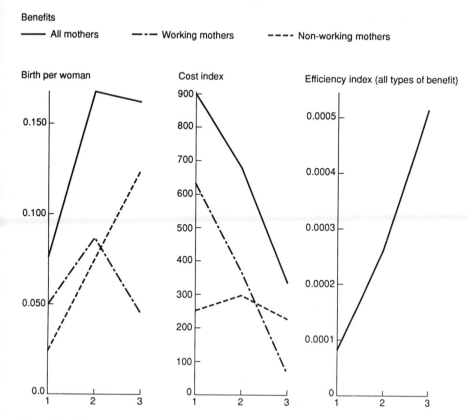

Fig. 4.3 The Impact of Various Measures of an Allocation of FF 1000 at Parities One to Three

of living between families of different sizes, and demographic policy, whose aim is to augment fertility, at least in low-fertility countries. As a whole, concentrating allowances on parities two and three could therefore represent an intermediate choice between demographic efficiency and equity.[6]

We can now use (11) to (17) and the empirical estimates of the previous section to evaluate the quantitative impact of family benefits. Consider an elementary allocation of about FF1000 at 1981 prices (i.e. around one-sixth of the average monthly wage-rate for men—see Table 3). Using values of b_i, p_i, and σ given or computed previously for the year 1981, we can construct Figs. 4.3*a* to 4.3*c* showing the impact of the various measures. We see that,

---

[6] Further reasons can be given to justify the concentration on parity three, as is frequently found in France. For instance, the standard of living of two-children families can be considered as a norm, family policy being designed to align larger families on this norm. One can also invoke the fact that the cost of the third child is higher than the cost of others (as shown, for instance, by Bloch and Glaude, 1983).

for instance, giving FF1000 to families with three children and nothing to others, would raise the percentage of people having a third child by 16 percentage points. The increase is only 4 points if this measure only applies to families with working mothers. It is 12 points if the measure only applies to families with non-working mothers. Fig. 4.3*b* gives indexes of total costs of family policy for the community, and Fig. 4.3*c* gives the index of efficiency obtained by dividing the numbers in Figure 4.3*a* by the numbers in Fig. 4.3*b*, an index which, as already mentioned, increases with parity and is independent of whether benefits are directed towards one- or two-earner families or both.

An Empirical Analysis of the Macro-Data

The model presented above suffers from some important limitations, concerning the estimation of some of its parameters as well as their distribution over the population. Yet, as it stands, it leads to quantitative predictions which can be tested with actual data. This is what we do in the following sections of this chapter, relying on macro-data from European countries in the late 1970s. We first give a brief survey of the various systems of family benefits in these countries, and then present an index of structure and intensity of family allowances accross these countries. It is this index which will be included in various regression analyses of fertility rates. It will then be possible to compare the empirical impact of this index with the predictions of the model outlined above.

Natalist Policies vs. Children's Rights

France and Belgium were the pioneers (in 1932) of family benefits among the democratic countries. Such systems were then established in most industrialized countries during the 1940s and 1950s: Cyprus and the United States are now the only countries in the developed world where universal family benefits do not exist, and where the state limits its interventions to poor families.

Such systems of family benefits can have three different motivations.

1. They can be of a pro-natalist nature, giving more importance to large families, the reason for doing so being the one stressed in the first part, i.e. the fact that allowances distributed at low parities will be expensive while having only a small demographic impact;

2. they can be based on the idea that there exists a kind of social obligation toward children irrespective of their birth order ('children's rights'), in which case total benefits per family will be strictly proportional to the number of children;

3. they can fill some objectives of social policy—such as income maintenance programmes—in which case benefits depend on both economic and demographic criteria.

These three aims are often confused in national legislation, and appear to differing degrees in the different kinds of actual allowances. Summarizing briefly, we distinguish four kinds of direct or indirect subsidies to children:

1. Some are completely independent of income (e.g. the French 'allocations familiales').

2. Some are income-tested. The level of the ceiling and the proportion of excluded families discriminates between allowances which belong more to family policy and measures which are more in the nature of social policy. For instance, the French 'complement familial', was originally income-tested to give more money to low-income families, but at parity three it is in fact received by 80 per cent of families.[7] On the other hand, in Japan the ceiling is equal to about one-half of the mean wage of workers, so that allocations are closer to a system of minimal income, given to families which are below a given poverty-level. Our study does not include this last kind of allowance. More precisely, we do not take into account any allowance which is limited to families whose income is less than one-half of the mean salary.

3. A third group of measures are related to special expenses, like housing, subventions for holidays, etc. They are also considered as being outside the scope of our study, mainly because of the complications they introduce, and because most of them are also limited to low-income families. In any case, this simplification is not of great importance, since these allocations are modest in relation to family allowances, and are closely correlated with them (Bradshaw and Piachaud, 1980). Taking them into account would not have altered the ranking of countries according to the intensity of family policies.

4. Last, some measures are positively linked with income, e.g. paid maternity leave and tax relief. Again for matters of tractability, we do not consider fiscal advantages for families.[8] At least for the French system (which is by the way the most generous for large upper-class families) some simulated results show that the amount of tax relief always represents less than 10 per cent of total family benefits (Coutière *et al.*, 1981; Ekert-Jaffé, 1984). Paid maternity leave has been included in the analysis, and has been evaluated for women earning the average female wage in each country.

Given these various assumptions, we estimated average amounts received monthly by children of various parities. They are given for 28 developed countries in Figs. 4.4*a* to 4.4*c* for parities 1 to 6 and after division by the average income of workers in each country.[9] The amounts received per child were computed as a monthly life-cycle average between birth and the

---

[7] The suppression of the ceiling is an objective of many liberal parties, and most of the 20 per cent of excluded families receive allowances when their children are students, so that the total amount received over the life-cycle is about the same (Ekert, 1983).

[8] Data were available for only one year for each country (about 1978) and for only three values of income: average income, twice the average income of one-earner families, and 1.33 times the average income of two-earner families (OECD, 1981).

[9] For OECD countries we took the average take-home pay of a single worker (OECD, 1981–7). For socialist countries we took the average salary of workers in the public sector.

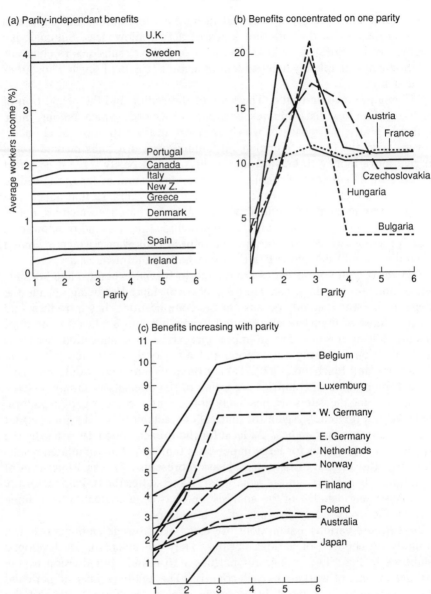

Panel A: Parity-Independent Benefits
Panel B: Benefits Concentrated on One Parity
Panel C: Benefits Increasing with Parity

Fig. 4.4 A Comparison of Benefits per Child by Parity in OECD and COMECON Countries

eighteenth birthday; allocations received for a shorter period than 18 years (e.g. birth grants) are artificially spread over this long time-period. We also assumed that eighteen is the mean age of leaving school for evaluating allocations related to schooling.

The progressiveness of family allowances in 1979 according to birth-order allowed us to classify the 28 countries into three groups, for 1979:

Group 1. All the Mediterranean countries (Spain, Greece, Italy, and Portugal) as well as the United Kingdom and its English-speaking former possessions of Canada—with the exception of Quebec—Ireland, and New Zealand, and two Nordic countries (Denmark and Sweden) gave the same amount to every child, irrespective of birth order. This suggests that their policies did not present any strong demographic motivation, but corresponded to the pure 'children's rights' logic. In this group, the benefit rates were usually low (less than 2 per cent of the salary); the most generous countries were Sweden and the United Kingdom, giving 4 per cent of the salary.

Group 2. Three countries of the former Austro-Hungarian empire (Austria, Hungary, and Czechoslovakia) as well as Bulgaria and France, focused their support on specific birth-orders (the second or third child). Demographic goals seemed predominant here, and the levels of child support were amongst the highest (10 to 19 per cent of the average salary for the third child).

Group 3. The last group offered some benefits which increase monotonically with birth order. But this group presents some important variations concerning the average level of these benefits as well as their progression with parity. Belgium and Luxemburg could be compared with France as far as levels and slope up to parity three are concerned. Benefits in West Germany were slightly lower, whereas in the former East Germany, the Netherlands, Norway, and Finland, the additional income ranged from 4 to 6 per cent of average earnings. Poland, Australia, Japan, and the USSR have never given more than 3 per cent of average earnings per child, and were closer to the countries of Figure 4.4*a*.

Thus, there seemed to be two conceptions of family policy, which have remained more or less valid since. The countries which give nearly the same amount to every child seem to be more preoccupied with equity aims, by fulfilling their social obligations towards already existing children. But, being universal, the amount of child support in these countries is quite modest (yet supplemented by taking into account the number of children in systems of income maintenance). On the other hand the countries with a pro-natalist orientation are more generous, yet, for efficiency purposes, their policies are also more selective.

The problem is therefore to produce an index which adequately combines these two factors of intensity and selectivity. The exact way to do so is not fundamentally important, since selectivity and intensity are more or less associated but it is preferable to use a weighting system which is justified on some a priori grounds. Following the results from the model outlined above we will therefore weight the allowances given to n-children families by $b_n(1 - b_n)$, where b_n is the proportion of couples having n children or more. Allowances weighted in that way will be summed up to an arbitrary limit which will be taken as equal to 6, and we know from (11) that for such an index we must expect an impact on total fertility of about $1.283/\sigma$, where σ is the common standard deviation of all the cost and resource parameters of the model, expressed in the same monetary unit as allowances. We will now examine various regression analyses which attempt to confirm this a priori prediction.

Simple Correlation Analysis

A first approach would be simply to examine the association between fertility and the index of family benefits in a simple correlation framework. This approach does not lead to any significant result: there does not seem to be any relation between the fertility pattern and the patterns of benefits shown in Fig. 4.4. It is in the first group of countries with low benefits that inconsistencies are the highest. Since some of these countries (Nordic and Commonwealth countries) had low fertility near or below replacement level in 1975, their non-interventionist attitude must be either ideological, or due to the fact that they consider their existing population density to be high enough. On the other hand, the Mediterranean countries still had very high fertility in 1975 (although it fell after that date: by 25 per cent in ten years), but in 1979 their traditional family policies were still made for high levels of fertility.[10]

In fact, there need not be any direct correlation between the family policy index and total fertility for at least three reasons:

1. In rationed economies such as those of the former Eastern Europe, the financial support may not have had the same value as in the Western world.

2. There are interactions between fertility and family policy: a low level of family benefits may be a sign of high fertility, considered to be sufficiently high by policy-makers; conversely, family benefits may be raised as an answer to low fertility. All this results in a negative association between family policy and fertility.

3. Lastly, in any case, family policy cannot be more than a partial explanatory factor, which acts alongside the main economic variables explaining fertility, such as wages and/or labour-force participation. Any correlation between the index of family policy and these variables will result in bias for simple correlation analysis. For instance, if fertility is falling with income and

---

[10] The fertility decline may have been viewed favourably in a context of rising unemployment and economic crisis. Some reactions have been observed since: in 1981, Greece introduced a small variation with the birth-order and its allowances reached the Finnish level; in 1984–5 Spain and Italy introduced allowances to poor families that varied with birth order.

if richer countries, all else being equal, give more for child support, then a negative correlation between family allowances and fertility may occur even if the former actually has a positive impact on the latter.

One way to control for these different sources of bias is to work with variations of TFRs and of the family policy index, which will eliminate all undesirable interferences resulting from constant characteristics of countries. For instance, if we make a regression of the variation of the TFR between 1977 and 1981 on the variation of the family policy index between 1975 and 1979 (the two-year lag accounting approximately for the average delay between the decision to have a child and its birth[11]), then we get a positive correlation of .72 (for 22 countries). The corresponding regression equation is:

$$\Delta \text{TFR} = -0.133 + 9.457 \ \Delta \text{FPI} \tag{18}$$
$$(4.73)$$

The family policy index has been divided by the average wage in each country so that the regression coefficient must be interpreted as $1.283/\lambda$ where λ will be the ratio of our general index of dispersion σ to average wages: we get $\lambda = 13.5$ per cent. This is not an implausible value, but it is lower than that found with the previous analysis of French data. In any case this regression is somewhat unstable. It improves if we remove the Eastern-bloc countries and high-fertility countries, but it worsens if we change the time-period (Ekert-Jaffé, 1986). A better specified model therefore seems preferable.

Multiple Regression

The model described in the first part of this chapter justifies the introduction of women's wages as the main economic variable affecting fertility. Such series of wages are available for the period under consideration for nine EC countries (i.e. the present members minus Spain, Portugal, and Ireland) plus Norway and Finland. They can be made comparable from country to country by using indexes of purchasing power parities as computed by the Statistical Office of the European Community, and the OECD (Ward, 1986).[12]

The model shows how such a wage variable should be introduced in a model of TFRs. If we consider the fertility at parity n in country i and at time t, then an expansion at order one around an average situation characterized by the superscript * yields:

$$b_n(i, t+2) = b_n^* + \frac{\sigma_0}{\sigma^*} b_n^*(1 - b_n^*)\Big[(s_n(i,t) - s_n^*) - p_n^*(c_{a,n}(i,t) - c^*_{a,n})$$
$$- (1 - p_n^*)(c_{i,n}(i,t) - c^*_{i,n})\Big] \tag{19}$$

[11] A simulation model on French longitudinal data shows an average delay of eighteen months (Deville, 1976).

[12] As is well known, such a procedure of normalization is preferable to conversion into a common monetary unit using simple exchange rates, which do not reflect the relative purchasing powers of national currencies for current consumption goods.

If we make the assumption that $c_{i,n}(i,t)$ is of the form $W_f(i,t) - W_{res}$, as we did above, and if we assume that the only other time-varying parameter is family allowances a_n at parity n, which appears negatively in $s_n(i,t)$, then we get, after the grouping of all the fixed effects:

$$b_n(i,t+2) = q_n(i) + \frac{\sigma_0}{\sigma^*}b_n^*(1 - b_n^*)a_n(i,t) - \frac{\sigma_0}{\sigma^*}b_n^*(1 - b_n^*)$$
$$(1 - p_n^*)W_f(i,t) \tag{20}$$

so that, since the TFR is the sum of the b_ns:

$$\text{TFR}(i,t) = Q(i) + \frac{\sigma_0}{\sigma^*}\text{FPI} - \frac{\sigma_0}{\sigma^*}\sum_{n=1}^{6}b_n^*(1 - b_n^*)(1 - p_n^*)W_f(i,t) \tag{21}$$

We therefore justify a linear model of TFRs with dummy variables for each country, and with the index of family policy and the female wage-rate as covariates. But, more importantly, the model also predicts the values of the coefficients for these last variables. For FPI, this coefficient should be, as already seen, σ_0/σ^*. For the female wage rate, provided it is expressed in the same units, it should be equal to this ratio multiplied by a factor, which for average values of the p_n amounts to about .3.

Table 4.5 shows the result of the regressions, while data is displayed in Table 4.4 (note that all monetary variables have been expressed in purchasing parity of 1980 US dollars). The first two columns show two ordinary least-squares regressions, without and including the FPI variable. The first one shows a good fit (although the use of dummy variables plays a large role in this result). The impact of the female wage-rate appears very significantly negative, and, most important, has an order of magnitude consistent with expectations. Given that it must be approximately equal to minus $.3 \times 1.283/\sigma$, we see that its value of -0.0017 implies a σ of about US\$ 225 which is a plausible value and corresponds to that found above for the French case.

When the FPI is introduced in the regression, its effect is both positive and significant. For a σ of \$225, its coefficient should be $1.283/225 = 0.0057$. The empirical result of 0.0048 is once again in rough agreement with this prediction.

Columns 3 and 4 of Table 4.5 examine whether this result holds when controlling for female labour-force participation rates. Introducing such rates is common practice in models of fertility behaviour, since the contribution by Butz and Ward (1979). Yet, the method of and motivations for doing so are not straightforward (see for instance the discussion of Butz and Ward by Kramer and Neusser, 1984). In fact, labour-force participation rates can be interpreted here as a proxy for unobserved elements of our micro-model. For instance, if there are some cross-national differences in the reservation wage W_{res} (for cultural reasons or so on), they will not be directly observed, but they will be indirectly shown by the variations of the p_ns at given levels of W_f. On the other hand, these labour-force participation rates will themselves be

Table 4.4. Data for Some EC and Nordic Countries

Country	Year($=t$)	$W_f(t)$	FPI(t)	TFR($t + 2$)
Belgium	1969	444.75	40.6008	2.209
	1970	475.46	42.8640	2.089
	1972	571.06	44.6537	1.825
	1974	686.65	47.4546	1.720
	1975	734.64	49.4913	1.705
	1976	751.52	52.1260	1.692
	1977	761.26	50.6338	1.689
	1978	772.69	51.5552	1.683
	1979	792.34	51.2435	1.659
	1980	812.66	52.3221	1.600
	1981	835.87	50.4723	1.560
	1982	834.12	51.4850	1.520
	1983	819.29	57.5497	1.490
Denmark	1974	966.36	21.5083	1.747
	1975	1,049.84	21.5078	1.660
	1977	1,079.38	19.7014	1.602
	1978	1,072.33	19.5769	1.546
	1979	1,083.18	18.7617	1.437
	1980	1,054.11	15.5883	1.430
	1981	1,028.71	17.6766	1.380
	1982	1,022.60	17.3356	1.400
	1983	1,025.77	16.9833	1.450
Finland	1975	601.95	15.1436	1.679
	1977	594.45	18.9657	1.635
	1979	622.38	19.4848	1.644
	1981	639.29	21.9071	1.740
	1983	657.73	27.2468	1.650
France	1969	370.87	43.5937	2.490
	1970	391.85	43.5514	2.412
	1971	420.69	43.4980	2.303
	1972	452.77	44.5133	2.107
	1973	482.22	45.2984	1.927
	1974	506.75	44.4850	1.830
	1975	527.98	45.0400	1.868
	1976	552.66	44.5304	1.832
	1977	572.33	44.8861	1.869
	1978	593.49	53.2723	1.964
	1979	601.69	55.1235	1.968
	1980	610.70	57.0640	1.910
	1981	627.80	60.4578	1.790
	1982	634.63	59.5225	1.810
	1983	657.02	59.5508	1.820

Table 4.4. (Cont.)

Country	Year(=t)	$W_r(t)$	FPI(t)	TFR($t + 2$)
Germany (West)	1969	502.348	14.9302	1.922
	1970	552.606	15.7362	1.718
	1971	580.640	15.1844	1.544
	1972	593.341	14.4999	1.513
	1973	629.582	14.0175	1.452
	1974	659.563	13.4421	1.459
	1975	669.236	28.1923	1.405
	1976	687.467	27.2947	1.381
	1977	710.862	26.4851	1.379
	1978	731.263	30.0471	1.449
	1979	734.616	35.8192	1.440
	1980	749.667	34.3086	1.410
	1981	749.208	39.5095	1.320
	1982	740.391	34.6408	1.290
Greece	1975	319.350	11.3549	2.280
	1977	365.019	9.1601	2.290
	1979	412.066	7.0952	2.095
	1980	411.099	21.7042	2.020
	1981	415.953	18.1361	1.940
	1982	505.425	30.3116	1.820
Italy	1969	367.031	19.4373	2.411
	1970	432.940	18.9625	2.359
	1971	484.866	18.4141	2.330
	1972	508.470	17.5215	2.313
	1973	587.924	16.5487	2.185
	1974	596.660	17.8592	2.084
	1975	645.131	17.1775	1.950
	1976	724.023	18.3967	1.845
	1977	755.450	16.4786	1.738
	1978	775.438	13.6420	1.680
	1979	800.420	14.2456	1.620
	1980	790.332	20.3969	1.590
	1981	826.515	18.1507	1.530
	1982	842.310	16.4071	1.460
	1983	868.665	15.3327	
Luxemburg	1970	493.213	28.4698	1.750
	1972	583.635	31.0757	1.570
	1974	700.363	39.5515	1.480
	1975	721.373	37.0926	1.490
	1976	795.867	42.6848	1.470
	1977	790.153	43.1134	1.470
	1978	787.184	45.1522	1.490
	1979	767.064	47.0953	1.580

Table 4.4. (Cont.)

Country	Year(=t)	$W_f(t)$	FPI(t)	TFR(t + 2)
	1980	804.894	53.7326	1.490
	1981	767.984	51.0737	1.450
	1982	762.030	54.3702	1.430
	1983	777.276	53.6081	1.400
Netherlands	1970	458.986	22.8116	2.150
	1972	566.013	28.3338	1.774
	1974	694.776	30.3017	1.632
	1975	743.647	28.8522	1.579
	1976	748.586	30.1206	1.583
	1977	772.491	29.1801	1.563
	1978	785.795	31.3340	1.602
	1979	787.186	30.3225	1.570
	1980	783.929	35.3621	1.500
	1981	767.507	34.1090	1.470
	1982	777.286	34.5668	1.490
	1983	781.907	34.4407	1.510
Norway	1975	804.536	22.1733	1.753
	1977	893.049	23.2052	1.750
	1979	881.004	23.6854	1.701
	1981	864.661	30.3697	1.660
	1983	870.745	32.9116	1.680
United Kingdom	1972	510.27	13.4460	1.931
	1973	553.85	12.7659	1.823
	1974	609.05	11.3339	1.757
	1975	632.30	14.3533	1.701
	1976	629.51	12.5611	1.770
	1977	597.04	12.6864	1.882
	1978	618.69	18.1759	1.918
	1979	640.42	27.3212	1.840
	1980	634.57	23.4541	1.760
	1981	628.21	24.3758	1.750
	1982	630.61	24.6944	1.770
	1983	647.14	26.2822	1.790

endogenous to the model. This will be especially true of the aggregate LFPRS which are weighted averages of the p_ns with weights which depend on the intensity and structure of fertility.

For this reason the results given in Table 4.5 use instrumental variable estimators, where the instruments are the national dummies, W_f, FPI and two variables related to female educational level, which are the upper-level schooling rates lagged two and five years respectively. In fact, the endogeneity

Table 4.5. Multiple Regression Results with the Total Fertility Rate as the Dependent Variable

	OLS	OLS	2SLS	2SLS
Intercept	2.573	2.5801	2.8362	2.9551
	(36.3)	(37.7)	(11.5)	(12.4)
W_f	−0.0017	−0.0019	−0.0015	−0.001
	(−17.0)	(−16.1)	(−8.0)	(−9.4)
LFPR			−0.77	−1.1
			(−1.1)	(−1.6)
Belgium	0.3453	0.2388	0.3067	0.1656
	(9.6)	(4.7)	(6.2)	(2.5)
Denmark	0.6865	0.7866	0.7669	0.9180
	(13.0)	(12.8)	(8.6)	(9.2)
Finland	0.1381	0.1508	0.3034	0.3883
	(2.9)	(3.3)	(1.9)	(2.5)
France	0.2959	0.1538	0.3390	0.1908
	(8.1)	(2.5)	(6.4)	(3.0)
Greece	0.1775	0.1695	0.1079	0.0691
	(3.4)	(3.4)	(1.3)	(0.8)
Italy	0.4533	0.4915	0.3525	0.3545
	(13.1)	(13.7)	(3.6)	(3.9)
Luxemburg	0.1517	0.0733	0.0616	−0.068
	(4.2)	(1.6)	(0.7)	(−0.7)
Netherlands	0.2529	0.2355	0.1192	0.0422
	(7.1)	(6.7)	(0.9)	(0.3)
Norway	0.5780	0.6076	0.6339	0.6922
	(11.6)	(12.3)	(9.0)	(9.9)
UK	0.2557	0.2762	0.3168	0.3665
	(7.1)	(7.8)	(4.8)	(5.6)
FPI		0.00475		0.00556
		(2.9)		(3.3)
R^2	.8906	.8991	.8959	.9074
Adj. R^2	.8787	.8870	.8834	.8952
d.f.	102	101	101	100

as well as the explanatory power of LFPR is weak. Endogeneity has been tested through a Lagrange multiplier test of an extended regression[13] and is not significant, which may be due to the fact that, as are other explanatory variables, LFPR is lagged two years in the regression.[14] Indeed, OLS estimators (not reported) are very close to these instrumental variable results. However the

---

[13] This test is locally asymptotically equivalent to the Hausman test (Holly, 1983).

[14] There can of course be a link between past activity and current fertility but, as shown by Lagarde (1981) or Desplanques (1987) from French data, it seems to exist only for the third birth.

most important findings is that, in both cases, this control by LFPR does not reduce the significance of the FPI, nor does it modify the magnitude of its impact.

Another check of the robustness of the model is given by regressions including time-dummies. These dummies provide a way to control for global non-stationarity in all the series, while retaining all the information brought by differential trends between countries. Table 4.6 shows regressions with these dummies, and with or without the FPI. We see that the FPI retains its significant explanatory power when dummies are introduced, and its coefficient is larger than in the previous regressions. Dummies themselves are generally much more significant after the intoduction of the FPI than before: the FPI and dummies therefore interact to produce a much better fit to the data (in terms of adjusted R^2).

Some other regressions have also been estimated. Regressions in log-linear form behave at least as well as those presented here. This is not the case with regressions on first-order differences, which theoretically constitute an alternative to time-dummies for removing global time-trends from the series, and also correct partial autocorrelation of residuals: T-statistics fall between 1.0 and 1.4.[15] In fact these regressions raise many problems. The main one is that, due to non-linearities, differentiated series are no more stationary than the original ones. Second, in a model whose dynamic structure is poorly specified, as is necessarily the case here, the interpretation of regressions on differences is difficult. This difficulty is amplified here by the fact that, due to missing data, we have not been able to compute differences between successive time-periods, but only between values in t and $t + 2$.

As a whole, it appears that our results are not spurious and do not result from some common time-trends in FPI and fertility when these trends are removed through dummies, but may be considered as such when these trends are removed by differentiation. Appreciation of their robustness depends on the a priori values we give to these two detrending methods.

Conclusion

Assuming that we trust their statistical significance, what is the practical importance of the results of Tables 4.5 and 4.6? Let us compare two countries with low and high levels of family benefits in 1981: the United Kingdom and France, whose family policy indexes are respectively 25 and 60. This would account for a difference of 0.17 child per women with the first regressions (or of 0.31 if we consider the regression with time-dummies included). Such estimates are roughly in agreement with those given, for instance by Ermisch

---

[15] This depends on whether or not we keep country dummies in the regression. In the former case, this amounts to removing all information on differential trends between countries, which leaves almost nothing to be explained by the model!

Table 4.6.   Multiple Regression Results Including Time-Dummies

	OLS	OLS
Intercept	2.588	2.1236
	(12.9)	(10.9)
W_f	−0.0017	−0.001
	(−6.5)	(−6.6)
Belgium	0.3497	0.1219
	(10.0)	(2.34)
Denmark	0.697	0.7320
	(7.9)	(9.58)
Finland	0.130	0.2297
	(2.4)	(4.54)
France	0.292	0.0904
	(6.1)	(1.62)
Greece	0.170	0.3565
	(1.7)	(3.89)
Italy	0.453	0.5299
	(14.)	(16.8)
Luxemburg	0.155	−0.011
	(4.5)	(−0.2)
Netherlands	0.256	0.2146
	(7.5)	(7.01)
Norway	0.579	0.5753
	(10.)	(11.9)
UK	0.261	0.3616
	(6.2)	(8.78)
1970	0.037	0.2337
	(0.4)	(2.79)
1971	0.067	0.2347
	(0.8)	(3.05)
1972	−0.05	0.1071
	(−0.8)	(1.62)
1973	−0.03	0.1200
	(−0.5)	(1.94)
1974	−0.02	0.0925
	(−0.5)	(1.91)
1975	−0.00	0.0935
	(−0.01)	(2.28)
1976	0.003	0.0915
	(0.01)	(2.16)
1977	0.046	0.1322
	(1.1)	(3.51)
1978	0.078	0.1373
	(1.8)	(3.59)
1979	0.053	0.1048
	(1.3)	(3.00)

Table 4.6. (Cont.)

	OLS	OLS
1980	0.013	0.0324
	(0.3)	(0.90)
1981	−0.02	−0.009
	(−0.7)	(−0.2)
1982	−0.04	−0.041
	(−1.2)	(−1.1)
FPI		0.0094
		(5.38)
R^2	.91	.94
Adj. R^2	.89	.92
d.f.	89	88

(1988), who calculated an increase in the TFR in the UK of 0.17 if child benefit had been doubled in 1986. Such an impact is not insignificant, even if it shows that we cannot expect some major fertility upswings from family policies which are already expensive.

Of course, the model and statistical analysis we relied on to arrive at these results remain preliminary. The micro-model of the first part was only designed to show how family benefits could act at the individual household level and it leaves many points unresolved. A more detailed micro-model which could be treated by simulation analysis would be preferable and this would allow for a better tuning of parameters and of stochastic assumptions. Concerning the macro-analysis presented above, its results should be validated on longer time-periods and on a wider sample of countries. This implies an important task in compiling national systems of family benefits, as well as a better understanding of the factors which, besides family policy, explain the cross-national differences in fertility levels and trends.

References

Blanchet, D. (1987), 'Les effets démographiques de différentes mesures de politique familiale', *Population*, 1, 99–128.

—— and Blum, A. (1984), 'Naissance, coût de l'enfant et activité de la mère: un modèle', *Population*, 2, 281–94.

Bloch, L. and Glaude, M. (1983), 'Une approche du coût de l'enfant', *Economie et Statistique*, 135, 51–67.

Bradshaw, J. and Piachaud, D. (1980), *Child Support in the European Community*, London: Bedford Square Press.

Butz, H. P. and Ward, W. P. (1979), 'The Emergence of Countercyclical U.S. Fertility', *American Economic Review*, 69, 318–28.

Coutière, A., Pontagnier, C., and Godderidge, W. (1981), 'Le modèle d'impôt sur le revenu', *Economie et prévision*, 46, 5–30.

De Cooman, E., Ermisch, J., and Joshi, H. (1987), 'The Next Birth and the Labour Market: A Dynamic Model of Births in England and Wales', *Population Studies*, 41/2, 237–68.

Desplanques, G. (1987), 'Activité féminine et fécondité', in *Données sociales 1987*, Paris: INSEE, 497–501.

Deville, J. C. (1976), 'Reflexions sur les liaisons entre l'activité féminine et la fécondité des femmes mariées. Présentation d'un modèle de simulation', Technical Report 2234/427, Paris: INSEE.

Ekert-Jaffé, O. (1983), 'Activité féminine, prestations familiales et redistribution', *Population*, 3, 503–26.

—— (1984), 'Prestations familiales, fiscalité et redistribution', *Revue française des affaires sociales*, special issue (June), 127–49.

—— (1986), 'Effets et limites des aides financières aux familles: une expérience et un modèle', *Population*, 2, 327–48.

Ermisch, J. (1988), 'Economic Influences on Birth Rates', *National Institute Economic Review* (Nov.), 71–81.

Kramer, W. and Neusser, K. (1984), 'The Emergence of Countercyclical U.S. Fertility: Note' *American Economic Review*, 74, 201–2.

Holly, A. (1983), 'Une présentation unifiée des tests d'exogénéité dans les modèles à équations simultanées', *Annales de l'INSEE*, 50, 3–24.

Lagarde, F. (1981), *Liaison activité féminine-fécondité: Un essai de chiffrement*, Technical Report, Paris: Ministère des Finances, Direction de la prévision, Bureau des Transferts Sociaux.

Moffit, R. (1989), 'Demographic Behavior and the Welfare State: Econometric Issues in the Identification of the Effects of Tax and Transfers Programs', *Journal of Population Economics*, 1/4, 237–50.

OECD (1981), *La Situation au regard de l'impôt et des transferts sociaux de certains groupes de revenu dans les pays membres de l'OCDE. 1974–1979*, Technical Report, Paris: OECD.

Ward, M. (1985), *Parités de pouvoir d'achat et dépenses réelles dans les pays de l'OCDE*, Paris: OECD.

Appendix

Since the model developed in the first part of the paper does not exactly correspond to the standard multinomial logit, it is useful to give details on the computations which lead to formulae (5) and (6). Using the same notation as in the text, the share of parents whose number of children will be n or more is:

$$b_n = \Pr(s_n > c_{a,n} \text{ or } s_n > c_{i,n}, s_{n-1} > c_{a,n-1} \text{ or } s_{n-1} > c_{i,n-1}, \dots) \tag{22}$$

which is of the form $\Pr(y_n, \dots, y_1)$, if we note y_l the event:

$$y_l = (s_l > c_{a,l} \text{ or } s_l > c_{i,l}) \tag{23}$$

But, for a given couple, the fact that y_n is true implies that y_{n-1} to y_1 are also true, if we assume, as is natural, that $s_n - c_{i,n}$ and $s_n - c_{a,n}$ are both decreasing in n. The probability b_n therefore reduces to:

$$b_n = \Pr(s_n > c_{a,n} \text{ or } s_n > c_{i,n}) \tag{24}$$

or to:

$$b_n = 1 - \Pr(s_n > c_{a,n} \text{ and } s_n > c_{i,n}) \tag{25}$$

which is, using the repartition functions and omitting n for simplicity:

$$b_n = 1 - \int_{s=-\infty}^{s=+\infty} \left[1 - F_{c_a}(s)\right]\left[1 - F_{c_i}(s)\right] d\left[F_s(s)\right]$$

$$= 1 + \int_{s=-\infty}^{s=+\infty} \exp\left[-e^{k(s-\bar{c}_a+m_0)} - e^{k(s-\bar{c}_i+m_0)}\right] d\left\{\exp\left[-e^{k(s-\bar{s}+m_0)}\right]\right\}$$

with k as already defined in text and with m_0 being the mean of Gumbel's distribution.
Introducing the new variable:

$$z = -e^{k(s-\bar{s}+m_0)} \tag{27}$$

we get:

$$b_n = 1 - \int_{z=-\infty}^{z=0} \exp\left\{z\left[e^{-k(\bar{c}_a-\bar{s})} + e^{-k(\bar{c}_i-\bar{s})}\right]\right\} d(e^z)$$

$$= 1 - \int_{z=-\infty}^{z=0} \exp\left[z\left(e^{-k(\bar{c}_a-\bar{s})} + e^{-k(\bar{c}_i-\bar{s})} + 1\right)\right] dz \tag{28}$$

which leads directly to (5) in the text.
Labour-force participation p_n after an n_{th} birth can be written:

$$p_n = \Pr(c_{a,n} < c_{i,n}/s_n > c_{a,n} \text{ or } c_{i,n}, s_{n-1} > c_{a,n-1} \text{ or } c_{i,n-1}, \dots) \tag{29}$$

which can be written:

$$p_n = \Pr(x/y_n, y_{n-1}, \dots) \tag{30}$$

which reduces to $\Pr(x)$ since event x is independent from events y_n, y_{n-1}, etc. We can then write, omitting n once again:

$$p_n = \Pr(c_{a,n} < c_{i,n})$$

$$= \int_{c_i=-\infty}^{c_i=+\infty} F_{c_a}(c_i) d\left[F_{c_i}(c_i)\right] \tag{31}$$

or:

$$p_n = 1 + \int_{c_i=-\infty}^{c_i=+\infty} \exp\left[-e^{k(c_i-\bar{c}_a+m_0)}\right] d\left\{\exp\left[-e^{k(c_i-\bar{c}_i+m_0)}\right]\right\}$$

$$= 1 - \int_{z=-\infty}^{z=0} \exp\left[z(e^{-k(\bar{c}_a-\bar{c}_i)} + 1)\right] dz \tag{32}$$

with z being now:

$$z = -e^{k(c_i-\bar{c}_i+m_0)} \tag{33}$$

and which leads directly to (6) in the text.

5 Patrilocality, Childbearing, and the Labour Supply and Earning Power of Married Japanese Women

NAOHIRO OGAWA AND ROBERT WILLIAM HODGE

Introduction

At the end of World War II the Japanese economy was in shambles. Since then, however, its growth has been spectacular. By 1958 GNP per capita had recovered to its pre-war level, and by 1988 it was, at nearly US$ 21,000, among the highest in the world (World Bank, 1990). During the period 1958–88 real GNP per capita grew at an annual rate of 5.8 per cent, a remarkably high figure.

No less phenomenal was the unprecedented rapidity with which Japan moved through the final stages of demographic transition. After a short post-war baby boom (1947–9), Japan's fertility level declined dramatically. Between 1947 and 1957 the total fertility rate (TFR) fell more than 50 per cent, from 4.54 to 2.04 children per woman. After 1957 the TFR hardly changed until the first oil crisis of 1973, when it again headed downward; by 1988 it had fallen to 1.66. As fertility fell during the post-war period, mortality also fell. In 1947 life expectancy at birth was 50 years for males and 54 years for females; by 1988 it was 76 years for males and 81 years for females. At present, Japanese people have the highest life expectancy in the world.

As a consequence of these demographic shifts, the family life-cycle has also changed. Most Japanese women now finish their reproductive career with two children before they reach age 30 and therefore have a much longer 'empty nest' period than before (Otani and Atoh, 1988). As we shall show later, the changing family life-cycle pattern has a strong influence on women's labour-force participation.

Although Japan's current demographic situation is similar in many ways to that of other industrialized countries, there are noteworthy differences. For instance, Japan is the only industrialized society in which three-generation

Robert William Hodge co-authored an earlier version of this paper; sadly, he died in early 1989. We are grateful to the Population Problems Research Council of Mainichi Newspapers for permitting us to utilize data from the nineteenth Survey on Fertility and Family Planning. We also wish to acknowledge John Ermisch, Dennis Ahlburg, Robert Retherford, John Bauer, and Linda Martin for their valuable suggestions and comments.

households are still fairly common. Between 1955 and 1985, the proportion of three-generation households in all households decreased from 37 to 20 per cent (Preston and Kono, 1988). We shall show below that in 1988 30 per cent of married Japanese women of childbearing age lived with their own or their husband's parents and/or grandparents, and even larger fraction lived in such a household at some point during their marriages. A majority of such co-residence cases are of a patrilocal type, i.e. a woman takes up residence with her husband's parents.

The time-path of Japanese female labour-force participation also differs considerably from that of many industrialized nations (Ogawa, 1989*a*). In most industrialized nations, the female labour-force participation rate has risen sharply during the past two decades or so, but in Japan the rate for women aged 15 and over fell from about 51 per cent in the mid-1960s to about 46 per cent in the mid-1970s, and then rose to about 49 per cent in 1988 (Statistics Bureau, 1989). The absence of any substantial trend in the Japanese female labour-force participation rate during the past few decades is the product of off-setting trends in different types of female labour-force participation, as well as the sensitivity of female labour-force participation to short-run economic fluctuations such as the oil crisis of the early 1970s (Ogawa, 1987 and 1989*a*). The response of female labour participation in Japan to such factors supports the frequently heard claim that Japanese female workers are marginal workers.

In Japan, as in most other advanced societies, there has been a rise in the proportion of women who enter paid employment. Shimada and Higuchi (1985) claim that this rise has been the most rapid in the recorded experience of advanced economies. Among married women aged 15–49 the proportion working as paid employees rose from 23 per cent in 1972 to 38 per cent in 1988. This rise has been offset by declines in the proportion of married women participating in the labour-force as family workers. This proportion fell from 17 per cent in 1972 to 11 per cent in 1988 (Statistics Bureau, 1989). The fact that a considerable number of Japanese women continue to remain employed in the traditional sector sets Japan apart from the industrialized nations of North America and Western Europe. In 1984, for instance, only 1 per cent of the female labour-force in the United States were family workers (Hill, 1989).

The wages of women in Japan, as in other advanced economies, are con-siderably less than those received by male workers, and in fact the wages of women in Japan are notoriously low. Part of the sex differential in wages can be attributed to sex differentials in work experience, and part to the relatively high incidence of part-time employment among Japanese women. Relative women's wage-rates have recently been improving in most advanced economies, but not in Japan. According to a recent survey of sixteen countries by the International Labour Organization (1986), Japan was the only one among the countries surveyed where the difference between the salaries of men and women had widened between 1975 and 1984. Wage data compiled by the Ministry of Labour show that the ratio of women's to men's hourly wages declined almost continuously from 0.543 in 1975 to 0.514 in 1984, while between 1985 and 1988 it fluctuated considerably. It is expected, however, that the wage-ratio will rise substantially in the years to come, due to the implementation of the Equal Employment Opportunity Law in 1986 (Ministry of Labour, 1988).

These changes in female labour-force participation and the earnings differentials between the sexes appear to have contributed substantially to Japan's rapid fertility reduction over the past few decades. Ogawa and Mason (1986) have shown that an alternative specification of the Butz–Ward model (Butz and Ward, 1979), which uses the proportion of paid employees in the currently married female population and men's and women's real earnings to explain fertility change, tracks the course of the TFR quite satisfactorily over the period 1966–84.

This paper analyses the way in which the supply of female labour and the wages of women are intertwined, not only with each other, but also with selected demographic and socio-economic factors such as Japanese family structure and life-cycle stage. The data are primarily from a survey conducted in June of 1988 by Mainichi Newspapers. This survey is the nineteenth round in a series of inquiries concerning fertility and family planning, carried out biennially since 1950 under the auspices of the Population Problems Research Council of Mainichi Newspapers. The nineteenth round used a stratified, multi-stage sampling procedure. Cities, towns, and villages throughout Japan were first stratified on the basis of population and local characteristics. As in previous rounds, the target population was married women of childbearing age. In all, 3,400 questionnaires were distributed and 2,560 completed, yielding a response rate of just over 75 per cent. We also utilize a nationwide study of family life and organization, conducted in April 1988 by Mainichi Newspapers in collaboration with Nihon University. This data-set, unlike our basic source, covers both men and women of all ages and marital statuses (Ozaki, 1988).

The analysis is structured as follows: section II examines wife's earnings relative to her husband's income, by type of her employment; section III analyses the earnings profile of married women working as full-time paid employees, and the determinants of full-time participation in the labour-force; section IV compares the differences between full-time paid workers and other married women with different work statuses in the determinants of their participation in the workforce. In order to gain a further insight into the analyses developed in the previous sections, section V discusses wives' reasons for participating in the labour-force.

Married Women's Earnings by Type of Employment

In order to facilitate the discussion that follows, we analyse the pattern of wife's earnings by her type of employment relative to her husband's earnings.

Table 5.1. Distribution of Earnings of Wives and Husbands, by Labour-Force Status of Women: Married Japanese Women of Childbearing Age, 1988 (%)

Sex and Wife's Labour-Force Status	Annual Earnings in Thousands (Yen)				
	TOTAL	< 2,000	2,000–3,999	≥4,000	N
Working women	100.0	78.7	16.0	5.3	1,319
Full-time paid employees	100.0	58.7	31.4	9.9	477
Part-time paid employees	100.0	98.4	1.0	0.6	504
Traditional-sector workers	100.0	77.5	16.6	5.9	338
Husbands	100.0	7.8	42.9	49.2	2,303
With working wives	100.0	9.6	44.9	45.5	1,359
With non-working wives	100.0	5.2	40.1	54.7	944

In the nineteenth round of the Mainichi surveys of fertility and family planning, each respondent was asked about her occupation at the time of the survey. The pattern of responses to this question was as follows: 38.9 per cent were housewives; 13.6 per cent family workers; 19.3 per cent full-time paid employees; 20.8 per cent part-time paid employees; 2.4 per cent business proprietors; 1.1 per cent professional workers; 3.4 per cent in other categories; and 0.5 per cent gave no answer.

Many of the variables studied in this paper were based on questions asked for the first time in the nineteenth round. One of these variables is a wife's annual earnings. By using this variable, we can contrast the annual earnings of wives with those of their husbands, as shown in Table 5.1. It is readily apparent from Table 5.1 that the annual earnings of married working women are much lower than those of working husbands whose wives are of childbearing age. More than three-quarters of the women but less than one-tenth of the men have earnings of less than 2 million yen per annum. Less than 10 per cent of the women, but nearly half of the men, have earnings of 4 million yen or more. The broad details of this comparison are not changed by contrasting working wives with the husbands of working wives rather than with the husbands of all married women of childbearing ages.

Three other points emerge from Table 5.1. First, the earnings of women are related to their work status. Full-time paid employees have the highest earnings, followed by the heterogeneous category of traditional-sector workers, including family workers and self-employed proprietors of small shops. Part-time paid employees earn the least, well below those of the other two groups. This finding is accounted for by differentials by type of employment in the following three factors: hours worked, hourly wages, and bonuses. Regarding hours worked, data gathered in the afore-mentioned nationwide survey on family life and organization show that, on average, married women of childbearing age who participated in the labour-force as full-time paid employees worked 43 hours a week, as opposed to 41 hours for traditional-sector workers and 31 hours for part-time paid employees. Regarding hourly earnings, the same survey data indicate that hourly wages for part-time paid employees were 48 per cent of those of full-time paid employees and 62 per cent of those of traditional-sector workers. Furthermore, although full-time workers are entitled to receive substantial bonuses, one in the middle of the year and the other at the end of the year, only a small proportion of part-time workers receive bonuses. In 1988 married women of childbearing age who worked as full-time paid employees received bonuses equivalent to three months' salary. Bonuses for part-time workers were only 16 per cent of those received by full-time workers (Ministry of Labour, 1989).

Second, virtually all of the women working as part-time paid employees have earnings of less than 2 million yen per annum. Details not shown in Table 5.1 reveal that, in fact, more than three-quarters of these married, part-time workers earn 900 thousand yen or less. The explanation of the 900-thousand-yen cut-off is the Japanese income tax law, which takes effect when the annual income of working wives surpasses 900 thousand yen. Those who earn more than this must not only pay income tax but also lose their dependent status in their husbands' payroll and social security plans, including medical insurance and pension rights. Because the financial implications of losing dependent status are so serious, many wives who work part-time are careful to adjust their hours worked so that their annual earnings fall below 900 thousand yen.

Finally, there is a modest differential in the earnings distributions of husbands with and without working wives. Overall, the earnings of husbands whose wives do not work are higher than those of men with working wives. While the difference is not large, it is statistically significant (the value of χ^2 is 26.6, $p < .001$, with two degrees of freedom). This finding is consistent with the view that some wives work to supplement family income when their husbands have lower-paying jobs. Likewise, it is consistent with the proposition that the 'reservation wages' of women rise with husband's income, so that the wives of well-paid men are less likely to enter the labour-force.

Although female workers may be marginal, and receive relatively low wages, their earnings can be a significant supplement to household budgets. To examine the contributions of women to household finances, we have worked out the fraction of the joint earnings of married couples that come from wife's earnings. The results show that although women at different points in the life-cycle contribute on average rather different amounts to the joint earnings of couples, their proportional contributions are quite similar. The percentage share of working wives in the joint earnings of couples only ranges from 31.6 per cent among those with pre-school children to 24.8 per cent among those with only school-aged children.

Determinants of Full-Time Paid Employment

An instructive economic model for analysing a married Japanese woman's decision to participate in the labour-force and her choice among alternative types of employment if she participates has been advanced by Hill (1983; 1989). In this model a woman faced with mutually exclusive choices among non-participation in the labour-force and types of employment within it, compares the maximum utility attainable given each participation alternative and selects the alternative which yields the *maximum maximorum* (Hill, 1983). Based on this theoretical framework, Hill applied a multinomial logit model to data gathered in a small survey of women aged 20–59 living in the Tokyo Metropolitan Area in 1975, and has shown the differences between paid employees and family workers in the determinants of their labour-force participation. She also estimated, following the general framework of Heckman (1980) which corrects for sample selection bias, equations for both wages and hours of work for employees (based on 157 observations) and family workers (58 observations) respectively.

More recently, Ogawa (1989a) analysed determinants of labour-force participation of married women of childbearing age, using the eighteenth round of the Mainichi survey conducted in 1986. The underlying model resembles Hill's, but with one important difference. Ogawa modelled a woman's employment status as the outcome of a series of binary choices. The first choice is to work or not to work. Among those who choose to work, the second choice is to work part-time or full-time. Among those who choose to work full-time, the third choice is to work in the traditional sector or as a full-time paid employee. The end result of the hierarchical, binary decision-making process implicitly contained in the analysis of the Ogawa study differs little from the outcomes postulated in Hill's model. It should be stressed that the substantive analyses of the study done by Ogawa differ from Hill's because the former has employed alternative predictor variables, focused on residential patterns and life-cycle stages, and explicitly considered part-time employment. Unlike Hill's study, however, Ogawa could not estimate equations on wage and hours of work because these data were not collected.

Although we follow along a similar theoretical line to that taken in these previous studies, we take a considerably different analytical approach. In this section we estimate the wage equation for full-time paid employees, and identify the determinants of whether a woman chooses to be a full-time paid employee. One of the primary reasons for focusing our attention on full-time paid work is that, as discussed in the introductory section, it may be the wave of the future. Moreover, the growth of full-time paid employment has profound implications for the status of women in Japanese society, and it also has profound implications for fertility. In the next section, we contrast the determinants of being a full-time paid employee with those of choosing different work statuses.

The model used in the present study is framed in terms of market and reservation wages. The higher a woman's reservation wage, the less likely she is to work as a full-time employee; the higher her offered wage, the more likely she is to participate in the labour-force as a full-time employee. Based upon a number of previous empirical analyses (Heckman, 1980; Bauer and Shin, 1987), the variables assumed to affect her market and reservation wages have been chosen from the nineteenth round of the Mainichi survey. These variables include (a) a wife's education (junior high school*, senior high school, junior college, university) (b) her husband's education (junior high school*, senior high school, junior college, university) (c) the number of children at varying ages (children aged less than 1, children aged 1–5, children aged 6–17, children aged 18 and over) (d) a wife's potential work experience (e) her husband's annual income in millions of yen (f) type of place of current residence (urban area, or rural area*) (g) wife's experience of working as a full-time employee before marriage (yes, no*) (h) husband's occupation (paid employee, self-employed*) and (i) patrilocality of current residence (yes, no*). In the foregoing description of the predictor variables, some of them are of the classificatory nature, and the omitted category has been indicated by an asterisk. It should also be noted that because we have no data on wife's actual work experience, we have to use potential experience as a proxy for on-the-job experience. Potential work experience (EXP) is defined in the usual way as follows: EXP = wife's age – her years of schooling – 6. Among these predictor variables, both wife's potential work experience and education are assumed to affect her market wage. The reservation wage is assumed to be a function of all the predictor variables except for EXP.

By employing all these variables, we can estimate a reduced form probit for the wife's probability of labour-force participation as a full-time paid employee to generate Heckman's λ variable, which is used to correct for potential selectivity bias in the wage equation.

One of a few principal difficulties involved in this estimation was that because wife's annual earnings were reported in the class intervals, they were coded in millions of yen according to the mid-points of the class intervals with the exception of the lowest and highest categories. The category 'less than 900 thousand yen' was scored 0.75 and the open-ended upper category of '8 million or more' was scored 9.0.

The other difficulty concerns the deficiency of data on hourly wages. To cope with this data limitation we have used the wife's annual earnings as a proxy for a measure of earning-power per hour. This approximation seems reasonable for the reason that the hours of work for full-time paid employees are relatively homogeneous. Data from the survey on family life and organization indicate that the variance of hours of work among married Japanese women working as full-time paid employees is substantially smaller than that for married women with other work statuses.

Another difficulty which we encountered in the estimation of the wage equation was the absence of data on actual work experience. As mentioned earlier, we have employed potential work experience (EXP) as a proxy. Retrospective data gathered in one of the government fertility surveys conducted in 1987 show that when women progress from parity zero to parity one, about 30 per cent of full-time paid employees withdraw from the labour-force for the purpose of childbearing and child-rearing (Institute of Population Problems, 1988). When they progress from parity one to two, the corresponding figure drops further to approximately 15 per cent, but this level remains virtually unchanged throughout their reproductive stage, even though they might progress to higher parities. In view of these results, we introduce child variables into the wage equation in order to allow for wife's work experience lost to take up these child-related activities. It should be pointed out, however, that because about 15 per cent married women stay in the labour-force continuously regardless of their family-cycle positions, the resulting estimated wage equation including the child variables for the purpose of adjusting EXP may suffer from some statistical bias. The child variables are defined as follows: number of children at ages 0–5 (CHILD05), number of children aged 6–17 (CHILD617), and number of children aged 18 and over (CHILD18P).

Following a standard wage equation, the log of wages for full-time paid employees is assumed to be a function of the wife's work experience and educational attainment. The estimated result is:

$$\ln W = -\,0.0488 + 0.0354 \text{ EXP} - 0.0006 \text{ EXP}^2 - 0.0776 \text{ CHILD05}$$
$$(0.2116)\;(0.0218)\qquad(0.0006)\qquad(0.0534)$$

$$-\,0.0697 \text{ CHILD617} - 0.0707 \text{ CHILD18P} + 0.1364 \text{ WEDH}$$
$$(0.0377)\qquad\qquad(0.0546)\qquad\qquad(0.0903)$$

$$+\,0.4830 \text{ WEDJ} + 0.7840 \text{ WEDU} + 0.1310\ \lambda,$$
$$(0.0546)\qquad\quad(0.1358)\qquad\quad(0.0693)$$

$$N = 401;\ R^2 = 0.143 \qquad (1)$$

where W = wife's annual earnings in millions of yen, WEDH = 1 for a woman with senior high school education, and otherwise 0, WEDJ = 1 for a woman with junior college education, and otherwise 0, WEDU = 1 for a woman with university education, and otherwise 0. The standard errors of the coefficients are indicated in parentheses beneath their estimated values. All the estimated coefficients are consistent with a priori expectations, but only a few of them are statistically significant. That is, although the coefficient for WEDH is not significantly different from zero, the coefficients for both WEDJ and WEDU are statistically significant at the 5-per-cent level with a one-tail test. Nevertheless, these education variables are jointly significant as a group at the 1-per-cent level. Moreover, the estimated coefficients for CHILD18P and λ are statistically significant at the 10-per-cent level. Both EXP and EXP^2, which are key variables in the wage equation, are statistically insignificant, as revealed by their low *t*-values. These experience variables, however, are on the margin of significance as a group at the 5-per-cent level. Because the *t*-value for the estimated coefficient for EXP is fairly close to the critical value at the 10-per-cent significance level, we have re-estimated the wage equation without the squared term of EXP, as has been done in some of the previous studies (Heckman, 1980).

The estimated result for this alternative specification is shown as follows:

$$\ln W = 0.0683 + 0.0139 \text{ EXP} - 0.0723 \text{ CHILD05} - 0.0544 \text{ CHILD617}$$
$$\quad (0.1784) \quad (0.0062) \quad\quad (0.0532) \quad\quad\quad (0.0347)$$

$$\quad - 0.0841 \text{ CHILD18P} + 0.1724 \text{ WEDH} + 0.5177 \text{ WEDJ} + 0.8175 \text{ WEDU}$$
$$\quad\quad (0.0532) \quad\quad\quad (0.0833) \quad\quad\quad (0.1037) \quad\quad\quad (0.1319)$$

$$\quad + 0.1280 \; \lambda,$$
$$\quad\quad (0.0693)$$

$$N = 401; \; R^2 = 0.141 \quad (2)$$

A close comparison of (1) and (2) reveals that the estimated result for the latter is more satisfactory than that for the former. In (2) the two main variables, wife's work experience and educational attainment, are not only in agreement with theoretical predictions but also highly significant from a statistical point of view. Unlike the case of (1), all the dummy variables representing wife's educational attainment are statistically significant. As is the case with (1), the coefficient for Heckman's λ is significant at the 10-per-cent level with a one-tail test.

In (2) the estimated effect of an additional year of labour-market experience as a full-time paid employee is to raise the offered annual wage by 1.4 per cent. The magnitude of this effect is larger than that (1.0 per cent) computed from another wage equation without the child-related dummy variables. The effect of education on annual earnings is much more substantial than that of work experience. For example, compared with full-time paid employees with junior high school education, those with senior high school education are offered annual wages which are only 18.8 per cent higher. However, attending two years of junior college beyond senior high school raises a woman's annual wage by 41.2 per cent, and the corresponding figure for proceeding from junior college to university is 35.0 per cent. In absolute monetary values, women with junior college education receive higher annual wages by 525 thousand yen, compared with their counterparts who have received only a senior high school education. Women with university education are offered annual wages which are 628 thousand yen higher than those with only junior college education. These computed results imply that the returns on education increase markedly from senior high school to junior college or from junior college to university. It should be noted, however, that it would take several years to retrieve the earnings foregone by attending a higher educational institution beyond senior high school, let alone the costs of attendance.

We now turn our attention to the participation of married Japanese women of childbearing age in the labour-force as full-time paid employees. We eschew any extended discussion of the predictor variables entering the labour-force participation equation, both because the present endeavour is based upon some of the previous studies (Ogawa, 1987; 1989a; Hill, 1983; 1989; Shimada and Higuchi, 1985) where the factors affecting female labour-force participation in Japan are discussed at length, and because it is self-evident how most of the variables in the equation would either decrease or increase the propensity to work as full-time paid employees.

One of the key explanatory variables is the annual wage which a woman is expected to earn if she works as a full-time paid employee. The expected wage for each woman has been computed from (2). Because both wife's education and work experience are the main predictor variables in (2), the effect of these variables upon wife's labour-force participation is assumed to be mediated through the predicted annual wage. Wife's age is included as a predictor variable, and is expected to capture the effect of a woman's changing attitude towards participation through her life-course. This variable may also represent a change in tastes for work for each successive cohort of married women. Three dichotomous variables are introduced to indicate husband's educational attainment: senior high school, junior college, and university. The omitted category, to which these educational groups are contrasted, is junior high school. Husband's occupation is incorporated as a dichotomous variable representing whether or not he works as a paid employee. The reference category is the self-employed and those engaged in the primary sector. (Although an attempt has been made to introduce more detailed occupational categories of paid employment such as professional, managerial, clerical, sales, and blue-collar, the estimated coefficients for these occupational categories have been comparable in size.) Dummy variables are also included to indicate whether a woman resides in an urban area or worked as a full-time paid employee prior to marriage. Unearned income plays an important role in economic models of labour supply, but data on property income are not available in our data. Following many previous studies of female labour supply (Killingsworth, 1983), we use husband's earnings as a proxy. Husband's annual earnings are coded (in millions of yen) according to the mid-points of the intervals into which they were grouped. The lower interval of less than 2 million yen per annum is coded 1.5 and the open-ended upper interval of 12 million or more is assigned a score of 13.0.

Apart from these predictor variables, we include the following two additional variables: number of children at varying ages, and patrilocality of current residence. As regards the former, four variables are introduced: (*a*) number of children aged less than 1 (*b*) number of children aged 1–5 (*c*) number of children aged 6–17, and (*d*) number of children aged 18 and over. In so far as the latter is concerned, it is another dummy variable which takes on the value 1 if a woman co-resides with her husband's or her own parent(s), and otherwise 0. Because almost 85 per cent of co-residence cases belong to the patrilocal household type in contemporary Japan, this dummy variable can be considered to represent patrilocality of current residence.

It is important to note, however, that both of these variables may be endogenous. The presence of young children is likely to be affected by a woman's labour-force participation (Cogan, 1980; Heckman, 1980; Hanoch, 1980; Bauer and Shin, 1987). Overlooking the endogeneity of these variables would tend to bias the impact of life-cycle stage upon the labour-force participation among married Japanese women. Unfortunately, due to the fact that the available data did not provide a sufficient number of good instruments to carry out estimation, no practical solution to this potential estimation problem is available in the present study. In addition, Blundell and Walker (1984) argue that in the household production framework, children may be assumed to be predetermined.

With respect to the causal relationship between patrilocality and female labour-force participation, the afore-mentioned nationwide survey on family life and organization provides useful information pertaining to the reasons for co-residence. In this survey, 32 per cent of currently married women of childbearing age were maintaining patrilocal residences. Approximately 53 per cent of those with patrilocal households stated that because their husbands were the oldest amongst their siblings, they were co-residing with their parents-in-law; about 15 per cent of them were in patrilocal residences due to the wishes of their parents-in-law; more than 10 per cent of them stated that they wanted to stay close to their parents-in-law; only 4 per cent of them moved into patrilocal residences with the expectation that their parents-in-law could take care of their children and household chores. These results seem to suggest that the most important motives for co-residence in contemporary Japan are highly cultural, and that it is unlikely that women start to share residences with their parents-in-law in order to pursue or continue their professional careers. Thus, the causational relationship appears to be predominantly one-way, from patrilocality to women's labour-force participation, the former facilitating the latter.

The results of a probit structural equation for wife's participation in the labour-force as a full-time paid employee are presented in Table 5.2, where it may be seen that a number of the predictor variables entered into the labour-force participation equation have estimated coefficients which are statistically significant. The presence of infant children and/or pre-school children aged 1–5 inhibits a woman's entry into the workforce as a full-time paid employee. Although the presence of children aged 6–17 has a considerable negative effect on wife's labour-force participation, its estimated coefficient is only statistically significant at the 10-per-cent level with a one-tail test. The presence of children aged 18 and over does not have any impact.

Table 5.2. Probit Analysis of Wife's Labour-Force Participation as a Paid Employee for Married Japanese Women of Childbearing Age, 1988

Independent Variables	Parameter Estimates and Significance Tests		
	Coefficients	Standard Errors	*t*-Ratio
Intercept	−1.5243	0.3599	−4.236
Children aged:			
<1	−0.5647	0.1839	−3.070
1–5	−0.2739	0.0688	−3.981
6–17	−0.0892	0.0473	−1.886
≥18	0.0474	0.0735	0.645
Husband's annual earnings	−0.1228	0.0195	−6.305
Husband's education			
Senior high school	−0.0367	0.1018	−0.360
Junior college	−0.1009	0.1419	−0.711
University	−0.2641	0.1361	−1.940
Urban residence	−0.4671	0.0926	−5.044
Wife full-time employee before marriage	0.5171	0.0988	5.235
Husband working as a paid employee	0.4167	0.0951	4.380
Patrilocality of residence	0.4738	0.0765	6.196
Wife's age	0.0028	0.0086	0.326
Wife's predicted wage	0.5334	0.1165	4.577

Notes: Both means and standard deviations of all the predictors are listed in Table A1. N = 1915; Log-likelihood = −857.95.

As regards husband's occupation, the wives of men working as paid employees are more likely to be in the labour-force as full-time paid employees than are the wives of self-employed and agricultural workers. As expected, the higher the husband's annual income, the lower the probability of his wife's participation in the labour-force as a full-time paid employee. While all the estimated coefficients for dummy variables representing husband's educational attainment have negative signs as theoretically expected, none of them are statistically significant at the 5-per-cent level. This result suggests that, as has been the case for wife's earnings, the effect of husband's education is largely captured by the variable for husband's annual earnings.

The behaviour of married women living in urban areas is substantially different from that of their counterparts residing in rural areas. They are less likely to work full-time, probably because part-time positions, which are one of the major alternatives to full-time positions, are concentrated in urban areas (Ogawa, 1987; 1989*a*). Wife's work in a similar position prior to marriage has the expected positive impact, but wife's age is statistically insignificant.

Table 5.3. Estimated Probabilities of Working as Full-Time Paid Employees

Number of Children at Varying Ages			Current Residence	
0	1–5	6–17	Patrilocal	Neolocal
0	0	0	0.425	0.246
1	0	0	0.226	0.110
1	1	0	0.152	0.067
1	2	0	0.097	0.038
0	2	1	0.205	0.099
0	1	1	0.291	0.153
0	0	1	0.391	0.226
0	0	2	0.357	0.200

The latter result makes a marked contrast to the findings obtained from some of the earlier studies on the female labour supply in the other industrialized countries (Cogan, 1980; Smith, 1980; Joshi, 1986).

The patrilocality of residence has a substantially positive impact upon wife's participation in the workforce as a full-time paid employee. This result indicates that because women with patrilocal residences potentially have a child-care system supported by their parents-in-law built into their household structures, they are more likely to work as full-time paid employees than those with neolocal residences. It should be noted, however, that because there is, as discussed earlier, a long-term decline underway with respect to patrilocality of residence, an important source of full-time paid employees may dry up in the years to come, if this trend continues. In addition, it is conceivable that because middle-aged Japanese women often take care of their frail elderly parents-in-law at home, the positive effect of patrilocality of residence upon the former's participation in full-time paid employment may become weaker as the ageing process in Japan advances in the 1990s and beyond (Ogawa, 1989*b*).

To assess further the effect of patrilocality of residence as a built-in child-care system, we have computed the probabilities of working as full-time paid employees for women living in patrilocal and neolocal households and having a different number of children at varying ages, as displayed in Table 5.3. These probabilities have been calculated for women having no children aged 18 and over, residing in urban areas, having work experience as full-time paid employees prior to marriage, and being married to husbands who work as paid employees with senior high school education; the mean values have been used for husband's annual earnings, wife's predicted annual wage, and her age. Obviously, the probabilities of working are substantially higher among women with patrilocal residences than among those with neolocal residences, regardless of the number of children at different ages. It is important to observe, however, that the differentials in the probabilities of participation are large for women either with no children or with one school-aged child, but the differentials shrink as the number of infant and pre-school children increases. For women with one infant and two pre-school children, for instance, the differential is only 0.06 between women with patrilocal residences and those with neolocal residences. In relative terms, however, the probability for the former is 2.5 times as high as that for the latter, which is substantial.

Wife's predicted annual wage, which she would receive if she worked as a full-time paid employee, has a positive effect on her participation. As full-time wages continue to grow in the future, higher proportions of married Japanese women are expected to work as full-time paid employees. The computed elasticity of wife's participation as a full-time employee with respect to her predicted annual wage is 1.10. Note that it is the elasticity of the probability of participation in the neighbourhood of the means in the explanatory variables. This computed elasticity seems reasonable. Compared with the wage elasticities (ranging from 3.85 to 4.34) for the participation of Japanese urban women as employees estimated by Hill (1989), it is substantially lower. However, it is comparable to the average wage elasticity (1.02) for female participation reported by Mincer (1985) in his review of studies from industrialized countries.

We have also computed, using the estimated coefficient for husband's annual earnings, the income elasticity. The computed value is −0.70, which is considerably smaller in absolute value than the calculated wage elasticity. Hence, these results on wage and income elasticities suggest that if annual wages for both husbands and wives increase at the same rate, the net effect is a rise in the probability of the latters' participation as full-time paid employees. It should be borne in mind that as a result of the enactment of the Equal Employment Opportunity Law in 1986, which has been discussed earlier, women's wages are likely to grow at a rate faster than men's in the years to come. Thus, it is highly probable that Japanese women's participation in the labour-force as full-time paid employees will rise considerably in the future.

Determinants of Labour-force Participation of Married Women with other Work Statuses

In the foregoing section, we have identified the factors determining whether or not a woman works as a full-time paid employee. It should be emphasized, however, that among those who do not work as full-time paid employees, about half of them are non-participants, but the other half of them participate in the labour-force as part-time paid employees or family workers. In this section, therefore, we shed light upon the choice of other work statuses, and attempt to contrast their determinants with those for full-time paid employment.

To achieve this objective, we conduct a multinomial logit analysis. The dependent variable is defined as follows: it takes a value of 1 if a woman works as a part-time paid employee, the value 2 if she works as a family worker, and a value of 3 if she is a non-participant. The category of full-time paid employees is treated as a reference group. Due to their small number of observations, women working in a professional or self-employed capacity are excluded from the present analysis. The predictor variables introduced are the same as those used for the analysis of full-time paid employees.

Table 5.4 presents the estimated results. A brief comparison of the results for the three different outcomes reveals that the following four predictor variables are statistically significant for all the three outcome cases: husband's annual earnings; wife's predicted annual wage in full-time paid employment; wife's pre-marital work experience as a full-time paid employee; and the patri-locality of current residence.

Husband's higher earnings induce his wife to work as a part-time employee or family worker, or to stay at home as a housewife, rather than to participate in the labour-force as a full-time paid employee. More importantly, as indicated by the difference in the size of the estimated coefficients, as her husband's earnings rise a wife is more likely to choose to be a non-participant than a part-time employee or family worker. In contrast, a higher annual wage offered for full-time paid employment reduces the odds of being a part-time employee, family worker, or non-participant relative to being a full-time paid employee by roughly comparable amounts.

Women who worked as full-time paid employees before marriage are more likely to retain the same work status. Compared with those who did not work as full-time paid employees prior to marriage, those who worked as full-time paid employees during their pre-marital period have 53 per cent higher odds of choosing full-time paid jobs over part-time jobs; 58 per cent higher odds over family employment; and 65 per cent higher odds over non-participation.

In comparison to women residing in neolocal households, women living in patrilocal households are less likely to work as full-time paid employees than as part-time employees or family workers, or to stay out of the labour-force as housewives. Women with patrilocal residences have 63 per cent higher odds of choosing full-time paid employment over part-time employment; 36 per cent higher odds over family employment; and 61 per cent higher odds over no employment, than women with neolocal residences.

Judging from the recent trends for each of these four variables, the foregoing analysis seems to suggest that changes in both wife's predicted wage and her pre-marital work experience are likely to contribute to a further shift to full-time paid employment from part-time or traditional-sector employment among married Japanese women, whereas increases in husband's annual earnings and the decline in patrilocality tend to counteract such a shift.

Apart from these four predictor variables, each outcome is affected by a different set of predictors. For instance, women who have children aged

Table 5.4 Multinomial Logit Regression Coefficients for Labour-Force Participation of Married Japanese Women among Alternative Types of Employment

| | Multinomial Logit Coefficient (T-Ratio) | | |
| | Part-time Paid Employee | Family Worker | Non-Participant |
Independent Variables	Full-Time Paid Employee	Full-Time Paid Employee	Full-Time Paid Employee
Intercept	−0.1846	2.2371	1.4169
	(−0.227)	(2.057)	(1.969)
Children aged:			
<1	−1.9406	0.5271	1.3683
	(−1.831)	(0.812)	(3.818)
1–5	−0.2056	0.4258	0.7777
	(−1.115)	(2.039)	(5.727)
6–17	0.3365	0.4360	0.0196
	(3.332)	(3.260)	(0.204)
≥18	−0.0573	0.2042	−0.2031
	(−0.376)	(1.011)	(−1.315)
Husband's annual earnings	0.1418	0.1838	0.3240
	(3.223)	(3.731)	(7.924)

Husband's education			
Senior high school	0.0022	0.2679	0.1220
	(0.011)	(0.965)	(0.572)
Junior college	−0.0053	0.3703	0.4206
	(−0.017)	(0.951)	(1.478)
University	0.3535	0.2612	0.6769
	(1.227)	(0.677)	(2.474)
Urban residence	0.9180	−0.1020	1.1039
	(4.477)	(−0.412)	(5.648)
Wife full-time employee before marriage	−0.7539	−0.8679	−1.0444
	(−3.488)	(−3.311)	(−5.119)
Husband working as a paid employee	0.4919	−3.0894	0.1908
	(2.079)	(−13.473)	(0.897)
Patrilocality of residence	−0.9883	−0.4392	−0.9390
	(−5.893)	(−1.974)	(−6.145)
Wife's age	0.0247	−0.0021	−0.0269
	(1.312)	(−0.082)	(−1.578)
Wife's predicted wage	−1.1780	−1.1149	−1.0208
	(−4.482)	(−2.966)	(−4.503)

Notes: Both means and standard deviations of all the predictors are listed in Table A2.
N = 1849; Log-likelihood = −1835.7.

6–17 or who are married to husbands working as paid employees are more likely to choose part-time jobs over full-time jobs. Also, women living in urban areas have 150 per cent higher odds of choosing part-time employment over full-time employment. As discussed in the previous section, this result is accounted for partly by the fact that part-time jobs are concentrated in urban areas. It can also be explained partly by the hypothesis that although there are more job opportunities available in urban areas, due to their urban life-style and commuting difficulties, urban women prefer to work as part-time employees rather than to be employed on a full-time basis (Ogawa, 1987; 1989a).

Wives whose husbands are self-employed are much more likely to be employed as family workers. This is in agreement with a priori expectation: in a patriarchal society like Japan, if her husband is self-employed a wife hardly has any choice but to help in his business. These women have 95 per cent higher odds of choosing family employment over full-time paid employment. These computed odds increase further when they have children aged 1–5 and/or 6–17. This is presumably because the family business can often be run while they are simultaneously caring for their young children.

Women with infants and children aged 1–5 and living in urban areas are more likely to stay at home as housewives than to work as full-time paid employees. Moreover, one of the dummy variables for husband's education is statistically significant. The women married to husbands with university education have 97 per cent higher odds of choosing the non-participant status over full-time paid employees. This result, consistent with the finding of some of the previous studies (Shimada and Higuchi, 1985; Ogawa, 1987; 1989a), implies that Japanese husbands with a higher educational status want their wives to stay at home rather than to work outside the home.

To shed light upon the effect of the family structural variables upon women's employment choice, we have calculated the probabilities of being in one of the four alternative employment categories for women living in patrilocal and neolocal households and having a differing number of children at various ages, as presented in Table 5.5. These probabilities have been computed by using the mean value for each covariate (except for the patrilocality of residence and the number of children at varying ages) included in the analysis. Irrespective of the number of children at different ages, the probabilities of working as full-time paid employees or family workers are considerably higher among women with patrilocal residences than among those with neolocal residences, while the opposite pattern is observable with respect to the probabilities of working as part-time paid employees or staying at home as housewives. In addition, although the probabilities of Japanese married women being in one of the three participant categories decline pronouncedly with an increase in the number of children at ages less than 6, the extent to which their probabilities fall varies considerably by type of employment as well as type of residence. There is a particularly large decrease in the

Table 5.5. Computed Probabilities of Being in Alternative Employment Statuses by Type of Household

Number of Children at Varying Ages			Employment Type			
0	1–5	6–17	Full-time paid employee	Part-time paid employee	Family worker	Non-participant
Patrilocal						
0	0	0	0.441	0.178	0.047	0.333
1	0	0	0.238	0.014	0.043	0.706
1	1	0	0.129	0.006	0.035	0.830
1	2	0	0.064	0.002	0.027	0.906
0	2	1	0.185	0.069	0.071	0.675
0	1	1	0.295	0.136	0.074	0.495
0	0	1	0.400	0.226	0.066	0.308
0	0	2	0.353	0.280	0.090	0.277
Neolocal						
0	0	0	0.239	0.260	0.039	0.462
1	0	0	0.111	0.017	0.031	0.841
1	1	0	0.055	0.007	0.024	0.914
1	2	0	0.027	0.003	0.017	0.953
0	2	1	0.084	0.084	0.050	0.782
0	1	1	0.145	0.179	0.056	0.620
0	0	1	0.211	0.320	0.054	0.415
0	0	2	0.181	0.385	0.071	0.363

probabilities of women with neolocal residences participating in the labour-force as full-time or part-time paid employees, or family workers.

The results derived from the multinomial logit model reveal that despite the relatively sizeable number of wives working in the informal sector, the labour-market behaviour of married Japanese women is heavily influenced by the factors similar to those for other developed countries. These factors include wife's predicted wage offer for full-time paid employment, husband's annual earnings, wife's work experience before marriage, and number of children at different ages. It should be stressed, however, that the behaviour of Japanese women is substantially affected by the pattern of residence, a feature which cannot be observed in other industrialized societies where neolocal households are widely prevalent. In addition, there are considerable differences in the determinants of labour-force participation among the alternative types of employment. For this reason, as pointed out by Hill (1983; 1989), economic models of labour-force participation which treat these alternative choices as identical will incorporate a specification bias.

Table 5.6. Reasons for Working by Current Work Status: Married Japanese Women of Childbearing Age in the Labour-Force, 1988 (%)

		Current Work Status			
Reason for working	TOTAL	Full-Time Employee	Part-Time Employee	Family Worker	Business Proprietor
Educational expenses for children	33.9	36.3	43.9	16.0	21.4
Pay off housing loan	12.1	15.8	14.0	4.3	12.5
Family business	21.3	5.2	1.4	81.1	25.0
Make use of abilities	9.2	15.5	4.3	0.7	25.0
Money for myself	20.3	19.4	31.4	5.0	8.9
Finished child-rearing free time	12.5	8.6	21.9	5.0	0.4
Husband's income low	20.5	30.0	22.1	5.0	14.3
Personal self-satisfaction	15.8	19.8	9.3	14.2	39.3
Broaden social perspectives	19.3	23.6	22.3	10.3	7.1
Number of responses	2,146	773	842	398	88
Number of respondents[a]	1,301	444	494	281	56

Notes: Up to two responses were allowed; hence percentages do not add to 100.
[a] Base for percentages.

Reasons for Working

We have observed in the foregoing section that the decisions by married Japanese women to enter alternative types of employment are governed by different sets of factors. In a situation such as this, the reasons why married Japanese women work must be as heterogeneous as the factors which affect their decisions about choosing a particular type of employment. Previous research has, however, provided scant insight into the reasons that Japanese women have for working and virtually no empirical evidence to back up the few conjectures which have been offered. Some data concerning reasons for working were, however, collected in the nineteenth round of the Mainichi survey. Working women were presented with a checklist of reasons that they might have for working and asked to select up to two of them.

The relationships between the various reasons for working and wife's current labour-force status are shown in Table 5.6. Before turning to the breakdown by labour-force status, we may note from the first column of Table 5.6 that fairly substantial numbers of women are attracted to all of the response alternatives. The least chosen response, 'make use of my abilities', is selected by just under 10 per cent of the respondents. The most popular alternative, 'educational expenses for children' attracts one-third of working wives. There is some irony in the fact that although child-rearing inhibits labour-force participation when children are young, many women end up working to secure their children's education. Four other responses—'family business', 'make money for myself', 'low income of husband', and 'broaden social perspectives'—attract about one-fifth of the respondents each. There are no surprises in these proportions. Because the traditional sector still remains a significant part of the Japanese economy, 'family business' would be expected to emerge as an important reason for working. The Japanese family is patriarchal and many husbands control the household budget by providing their wives with only sufficient funds to keep the household running; it is, therefore, not surprising that women might want some financial resources for themselves. As we have already observed in section II, because the husbands of working women earn less, on average, than the husbands of those not working, it is natural that a substantial number of women should mention their husband's income as a motivation for working. Finally, we noted that relatively few women selected 'make use of my abilities' as a reason for working. That is consistent with the evidence that the returns on education are relatively modest particularly among those with lower educational attainment, who comprised the majority of the women sampled in the nineteenth round of the Mainichi survey. The remaining responses attract between 12 and 16 per cent of the respondents. Two of these simply reflect matters of fact: you either do or do not have to work to pay off a housing loan, and you either have or have not finished child-rearing and have nothing to do. The last category, 'personal self-satisfaction', is itself somewhat nebulous, since it conceals wide variations in taste.

If we now turn to breakdowns by the current work status of women, we see that 'educational expenses for children' is chosen most frequently by paid employees, whether full- or part-time. This may well be an important clue to the expansion of paid employment in Japan, since it has gone hand-in-hand with the expansion of educational expectations and opportunities (Martin and Ogawa, 1988). 'Low income of husbands' and 'broadening social perspectives' also exhibit a response pattern rather similar to that observed for 'educational expenses'.

'Paying off housing loans' exhibits little variation across the various work statuses of women, save that family workers are least likely to choose it. Family workers are likely already to own a family farm or a house above or adjacent to a business. Because everyone needs shelter, it is not surprising that variation across the remaining categories of work status is minimal. 'Family business', as one would expect, is chosen overwhelmingly by family workers. The only group that chooses 'making use of my abilities' in large numbers is the small group of women who are professional workers. This response is also chosen relatively more frequently by women who own their own business or work as full-time paid employees. Some women with their own business have doubtless organized it around their abilities. The few women in female careers like education and nursing will be numbered among the full-time employees.

The one group that chooses 'money for myself' in sizeable numbers is part-time employees, which is consistent with the view that some women accept low wages and menial jobs because they intend to work only part-time for pocket money. Full-time employees also give this response rather frequently, but less so than part-time workers. Like 'money for myself', the response 'finished child-rearing and have free time' is chosen in relatively large numbers only by part-time employees. This is as expected, since older women returning to work after child-rearing may still have to be at home to look after their children when they have returned from school; many Japanese mothers spend a considerable amount of time helping their children with their homework (Prais, 1987). The remaining category to be discussed is 'personal self-satisfaction', which is selected in relatively large numbers only by women who have their own business, and professional workers.

From the examination of Table 5.6, it seems clear that married Japanese women have a variety of reasons for working. Although reasons are quite heterogeneous, they are clearly linked to the familial and work situations in which women find themselves. Consistent with the results obtained in sections III and IV, both full-time and part-time paid employees work mainly for economic reasons such as 'educational expenses for children', 'money for myself', and 'husband's low income', while family workers participate in the labour-force primarily to support the 'family business'.

Summary and Conclusions

In the initial portion of this paper, we have drawn heavily on data gathered in the nineteenth round of the Mainichi survey on fertility and family planning, to discuss the pattern of wife's earnings by type of employment, and compared it with that of husband's earnings. The results have shown that although wife's earnings, regardless of her work status, are substantially lower than husband's earnings, there are considerable differentials in wife's earnings among various employment alternatives. Full-time paid employees have the highest income level, followed by the group of traditional-sector workers, and over three-quarters of part-time paid employees have earnings of less than 900 thousand yen. This low earning level for part-time employees is largely attributable to both the income-tax law and lower bonus payments offered to them. Although women's earnings are generally low, they still work to supplement family income and bring in a significant amount of a couple's joint earnings. Among women who work, wife's earnings are, on average, about one-quarter of total household earnings.

In the second half of the present paper, we have estimated the wage equation for full-time paid employees, and identified the determinants of wife's participation in the labour-force as a full-time paid employee. The estimated result has shown that the wage for full-time employees is influenced considerably by wife's work experience and her educational attainment, which confirms a priori expectations. The factors affecting the probabilities of women's participation in the labour-market as full-time paid employees are comparable to those for other industrialized countries. These include the presence of young children, wife's pre-marital work experience, husband's earnings and occupation, the current place of residence, and wife's expected wage offer. It should be emphasized, however, that patrilocality of current residence, which is a unique feature of Japanese society, has been observed to have a positive impact on pursuit of full-time paid employment.

As a result of the implementation of the Equal Employment Opportunity Law in 1986, it is expected that women's wages will continue to improve more rapidly than men's in the years to come. Moreover, as has been observed in other developed societies, the demand for female labour is expected to increase due to the slower growth of the male labour-force induced by both the maturity of public pension schemes and the secular decline of fertility (Ogawa, 1989*b*). Hence, it is conceivable that the growth of women's wages will accelerate. Under these circumstances, a greater proportion of married Japanese women will be likely to participate in the labour-force as full-time paid employees in the years ahead. However, if the long-term downward trend with respect to patrilocality of residence continues in the future, this wage effect upon participation is likely to be offset to some extent.

We have also analysed the differences in the determinants of participation between full-time paid employment and other work statuses. Although the different strengths of a given set of determinants have been identified for each employment type, the following four variables have been statistically significant in accounting for women's choice among the four employment alternatives: husband's annual earnings, wife's predicted wage for full-time paid employment, wife's pre-marital work experience, and patrilocality of residence. Husband's higher annual earnings raise his wife's probability of working as a part-time employee or family worker, or staying at home as a housewife rather than working as a full-time employee. The opposite force is generated by a higher expected wage offer in full-time employment, pre-marital work experience as a full-time employee, and patrilocality. It should be noted, however, that these four variables have different strengths for each employment type. Depending upon the extent to which these variables change in the future, the allocation of married Japan women among the alternative employment statuses will vary pronouncedly. In addition, if the Japanese income-tax law related to the upper limit imposed upon the income of part-time employees is either drastically changed or abolished, more married women may shift their work status from part-time to full-time employment.

In order to gain a further insight into the above analyses, we have also analysed wife's reasons for working. Although married Japanese women have a host of reasons for working, both full-time and part-time paid employees, by and large, work for 'educational expenses for children', 'money for myself', or because of 'husband's low income', whereas family workers participate in the work force mainly to support a 'family business'.

References

Bauer, J. and Shin, Y.-S. (1987), 'Female Labor Force Participation and Wages in the Republic of Korea', East–West Population Institute Working Paper No. 54.

Blundell, R. and Walker, I. (1984), 'A Household Production Specification of Demographic Variables in Demand', *Economic Journal*, supp. to vol. 94, 59–68.

Butz, W. P. and Ward, M. P. (1979), 'The Emergence of Counter-cyclical U.S. Fertility', *American Economic Review*, 69/3, 318–28.

Cogan, J. (1980), 'Labor Supply with Costs of Labor', in J. P. Smith (ed.), *Female Labor Supply: Theory and Estimation*, Princeton, NJ: Princeton University Press, 327–64.

Hanoch, G. (1980), 'Hours and Weeks in the Theory of Labor Supply', in J. P. Smith (ed.), *Female Labor Supply: Theory and Estimation*, Princeton, NJ: Princeton University Press, 119–65.

Heckman, J. (1980), 'Sample Selection Bias as a Specification Error', in J. P. Smith (ed.), *Female Labor Supply: Theory and Estimation*, Princeton, NJ: Princeton University Press, 206–48.

Hill, M. A. (1983), 'Female Labor Force Participation in Developing and Developed Countries—Consideration of the Informal Sector', *Review of Economics and Statistics*, 65/3, 459–68.

—— (1989), 'Female Labor Supply in Japan: Implications of the Informal Sector for Labor Force Participation and Hours of Work', *Journal of Human Resources*, 24/1, 143–61.

Institute of Population Problems (1988), *Marriage and Fertility in Present-Day Japan*, Tokyo: Institute of Population Problems.

International Labour Organization (1986), 'Equality on Pay Day Still an Elusive Goal', mimeographed.

Joshi, H. (1986), 'Participation in Paid Work: Evidence from the Women and Employment Survey', in R. Blundell and I. Walker (eds.), *Unemployment, Search and Labor Supply*, Cambridge: Cambridge University Press, 217–42.

Killingsworth, M. R. (1983), *Labor Supply*, Cambridge: Cambridge University Press.

Martin, L. G. and Ogawa, N. (1988), 'The Effect of Cohort Size on Relative Wages in Japan', R. D. Lee, W. B. Arthur, and G. Rodgers (eds.), *Economics of Changing Age Distributions in Developed Countries*, Oxford: Clarendon Press, 59–75.

Mincer, J. (1985), 'Intercountry Comparisons of Labor Force Trends and of Related Development: An Overview', *Journal of Labor Economics*, 3/1, pt. 2, 1–32.

Ministry of Labour (1988), *Fujinrodo no Jitsujo* ('The Situation of Female Labor'), Tokyo: Government Printing Office.

—— (1989), *Basic Survey on Wage Structure 1988*, Tokyo: Rodo Horei Kyokai.

Ogawa, N. (1987), 'Sex Differentials in Labour Force Participation and Earnings in Japan', *Women's Economic Participation in Asia and the Pacific*, Bangkok: United Nations ESCAP, 305–32.

—— (1989*a*), 'Female Labor Supply and Family Size Aspirations in Contemporary Japan', unpublished manuscript.

—— (1989*b*) 'Population Ageing and Household Structural Change in Japan', in J. M. Eekelaar and D. Pearl (eds.), *An Ageing World: Dilemmas and Challenges for Law and Social Policy*, Oxford: Clarendon Press, 75–97.

—— and Mason, A. (1986), 'An Economic Analysis of Recent Fertility in Japan: An Application of the Butz–Ward Model', *Journal of Population Studies ('Jinkogaku Kenkyu')*, 9, 5–14.

Otani, K. and Atoh, M. (1988), 'The Social Consequences of Rapid Fertility Decline in Japan', paper presented at the IUSSP on Fertility Transition in Asia: Diversity and Change, Bangkok.

Ozaki, M. (1988), 'Introduction and Summary of the Survey on the Family', paper presented at the Workshop on Crossnational Analysis of the Family, Nihon University, Tokyo.

Prais, S. J. (1987), 'Educating for Productivity: Comparisons of Japanese and English Schooling and Vocational Preparation', *National Institute Economic Review* (Feb.), 40–56.

Preston, S. H. and Kono, S. (1988), 'Trends in Well-Being of Children and the Elderly in Japan', in J. L. Palmer, T. Smeeding, and B. Boyle Torrey (eds.), *The Vulnerable*, Washington DC: The Urban Institute Press, 277–307.

Shimada, H. and Higuchi, Y. (1985), 'An Analysis of Trends in Female Labor Force Participation in Japan', *Journal of Labor Economics*, 3/1, pt. 2, 355–74.

Smith, J. P. (1980), 'Assets and Labor Supply', in J. P. Smith (ed.), *Female Labor Supply: Theory and Estimation*, Princeton: Princeton University Press, 166–205.

Statistics Bureau, Government of Japan (1989), *Annual Report on the Labour Force Survey*, Tokyo.

World Bank (1990), *World Development Report 1990*, New York: Oxford University Press.

Appendix

The appendix presents illustrative statistics for the variables used in the analysis.

Table 5.A1. Means and Standard Deviations of Explanatory Variables of Wife's Labour-Force Participation as a Paid Employee for Married Japanese Women of Childbearing Age, 1988

Explanatory Variables	Mean	Standard Deviation
Number of children aged:		
<1	0.062	0.243
1–5	0.401	0.676
6–17	1.112	0.990
≥18	0.366	0.730
Husband's annual earnings		
(millions of yen)	4.570	2.333
Husband's education		
Junior high school	0.154	0.361
Senior high school	0.448	0.497
Junior college	0.109	0.311
University	0.289	0.453
Urban–rural residence		
(urban = 1, rural = 0)	0.839	0.368
Wife full-time employee before marriage		
(yes = 1, no = 0)	0.805	0.397
Husband working as a paid employee		
(yes = 1, no = 0)	0.804	0.397
Patrilocality of residence		
(yes = 1, no = 0)	0.292	0.455
Wife's age	37.574	6.623
Wife's predicted wage		
(millions of yen)	1.665	0.390

Note: N = 1915.

Table 5.A2. Means and Standard Deviations of Explanatory Variables of Labour-Force Participation of Married Japanese Women among Alternative Types of Employment

Explanatory Variables	Mean	Standard Deviation
Number of Children aged:		
<1	0.062	0.244
1–5	0.404	0.679
6–17	1.115	0.992
≥18	0.367	0.730
Husband's annual earnings (millions of yen)	4.560	2.325
Husband's education		
Junior high school	0.153	0.360
Senior high school	0.451	0.498
Junior college	0.109	0.311
University	0.287	0.452
Urban–rural residence (urban = 1, rural = 0)	0.836	0.370
Wife full-time employee before marriage		
(yes = 1, no = 0)	0.812	0.391
Husband working as a paid employee		
(yes = 1, no = 0)	0.813	0.390
Patrilocality of residence (yes = 1, no = 0)	0.292	0.455
Wife's age	37.515	6.641
Wife's predicted wage (millions of yen)	1.656	0.381

Note: N = 1849.

Part II

**Intergenerational Transfers in
Theory and Practice**

6 Fertility, Mortality, and Intergenerational Transfers: Comparisons across Steady States

RONALD LEE

Introduction

Biological changes over the life-cycle interact with economic incentives and socio-cultural values and institutions to produce life-cycle patterns of earning and consumption. These patterns, while by no means identical in detail across populations, share the general features of consumption in excess of labour earnings in youth and old age. Consumption in excess of labour earnings at these ages is funded, at least in part, from the excess of earnings in the working ages, through what may be called intergenerational transfers. Such transfers take place through the family, the public sector, and the market.[1]

In steady state, age-patterns of intergenerational transfers are repeated generation after generation, and we may view them as a means for individuals to smooth their own consumption streams through inter-temporal transfers to themselves. In this sense, the consumption needs and labour efforts of the different age-groups in a population at any instant are a kind of surrogate for those same needs and efforts over the individual life-cycle. When the population is stationary, the correspondence is exact: the proportion of the population at each age is identical to the average proportion at each age over the individual life-cycle (see Preston, 1982). When the population is either growing or declining, however, the correspondence is systematically distorted, and this distortion affects the terms on which individuals can effectively transfer

The research assistance of Tim Miller is gratefully acknowledged, as are helpful suggestions from Robert Willis, Kenneth W. Wachter, and the seminar participants. The research on which this project was based was supported by a grant from the Sloan Foundation.

[1] Reference to saving and dissaving over the life-cycle as an intergenerational transfer through the market is a departure from common language, but one which is theoretically convenient, and consistent with a growing literature (see Samuelson, 1958; Arthur and McNicoll, 1978; Lee, 1980; Willis, 1980; 1987; 1988; and Lee and Lapkoff, 1988). It is likewise a departure from common usage that inheritances and gifts, which are gross familial intergenerational transfers, do not alter the net transfers with which I am here concerned unless they lead recipients and donors to alter their consumption patterns. But under the steady-state assumption, one passes on to one's children an amount in bequests exactly equal to those one receives, inflated by the steady-state population growth rate, so the net transactions with other generations are unaffected.

resources inter-temporally to themselves by engaging in contemporaneous transfers with other age-groups. In steady state, the effects of the distortion are summarized by the implicit rate of return to all transfers, which equals the population growth-rate, as was discovered by Samuelson (1958) and is well known for pay-as-you-go pension systems.[2] Evidently, the effect of the distortion—and of the implicit rate of return—may be favourable or unfavourable, depending on the average ages at which consumption and labour earning take place in the population and over the life-cycle.

Variations in fertility always strongly affect the population growth-rate and age-distribution, and therefore lead to such distortions.[3] In low mortality countries, however, typical variations in mortality have very little effect on the growth-rate, and therefore have little effect on the implicit rate of return on intergenerational transfers. For this reason, while recent mortality declines in developed countries have indeed tended to raise the proportion of elderly, this effect is roughly equal for the steady-state population age distribution and for the distribution of person-years lived over the life-cycle. In high mortality settings, however, mortality change has a powerful effect on the population growth-rate, since many women die before reaching reproductive age. For this reason, mortality differences alter the population age distribution and the individual life-cycle in very different ways: higher life expectancy causes younger populations.

But if mortality change in low mortality countries has little effect on the implicit rate of return earned on transfers, it none the less has a strong effect on the transfers themselves, for the obvious reason that mortality decline affects the shape of the life-cycle by prolonging the period of old-age dependency. In recent decades, both declining fertility and declining mortality have had important effects on age distribution, and therefore have had implications for intergenerational transfers. In steady state, these changes would require some combination of reduced consumption or increased labour effort age-for-age. But it is important to realize that these consequences of fertility and mortality change are significantly different from a theoretical point of view. Declining fertility reduces the implicit rate of return to intergenerational transfers; declining mortality increases the need of individuals for transfer income at later stages of the life-cycle, in addition to any effects it has on the implicit rate of return.

From the point of view of workers paying higher payroll taxes this may appear to make little difference, yet the distinction is important. When payroll taxes are higher in a lower fertility population, it is because the implicit rate of return on intergenerational transfers is lower. If fertility is below replacement, and the growth-rate and implicit rate of return are negative, then a worker actually pays to support more person-years of elderly retirement

---

[2] This is true when technology is stationary, so per capita income is constant over time.

[3] Indeed, to a close approximation, the effect of fertility differences on the growth-rate is independent of the level of mortality.

than s/he will receive in turn. Resentment is then understandable. When, however, payroll taxes are higher in a population with lower mortality, this is because each individual will spend a longer time in retirement; workers are paying more to themselves, and earning an implicit rate of return on their contributions that is actually slightly higher than in a comparable population with higher mortality. Over the life-cycle, individuals in a lower mortality regime will consume more, whereas those in a lower fertility regime will perhaps consume less, depending on some empirical issues to be discussed below. Politically, morally, and economically, the situation is quite different.

The first part of this chapter reviews recent research on fertility change, intergenerational transfers, and life-cycle consumption. This discussion briefly considers the assumptions made, the advantages of a household accounting framework, the empirical findings for some developed and developing countries, and their interpretation. I will then discuss the effect of mortality change on life-cycle consumption. First I set out the analytical framework, and then I make a more detailed assessment of actual patterns of mortality change and their implications for consumption. As a first and simpler case, I examine the effect of different mortality rates when fertility changes at the same time so as to keep the population growth-rate fixed at zero; in this way the pure effect of mortality on life-cycle is isolated. I then consider the full effects of mortality change when induced changes in population growth-rates occur as well.

The Consequences of Reduced Fertility for Intergenerational Transfers

The Approach and Special Assumptions

This paper will only consider economic–demographic steady states, which is a serious limitation. Furthermore, only a particular kind of steady state will be considered, namely 'golden-rule' steady states. In these, for any given demographic structure, the saving rate and capital stock are such that average consumption at each instant is maximized. If there is no technical progress, the rate of interest equals the population growth rate, and the aggregate proportion of output consumed equals labour's share, while the proportion of output saved equals capital's share.[4] The question to be addressed here is how demographic differences in fertility and mortality affect the possibilities for life-cycle consumption in such golden-rule steady states, operating through the interaction of the population age-distribution with the age-structure of intergenerational transfers.

Earlier work by Arthur and McNicoll (1978) has shown that the effect of a variation in fertility, across golden-rule steady states, is proportional to the

[4] I will also assume that there is a single rate of interest which applies to both borrowing and lending.

difference between the mean age of consumption and the mean age of labour earning, less the capital/consumption ratio. Willis (1988) deepened and extended this work by showing how transfers through the family, the market, and the state interact to determine the overall pattern of net intergenerational transfers, and by demonstrating the close relation between the average age result and Gale's (1974) results on the aggregate credit balance. Willis (1987; 1988) has also shown that when fertility levels are chosen by parents with altruistic preferences, the resulting steady state will have less capital per head, and consequently higher interest rates, than in the golden-rule case. Eckstein and Wolpin (1985), however, found that with a non-altruistic utility function, the golden-rule outcome could occur. It is also important that Willis (1987) and Nerlove, Razin, and Sadka (1987) found that with an altruistic utility function, there are no externalities to childbearing, while Eckstein and Wolpin (1985) showed that with a non-altruistic utility function, externalities to childbearing could occur, and indeed when public transfers to the elderly are substantial, fertility might well be lower than optimal. Blanchet (1988) has shown that when capital has a finite life, the capital-dilution effect of more rapid population growth is less than the capital–consumption ratio, since growth reduces the average age of the capital stock and therefore reduces its rate of depreciation.

The Household Framework and the Role of Time Use

In Lee (1980; 1988a) I developed the idea that the household, rather than the individual, is the appropriate unit of accounting for studying intergenerational transfers. It is largely at the household level that consumption is managed, and economies of scale, public goods, and joint products within the household make it very difficult, if not impossible, to conceptualize satisfactorily, let alone measure, individual-level consumption. Furthermore, most (but not all) familial transfers take place within households, and fertility decisions are likewise made by adults living in households.[5] Familial transfers are presumably internalized as an individual cost or benefit of childbearing, while non-familial transfers through the market or the public sector may lead to externalities to childbearing.

Because of the non-linearities introduced by returns to scale, public goods, and joint production in the household, it does not suffice to base the analysis on the average mortality experience of individuals or households; instead, in principle, consumption under each possible combination of survival outcomes for household members should be calculated, and then a probability-weighted average formed (Lee, 1988). This would be very burdensome to operationalize.

[5] The principal difficulty with this generalization is that parents may transfer significant amounts to their adult children who have their own households, and adult children may transfer significant amounts to their parents after leaving home. To the extent that these later transfers are not taken into account by the parents as a 'cost' of children, the assertion about externalities is unaffected.

Empirical Findings and their Interpretation

When the population growth-rate increases, so does the implicit rate of return. Life-cycle consumption increases or decreases according to whether people on average earn before they consume, or vice versa. For this reason, it is informative to evaluate the average ages of consumption (A_c) and labour earning (A_{yl}). When A_{yl} is less than A_c, we will say that the net direction of intergenerational transfers is upwards, and conversely.

I have calculated values for A_c and A_{yl} for the United States in about 1980, based on the household framework, and I found A_c to exceed A_{yl} by about four years. Ermisch (1989) has found similar numbers for Great Britain and Japan, using the same framework. These indicate that if fertility increases (across steady states) so as to raise the population growth rate by 1 per cent (.01), the present value of life-cycle consumption would rise by 4 per cent through intergenerational transfers. This positive effect would probably be overwhelmed by the capital dilution effect, which could be of the order of 6 or 7 per cent (although see Blanchet, 1988); however, I will here focus on the intergenerational transfer effect.[6] These results indicate that the net direction of intergenerational transfers is upwards, from younger to older, in these three developed countries. Evidently, the combination of long life with a welfare state attending generously to the needs of the elderly, dominates the heavy public and private expenditures on health and education of the young. These findings bear out the concerns of many developed-country governments about the burden of old-age dependency in low fertility populations, and suggest that reduced expenditure on children is not fully off-setting. In another paper, Lee and Lapkoff (1988) incorporate time-use in the analysis, allocating it among home production (including time spent in child-care), leisure, schooling, and market work. Results are similar to those in Lee, 1988*a*.

I have also calculated average ages of consumption and labour earnings for one set of developing-country data. Mueller (1976) estimated age-profiles of consumption and earning for rural agricultural populations in the Third World, based on a review of survey data from a number of countries. Although the household framework is preferable, suitable data were not readily available, so I worked with Mueller's individual data.[7] Taking $e_0 = 25$, which I believe to be approximately correct for South Asia or China in the early twentieth century, I found A_c to about five years less than A_{yl}, despite the relatively early timing of labour supply. Doubtless the high mortality of children before reaching productive ages, combined with the slight probability of surviving past the active working years goes far to explain this pattern. Indeed, if

---

[6] Willis (1988) treats what I am calling the capital-dilution effect as a portion of the intergenerational transfer effect.

[7] Mueller also constructed synthetic household profiles based on these individual age-profiles, but these do not reflect the non-linearities that provide the entire rationale for using household data in this context.

identically shaped age profiles are applied to a stationary low mortality population, with $e_0 = 75$ instead of 25, the average age of consumption slightly exceeds that of earning. When $e_0 = 25$, the old-age dependency phase of the life-cycle is nearly non-existent, since at birth, there is only about one person-year of life expected after age 65.

These results apparently conflict with Caldwell's (1978) fertility theory, which asserts that in traditional societies, wealth flows upward from younger to older, and that fertility declines only when the wealth flows reverse. I find that wealth flows downward in a developing country with high mortality, and upward in three developed countries with low mortality. How can the anomaly be resolved? First, for fertility motivation, it is only internalized costs that matter, that is, those costs and benefits that are borne by the parents. The average ages given above refer to all transfers, through the market and public sector as well as through the family. It is clear that in developed countries, the intra-familial transfers are heavily downward, from parents to children. Inclusion of bequests would strengthen this claim. The overall upward direction results primarily from public sector transfers to the elderly, which are externalities to childbearing. Indeed, it is often suggested that fertility in developed countries is so low in part because society captures the financial benefits of children while leaving parents to bear most of the costs.

In developing countries, on the other hand, public-sector transfers play a relatively minor role. The Mueller data would not reflect any public-sector transfers, but I have elsewhere calculated age-specific Indian public expenditures for health, education, and pensions (Lee, 1991). In 1981 their present value over the entire life-cycle, US\$ 310, only slightly exceeded per capita income (US\$ 260). The flows were strongly downward, with an average age-difference (at current vital rates) of eleven years. Combining these public-sector transfers with Mueller's profiles would therefore only strengthen the finding that the flow is downward, rather than upward. Market transfers probably still play a rather minor role in intergenerational transfers in the Third World, since extended families and intra-household income transfers do much to smooth income and consumption over the individual life-cycle. Why then is fertility so high in these settings? My guess is that the absence of trusted institutions to provide insurance and long-term borrowing or loans at low (golden-rule) and secure rates raises the subjective value placed on the upward transfers from children well above the values imputed to such transfers by the model I am using.

Mortality and Life-Cycle Consumption

There is thus a growing literature examining the effects of fertility change on patterns of intergenerational transfers. This literature has yielded many useful insights, but aside from pioneering pieces by Arthur (1981) and Preston (1982), the role of mortality and its changes has been largely ignored. This is particularly true of the many analyses based on models which abstract entirely from mortality by assuming survival through the oldest age-group. Yet mortality change has become an increasingly important influence on population ageing in recent decades, and the convenient assumption of a 'neutral' age-pattern of mortality change (one which leaves the age-distribution unaltered), often used in the past to justify ignoring mortality's influence, is no longer tenable even as a rough approximation in developed countries.

Conceptual Problems

What do we want to know when we ask whether life-cycle consumption and leisure will rise or fall when mortality improves? If people live longer, then the parameters of their life-cycles are changed. Life-cycle consumption could be lower at every age, but higher in present value, because more years are now lived.

In fact, there are now three questions about the effects of a given variation in mortality. First, how much will the present value of consumption change, evaluated at the initial discount rate and probabilities of survival to each age, while allowing the planned level of consumption at each age to change? This question is well defined, since even when mortality is high, there is some probability of survival to the most advanced ages, and so the life-cycle consumption plan includes all ages. Second, how much will the present value of life-cycle consumption change, holding constant the planned age-profile of consumption at initial levels, and the discount-rate, while allowing survival probabilities to vary? The answers to these two questions can differ only to the extent that life-cycle earnings are altered by the mortality change. The third question, of course, asks how much the present value of life-cycle consumption will change, holding constant the consumption plan and survival, while allowing the population growth-rate and hence the discount-rate, to vary. Mathematical analysis categorizes the response to mortality change in exactly this way, producing expressions which can be explicitly evaluated.

I will turn to this task in a moment. First, however, I must point out that evaluation of the welfare implications of the change is not straightforward, and is beyond the scope of this paper (these issues are discussed in Arthur, 1981). In the case of an exogenously imposed change in fertility, the within-household transfers to children provided a convenient means for assessing the marginal utility of a birth, and therefore of netting out direct utility change due to the demographic shift (see Lee, 1988a). In the case of a mortality change, however, such a neat analytical solution is not available, although for nearly everybody the increase in expected length of life, particularly if accomplished through monotonic reductions in the force of mortality, would be highly valued (see Arthur, 1981).[8]

[8] Arthur (1981) uses the utility function $U[c(x), x]$ which assigns utility at age x separately for being alive and for consuming. Different values of the elasticity of substitution between these can cover a wide range of possibilities.

The remainder of this paper appraises the effects of mortality change on life-cycle consumption possibilities through intergenerational transfers, using a framework similar to that used by Arthur (1981).

The Social and Individual Budget Constraints

In a stable population, the density of the population at age x is proportional to $e^{-nx}p(x)$, where n is the intrinsic rate of natural increase, and $p(x)$ is the probability of surviving from birth to age x. Let $c(x)$ be the average rate of consumption by a person at age x, and let $y_l(x)$ be the average income from labour services at this age (earnings from capital are assumed to be saved and invested, in accordance with the golden-rule assumption). These age-profiles might be imposed exogenously by a central authority or by social norms, or they could result from life-cycle optimization decisions; their origin has no effect on the analysis which follows. It is helpful to view $y_l(x)$ as the product of the labour-force participation rate, $l(x)$, the efficiency of labour at age x, $e(x)$, and a wage per efficiency unit of labour, $w(k)$, where w is independent of age but depends on the amount of capital per (efficiency weighted) labour, k: $y_l(x) = l(x)e(x)w(k)$.

Along golden-rule paths, total consumption must equal total earnings of labour at every instant, so the population-weighted integrals of these age-profiles must be equal. The 'social budget' constraint expresses this requirement:

$$\int e^{-nx}p(x)y_l(x)\mathrm{d}x = \int e^{-nx}p(x)c(x)\mathrm{d}x. \tag{1}$$

Observe that this can also be interpreted as the individual life-cycle budget constraint, since the market interest rate for borrowing and lending equals the population growth rate, n, and the consumption, earning, and survival functions hold over the life-cycle as well as cross-sectionally. This simple but powerful analogy between population growth-rates and interest rates underlies Samuelson's biological interest-rate theorem, and greatly facilitates comparative steady-state analysis.

Now consider a different steady state associated with a marginal change in the survival function $p(x)$. The change can be of any form,[9] and need not be monotonic with age, but it will be convenient to view it as a change to a generally lower level of mortality and higher life expectancy (Arthur, 1981, examined changes resulting from the elimination of particular causes of death). How will this variation in mortality affect the possibilities for life-cycle consumption, including consumption of leisure? From a demographic point of view, a change in mortality affects the population through two routes: first

---

[9] Of course, since $p(x)$ is a survival function its level must be non-increasing in x, but the age-pattern of changes in $p(x)$ can have many forms, and may well be increasing in x over some range.

by altering the population growth-rate, or n in the above expression; and second by altering survival over the life cycle.[10]

From an economic point of view, these demographic changes entail several economic ones. First, individuals must now plan and save for a longer period of retirement, *ceteris paribus*; second, the market interest rate will change since mortality affects the population growth-rate; third, the implicit interest rate at which the family and the public sector can transfer income among age-groups changes, again because the population growth-rate changes; and fourth, the golden-rule capital–labour ratio declines, reducing wage-rates. In addition, there may be changes in disability and efficiency of labour, but we defer discussion of these. Responses to the changed social and private options may take various forms. People may choose to work longer hours and/or to post-pone retirement, or to consume less and save more in the working ages; or the public sector may alter the extent and terms of its transfer programmes; or intra-familial transfers may change.

Under the convenient golden-rule assumption, our analysis will summarize the necessary changes in the age-profiles of consumption and earning regardless of the combination of private and public responses that is chosen.[11] We can do this because the economic possibilities are so strictly constrained by the demographic changes. In this way, we can focus on that portion of the ageing problem which is common to all institutional arrangements.

Mortality Change and Life-Cycle Consumption Possibilities

Let i be an index of the age-schedule of mortality, representing its general level. We will write p as function of i as well as age: $p(x,i)$.[12] Let the left-hand side of the social budget constraint (1), representing the present value at birth of life-cycle labour earnings, be Y, and the right-hand side, representing the present value at birth of life-cycle consumption, be C. When mortality is different (i varies), $c(x)$ or $y_i(x)$ must also be different, or the identity would no longer hold.

Now consider the derivative of both sides of the natural logarithm of equation (1). Recall that $y_i(x) = l(x)e(x)w(k)$. When mortality varies, the population growth-rate varies, so k and $w(k)$ will vary as well. After some rearrangement, we find the following:[13]

---

[10] A change in fertility, by contrast, can affect the age-distribution only by affecting the popu-lation growth-rate.

[11] The golden-rule assumption assures us that the market interest rate faced by individuals equals the population growth-rate, which is the implicit rate of return yielded by a public-sector pay-as-you-go transfer programme or familial transfers.

[12] I assume both functions are differentiable with respect to i. It could be that the level of mortality, as expressed by e_0, for example, could be constant over i, while the shape of the mortality schedule varies with i. Typically both the shape and the level will vary, however.

[13] I do not give the details of this derivation here. Some details can be found in Lee, 1981 and Lee and Lapkoff, 1988. The average ages result from the fact that the derivative of e^{-nx} is xe^{-nx}, which when integrated forms the numerator of an average age. The capital-dilution term is identical to the corresponding term in an ordinary neoclassical growth model without age-distribution.

$$\int e^{-nx} p(x,i)(\partial c(x)/\partial i - \partial l(x)/\partial i)\mathrm{d}x = \tag{2}$$
present value of adjustments

$$(\partial n/\partial i)(A_c - A_{yl})C + \int e^{-nx}(\partial p(x,i)/\partial i)[y_l(x) - c(x)]\mathrm{d}x - \quad (\partial n/\partial i)(K/C).$$

rate-of-return effect   life-cycle effect   capital-dilution effect

where K is the aggregate capital stock.

This is the result we have been seeking for the effect of a mortality change on life-cycle consumption possibilities.

First consider the left-hand side, which is the quantity we wish to evaluate. It is the present value of the life-cycle changes in consumption and leisure which result from the change in mortality. (Note that the present value is evaluated at the initial levels of mortality and population growth-rate.) These changes can be of any form, provided only that their present value equals the quantity on the right. For example, if life expectancy rises (i increases) it might be that consumption stays the same at every age, while leisure is reduced (labour supply, $l(x)$, increased) either at every age, or just for ages that were previously retirement years. Alternatively, leisure could stay the same, while consumption was reduced at each age in order to save more for the now longer retirement, or in order to pay increased payroll taxes to a public pension programme. Preferences, policies, and institutions will determine which of these various adjustments occurs, but in any event the net outcome must equal the quantity on the right, to which we now turn our attention. Interpreting consumption broadly to include the value of leisure, I will refer to this left-hand-side quantity as the present value of adjustments in life-cycle consumption, or as the costs of mortality decline.

On the right side of the equation, the first portion, representing the indirect effect of mortality change operating through the population growth-rate, is familiar and intuitive: when the average age of consumption is older than the average age of earning, then a more rapidly growing, and therefore younger, population is beneficial. I will refer to this as the 'rate-of-return effect', since the implicit and market rates of interest equal the population growth-rate, and a higher rate is beneficial when the difference in average ages is positive. The second portion, representing the effects of mortality change on the life-cycle, is also very straightforward: it is a weighted sum of the increases or decreases in person-years lived at each age, times the excess or deficit of earnings relative to consumption at that age. For example, if (roughly speaking) life-cycle years lived during the working ages increase more than those lived during the dependent years, then life-cycle consumption possibilities increase. I will call this the 'life-cycle' effect. The third portion represents the reduction in the golden-rule capital–labour ratio resulting from more rapid population growth. I will refer to it as the 'capital-dilution' effect.

Our task is to evaluate the adjustment in life-cycle consumption required by a change in mortality, by evaluating each of the terms on the right: the rate-of-return effect, the life-cycle effect, and the capital-dilution effect. Before we can do that, however, we must consider the representation of mortality change. Readers not interested in this demographic topic may skip the next section.

Modelling Mortality Change

Let $\mu(x,i)$ be the force of mortality at age x, so that $p(x,i)$, the probability of surviving from birth to age x, is given by $p(x,i)=\exp(-\int\mu(s,i)ds)$. Let $\mu(x)$ and $p(x)$ represent initial levels, so that $\mu(x,0)=\mu(x)$, $p(x,0)=p(x)$. For small variations in i, $\mu(x,i) = \mu(x,0) + i\partial\mu(x,i)/\partial i$. Denote $\partial\mu(x,i)/\partial i$ by $\delta(x)$, so that $\mu(x,i) = \mu(x,0) + i\delta(x)$. Then $p(x,i)$ is approximately related to $p(x,0)$ by: $p(x,i) = p(x,0)\exp\{-i\int\delta(s)ds\}$. Letting $D(x) = \exp\{-\int\delta(s)ds\}$, we have:

$$p(x,i) = p(x)D^i(x). \qquad (3)$$

From this we can infer that for small i, $D(x)$ can be estimated as:

$$D(x) = [p(x,i)/p(x)]^{1/i}. \qquad (4)$$

We also have:

$$\partial p(x,i)/\partial i = p(x)D^i(x)\ln[D(x)] = p(x,i)\ln[D(x)]. \qquad (5)$$

Evaluating this at $i = 0$, to find the effect of a small variation in mortality about its initial level, we have:

$$\partial p(x,i)/\partial i(\text{evaluated at } i = 0) = p(x)\ln[D(x)] = -p(x)\int\delta(s)ds. \qquad (6)$$

So far this discussion has been very general. We can make it more specific by considering special cases. The simplest case is a so-called neutral mortality change, for which $\delta(x) = \delta$ at all ages, so that $D(x) = e^{-\delta x}$, and $p(x,i) = p(x)e^{-\delta ix}$. Another simple special case arises when variations in $\mu(x)$ are proportional to the level, so that $\delta(x) = -\mu(x)$. In this case, $p(x) = 1/D(x)$, and $p(x,i) = p^{-i}(x)$. Although analytically tractable, both of these cases are unrealistic, the second somewhat less so. We could go on to examine Brass logit forms and other special assumptions, but I prefer to move to a less constrained specification.

It is quite easy to avoid special assumptions; we need only calculate the function $D(x)$ from any pair of actual life-tables. For concreteness, I will use the Coale–Demeny Model West Female system (Coale and Demeny, 1983), with levels 22 and 23, corresponding to life expectancies at birth of 72.5 and 75. Let i equal the level minus 22. Then following (4), $D(x)$ is calculated as the ratio $p(x,1)/p(x,0)^{1/1}$, or the ratios of the $l(x)$s in the two tables. We have in effect created a one-parameter system of life-tables based on a standard age-pattern of the force of mortality and a standard age-pattern of changes in the force of mortality.[14]

Now consider the effect of mortality change on the population growth-rate. The intrinsic rate of natural increase is given approximately by $n = \ln[Fp(A_f)]/A_f$, where F is the gross reproduction rate, and A_f is the average age of childbearing in the stable population. A change in mortality can have some effect on F by reducing widowhood, but I will ignore this. It can also affect A_f, but any effect will be second-order and very small. The main effect is on the probability of survival to childbearing age, given by $\partial n/\partial i = (\partial p(A_f,i)/\partial i)/[A_f p(A_f,i)]$.

From the earlier results we have $\partial p(A_f,i)/\partial i$ (evaluated at $i = 0$) $= p(A_f)\ln[D(A_f)]$. Substituting, we find:

$$\partial n/\partial i = \ln[D(A_f)]/A_f \qquad (7)$$

When there is little change in the force of mortality below age A_f, $D(A_f)$ will be close to unity and its natural log will be close to zero, so this effect will be very small. Fig. 6.1 plots the change in the population growth-rate induced by an increase of one year in life expectancy, in the neighborhood of a zero population growth-rate, for initial life expectancies ranging from 20 to 80. Calculations are again based on the Coale–Demeny Model West Female system of life-tables. When $e_0 = 20$ and the growth-rate is initially zero, a one-year gain in e_0 raises the growth-rate by .0016, or one-sixth of 1 per cent. This is very substantial. By contrast, when e_0 is initially 77.5 and the growth-rate is zero, a one-year gain in e_0 raises the growth-rate by only .00011, one-hundredth of 1 per cent, which is almost nothing. The pattern shown in Fig. 6.1 is quite general, since the effect of mortality change on the growth-rate is approximately independent of the level of fertility.

The 'Life-Cycle Effect' of Mortality Change

Background

We have seen that mortality change has one set of effects that arises from the changed population growth-rate, and another that arises directly from the changed survival probabilities. This latter I have called the 'life-cycle effect', since it arises from the changed distribution of expected person-years lived over the life-cycle. When the gains in person-years occur predominantly at ages for which earnings exceed consumption, then the life-cycle budget constraint will be relaxed, and consumption and/or leisure can increase at each age. When the gains occur predominantly at dependent ages, the opposite is

---

[14] I have used this approach to modelling mortality change in other contexts, including inverse projection and mortality forecasts.

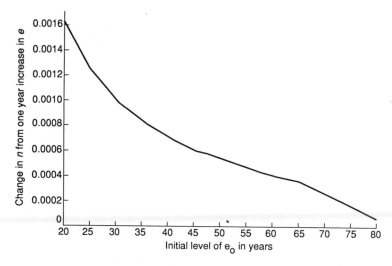

Fig. 6.1 The Effect on the Population Growth-Rate of a One-Year Gain in Life Expectancy at Birth

the case. The total effect of mortality change is the sum of the rate-of-growth effect, the life-cycle effect, and the capital-dilution effect. In the special case in which the population moves slowly along a zero-growth-rate isoquant while both fertility and mortality decline in tandem, the life-cycle effect is also the total effect.

I will begin by evaluating the life-cycle effect (see Blanchet, 1986, for a related attempt). This exercise is not without substantive interest, for in the (very) long run, the population growth-rate must be zero, with fertility adjusting to any difference in mortality. The age-distribution, and therefore the pattern of intergenerational transfers, will change as mortality and fertility vary along the zero-growth-rate isoquant. Of course, historical changes in fertility and mortality have not typically been of this form, since typically mortality decline precedes fertility decline, and rapid growth occurs. None the less, most populations have started at some time in the past two centuries close to the high fertility, high mortality, zero-growth region, and will move eventually to the low fertility, low mortality, zero-growth end of the isoquant. Note that along this isoquant, fertility and mortality decline together, so the population unambiguously ages.

Analytically, it is a simple matter to consider changes along the isoquant, since we are then dealing with population age-distributions which always correspond to the life-table or stationary-age distributions, and these are given by the $p(x)$ function and its changes, as already discussed. Of course, the life-cycle plans of earning and consumption will themselves change over

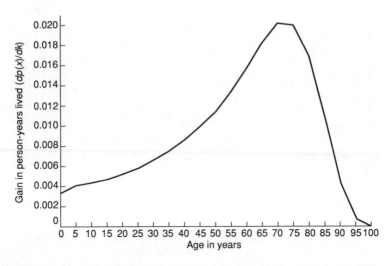

Source: Calculated from Model West Female life-tables derived from Coale and Demeny (1983).
Fig. 6.2   The Age Distribution of Gains in Person-Years Lived

the course of this transition, and such changes should be taken into account when evaluating the analytic expressions.[15]

Illustrations Based on Coale–Demeny Life-Tables

Coale–Demeny model life-tables can be used to calculate typical age-patterns of gains in expected person-years lived when mortality declines. Fig. 6.2 shows the distribution over the life-cycle of one additional year of life expectancy, when e_0 rises from 73 to 74.[16] Put differently, Fig. 6.2 plots $\partial p(x,i)/\partial i$ against x, where i has been scaled so that a unit change corresponds to one year gain in e_0. Clearly the gains in person-years lived are concentrated at the older ages, but this need not be so if we start from a different initial level of e_0.

The relation between the age-pattern of person-years of life gained and the initial level of mortality is shown in Fig. 6.3. The horizontal axis plots life expectancy at birth, ranging from 20 years to 80 years. The vertical axis shows the number of person-years of life gained in each of three broad age groups— 0 to 15, 15 to 65, and 65+—when life expectancy rises by a year. Since life expectancy is the sum of person-years lived at all ages, gains in these age-groups

---

[15] Also note that the analysis should be done in terms of household earning and consumption profiles, for reasons already discussed. However, the necessary data to carry out such an analysis are not available for developing countries, and are not yet analysed in the appropriate way for developed countries.

[16] This is based on Model West Female life-tables, and I have interpolated linearly between e_0 of 72.5 and 75.0.

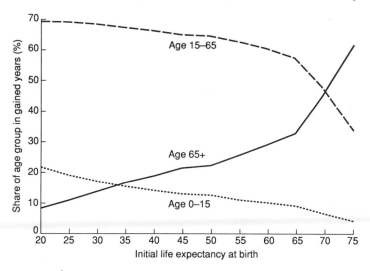

Fig. 6.3 The Percentage Distribution by Broad Age-Group of Gains in Person-Years Lived when e_0 Rises

must always sum to unity, and the lines can therefore also be interpreted as the proportionate distribution of gains in the different age-groups.

When initial life expectancy is 20 years, 22 per cent of the years gained are at ages 0 to 15; 69.5 per cent at ages 15 to 65; and only 8.6 per cent at ages over 65. By contrast, at an initial life expectancy of 75, only 3.9 per cent of the years accrue between 0 and 15; only 34 per cent between 15 and 65; and fully 62 per cent over the age of 65. As life expectancy continues to rise, the distribution of gains must become ever more skewed towards the last age-group, because the opportunities for gains before 65 will become progressively exhausted. The effects of mortality change on intergenerational transfers depend closely on the age-distribution of these changes in person-years lived, and therefore these effects should vary substantially depending on the initial level of mortality.

A different aspect of the age-pattern of mortality change is shown in Fig. 6.4, which plots the proportional gain in person-years lived for the same three broad age-groups as life expectancy rises from 20 to 80. Note that person-years lived in older age-groups always grow by a greater proportion than in younger age-groups; when the force of mortality decreases at each age, this pattern is a mathematical necessity. Thus the portion of the life-cycle spent in the working years always grows proportionately more than the portion spent in child dependency, and the portion of the life-cycle spent at older ages grows more rapidly still—in Fig. 6.4, always more than twice as rapidly

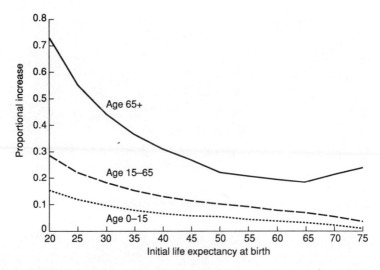

Note: The proportion is calculated on the basis of the original number of person-years lived in each broad age-group.
Source: Calculated from Model West Female life-tables derived from Coale and Demeny (1983).

Fig. 6.4 The Proportional Increase in Person-Years Lived in Broad Age-Groups when e_0 Rises by One Year

as the portion in the working ages. The absolute increments shown in Fig. 6.3 are more relevant for understanding the economic consequences than are the proportionate increments shown in Fig. 6.4.

An Example for a Less Developed Country

The economic implications of these mortality changes also depend on the shapes of the initial life-cycle profiles of earning and consuming. First, consider the life-cycle profiles presented by Mueller (1976). These are typical of the rural sector of many less developed countries. I have averaged these for the two sexes, and evaluated the effect of a one-year gain in life expectancy starting from $e_0 = 20$ and also from $e_0 = 75$.[17] In both cases the effect is very small. At $e_0 = 20$, mortality decline leads to an increase in consumption possibilities by about one-quarter of 1 per cent, because as noted above, nearly 70 per cent of the years gained are between 15 and 65, when there is net production. At $e_0 = 75$, mortality decline leads to a decrease in consumption possibilities by .22 per cent, because most of the gain is in years after age 65. The small effect at high mortality levels was to be expected, but not at low

[17] At each mortality level, I adjusted the level of consumption by a constant so as to make life-cycle consumption equal the life-cycle earnings of labour. The shape of the profiles was not altered.

levels. I suspect that the main reason that the ageing of the population has little effect even at low mortality is that in the Mueller profiles, people over 65 still have labour earnings equal to 60 per cent of their consumption.

A Stylized Example for a Developed Country

For developed countries, I will resort to a stylized example, assuming flat life-cycle profiles of earning and consuming, while maintaining realistic assumptions about mortality change. Individuals begin work at age 15, cease work at age 65, and earn a constant amount between these ages. They consume a constant amount per year from age 15 until death, and consume half this amount from birth until age 15. A one-year gain in life expectancy, starting from $e_0 = 75$, accrues 62 per cent after age 65, and 34 per cent in the working years. This entails a reduction by .7 per cent in life-cycle consumption evaluated over initial survival rates. That is, average consumption at each age must be reduced by .7 per cent. However, there is now an additional year of life in which to consume, and so total life-cycle consumption actually rises by .7 per cent. This increase in total life-cycle consumption is possible because the years lived in the working ages (15 to 65), increased by .34, or .7 per cent. Preliminary analysis of actual US age-profiles of earning and consumption leads to very similar results.

The Rate-of-Return Effect

When mortality declines, population growth-rates increase, as we saw earlier. When consumption on average precedes earning, people are on average implicit debtors over the life-cycle, and they are worse off with higher interest rates. When consumption on average follows earning, then they benefit from higher rates of return. Evaluation of these effects depends on the average ages of consumption and earning, and I will again report results for both developing and developed countries.

Pre-transitional Developing Countries

Mueller's (1976) profiles permit calculation of the average ages of consumption and earning. I have done this for a stationary population with e_0 of 25, which corresponds roughly to conditions in China in the 1920s and India in about 1900. In contemporary developing countries life expectancy is much higher, of course. Under these assumptions, A_c is 28.0 years and A_{yl} is 32.8 years, so consumption on average occurs about five years before earning. This may be surprising, since it is widely believed that in pre-transitional developing countries, children have positive asset value for their parents, or in Caldwell's (1976) terms, 'wealth flows upwards'. But when mortality is so high, the third stage of the life-cycle, old-age dependency, nearly vanishes. Out of a life expectancy at birth of 25 years, only one year is expected to be lived after age 65. Under these conditions, it is nearly inevitable that the average age of consumption will be dominated by child dependency, and will occur well before that of earning. The rate-of-return effect equals the change in the growth-rate times the difference in average ages. With the age-difference of five years reported above, an increase in the growth-rate by 1 per cent per year, or .01, would cause a 5 per cent decline in the present value of life-cycle consumption.

Developed Countries

For developed countries, I can here draw on my previous work on recent US data (Lee, 1988a), which suggested that consumption was on average later than earning by about four years. This result has subsequently also been found for Japan and for Great Britain by Ermisch (1989), using the same model and approach. In other words, in these three developed countries, the net direction of wealth flows is upward, from younger to older. Perhaps this is not surprising when about as many years are spent after 65 as before 15, and consumption is far higher in these later years than in childhood. In these countries, a 1 per cent increase in the population growth-rate would permit a 4 per cent increase in the present value of life-cycle consumption.

The capital-dilution effect (K/C) remains to be considered. For a developed country, under the golden-rule assumption, K/C is probably in the range of 5 to 10. For a high mortality, pre-transitional developing country, K/C may be as low as unity, since production is far less capital-intensive.

Miscellaneous Effects

Costs of Health Care and Terminal Illness

For the elderly, health care comprises a substantial portion of their consumption costs, and the costs of health care rise rapidly with age. However, it has been shown that the cost of the terminal illness, paired with an increasing probability of death in the older age-groups, accounts for much of the apparent age gradient for health costs. Thus as mortality declines, and the proportion of each age-group dying declines, age-specific health-care costs should also decline. This effect can readily be incorporated in the analysis.

Let $c(x)$ incorporate ordinary health-care costs at each age, and let $u(x)$ be the cost of terminal illness for someone dying at age x (of course, most of these costs will actually have accrued over the year or two preceding the moment of death). Then consumption per survivor to age x is $c(x) + \mu(x)u(x)$.

Differentiating this with respect to i, in addition to terms in $dp(x)/di$ and dn/di we will have $u(x)d\mu(x)/di = u(x)\delta(x)$. This provides a simple correction to the previous analysis. Note that when $u(x) = u$ for all x, that is when the costs of terminal illness do not vary by age of decedent, then the integral of this term in any stationary population is simply u, a constant, since everyone must die at some age. Lobitz and Prihoda (1984) provide data suggesting that u is roughly equal to US\$ 18,000 in the late 1980s.

Disability and Efficiency of Labour

We might naturally expect that declining mortality would be associated with less disability and increased efficiency of labour. Referring to the social budget constraint and the expression for y_l, we might therefore include derivatives of labour-force participation, $l(x)$, and efficiency, $e(x)$, with respect to the index of mortality, i. Such terms could easily be included in the differentiation. However, evaluating them is currently impossible. Indeed, it appears that mortality improvements often raise disability rates and reduce the efficiency of labour (Feldman, 1986). This happens when advances in medicine preserve the lives of frail individuals. Because of the substantial uncertainties, I have simply ignored all such potential effects, positive or negative.

Departures from Golden-Rule Paths

I have assumed that the economy is on a golden-rule path both before and after the mortality change. Even if we consider only steady states, this need not be true. Starting from a position off the golden-rule path, changing mortality might move the system either closer to or farther from it, and this would produce additional effects on life-cycle consumption. To study such possibilities we would need to leave the very general framework employed here, and introduce special behavioural and institutional assumptions. Examples of analysis of this sort include elaborations of the life-cycle savings model in a general equilibrium setting, such as Tobin (1967) or Mason (1987), or macro-simulation models including the public sector, such as Denton and Spencer (1976).

Combined Effects of Mortality Change

We are now in a position to evaluate the total effects of a mortality decline, based on the empirics just discussed. Before doing this, however, it will be useful to consider the special case of a neutral mortality change, which yields interesting insights into the interrelations of the life-cycle and rate-of-return effects.

Neutral Mortality Change

The assumption of neutral mortality change, while potentially misleading, provides a conveniently simple point of entry to the interacting effects of fertility and mortality. As discussed earlier, under this assumption $p(x, i) = e^{ix}p(x)$.[18] Let us first consider a movement along the zero-growth isoquant; that is, hold n constant while varying i. Inspection of the social budget constraint (1) shows that i is perfectly symmetric with n, but with an opposite sign.[19] For example, reducing every age-specific death rate by .01 per cent per year (additively) has exactly the same effect as increasing the population growth-rate by .01 per cent per year. The effect of a change in growth-rate is:

$$\mathrm{dln}C/\mathrm{d}n = A_c - A_{yl} - K/C \qquad (8)$$

Along the isoquant, n remains zero so the capital dilution term, $-K/C$, vanishes, and the sign of the transfer term is reversed, so:

$$\mathrm{dln}C/\mathrm{d}i = -(A_c - A_{yl}) \text{ (along the zero-growth isoquant).} \qquad (9)$$

Finally, if we consider the effect of mortality change while allowing the growth-rate to vary, the growth-rate change will exactly offset the intergenerational-transfer effect (since the age-distribution is unchanged), but we now acquire the capital-dilution effect. The result is simply:

$$\mathrm{dln}C/\mathrm{d}i = -K/C \text{ (allowing induced changes in the growth-rate).} \qquad (10)$$

This last equation can either be derived directly, or found by adding (8) and (9), and noting that under neutral mortality change, $\partial n/\partial i = 1$.

Consider this result solely from the point of view of intergenerational transfers, including both life-cycle saving and pay-as-you-go pension plans. Individuals in the longer-lived population are in the fortunate position of having their longer life financed entirely by higher rates of return to social transfers and private investments. They do not need to adjust either their labour supply or their savings rates to accommodate their longer period of retirement.[20]

In the real world, mortality changes are not neutral. In low-mortality populations, the neutral mortality assumption is very poor, since mortality changes are heavily concentrated in the older ages, and there is practically no off-setting increase in the population growth-rate. Then (9), for movement along the zero-growth isoquant, paints a more realistic picture. Based on the estimates by Lee (1988) and Ermisch (1989), A_c is a few years greater than A_{yl}, so the effect described in (9) is adverse: longer-lived populations must

[18] δ is here suppressed, since its value is indistinguishable from the scaling of i.

[19] I defined i so that higher i corresponded to lower mortality; otherwise, the negative sign would not be there.

[20] Although they will have to consume somewhat less due to capital dilution, the effects of this will be spread over earnings at all ages, which is consistent with the higher interest rate.

work longer, save more, and pay higher payroll taxes to provide for their longer old age. On the positive side, they do not suffer the effects of capital dilution.

By contrast, in high-mortality developing countries the induced increase in the growth-rate dominates, and (8) portrays better the consequences of mortality decline: populations get younger and suffer capital dilution. Since the Mueller profiles implied A_c less than A_{yl}, the transfer effect would again be disadvantageous.

The Total Effect for Typical Mortality Change

These patterns for developed and developing country populations can be established more accurately by dropping the assumption of neutral change, and instead treating realistic patterns of mortality change combined with the empirical estimates discussed earlier. In the low-mortality developed countries, a one-year gain in life expectancy required a reduction in the present value of life-cycle consumption of about .7 per cent. The one-year gain also raises the population growth-rate by about .0001. This leads to a positive rate-of-return effect of .0004, which is more than off-set by a negative capital-dilution effect of about .0007. Because the effect on the growth-rate is so small, the total effect is essentially equal to the life-cycle effect of −.7 per cent.

In the high-mortality developing country, a one-year gain in e_0 has a small but positive life-cycle effect of .0025. There is, however, a major effect on the population growth-rate, which rises by .0016. Because intergenerational transfers now flow upwards, this leads to a reduction in the present value of consumption by about .008. Furthermore, it causes a capital-dilution effect of about .002. The total effect is much like that in a developed country: per capita consumption must be reduced by about .7 per cent over the life-cycle.

Conclusion

The similarity in the net outcome in the two contexts should not lead us to overlook the fundamental difference between them, however. In the high-mortality setting, mortality decline is expensive mainly because it entails the support of greater numbers of surviving children. In the low-mortality setting, mortality decline is expensive because individuals live longer, and therefore must reduce their consumption in order to provide for their own increased years of post-retirement leisure.

As Keyfitz (1986) pointed out, declining mortality in developed countries has little effect on the implicit rate of return through pay-as-you-go pension programmes, since its effects on the population growth-rate are negligible. But to leave the matter there would be misleading, for mortality decline does have a potentially large effect on the level of contributions needed to provide for old-age consumption, and thus on the payroll tax-rate. Working-age people may well perceive a welfare loss if their current consumption is reduced to provide through transfers for more elderly retired people. And if instead private pension programmes play the dominant role, there may be similar perceptions of welfare loss when the premiums necessary to secure a given rate of post-retirement consumption rise in response to the increased number of retirement years. But the dominance of the life-cycle effect in developed countries means that people must pay more in only because they will survive to take more out. Such reductions in consumption should be accepted gladly, not resented.

References

Arthur, W. B. (1981), 'The Economics of Risks to Life', *American Economic Review*, 71/1, 54–64.
—— and McNicoll, G. (1978), 'Samuelson, Population and Intergenerational Transfers', *International Economic Review*, 19/1 (Feb.), 241–6.
Blanchet, D. (1986), 'Deux études sur les relations entre demographie et systèmes de retraite', dossiers et recherches no. 9 (Nov.), Paris: INED.
—— (1988), 'Age Structure and Capital Dilution Effects in Neo-Classical Growth Models', INED manuscript, Paris.
Caldwell, J. C. (1976), 'A Theory of Fertility: From High Plateau to Destabilization', *Population and Development Review*, 4/4, 553–78.
Coale, A. and Demeny, P. (1983), *Regional Model Life-Tables and Stable Populations*, 2nd edn., New York: Academic Press.
Eckstein, Z. and Wolpin, K. (1985), 'Endogenous Fertility and Optimal Population Size', *Journal of Public Economics*, 27 (June), 93–106.
Ermisch, J. (1989), 'Intergenerational Transfers in Industrialized Countries: Effects of Age Distribution and Economic Institutions', *Journal of Population Economics*, 1, 269–84.
Feldman, J. J. (1986), 'Work Ability of the Aged Under Conditions of Improving Mortality', in United Nations Secretariat, Population Division (ed.), *Consequences of Mortality Trends and Differentials*.
Gale, D. (1974), 'Pure Exchange Equilibrium of a Dynamic Economic Model', *Journal of Economic Theory*, 6, 12–36.
Keyfitz, N. (1986), 'The Demography of Unfunded Pensions', *Journal of European Population Studies*, 1/1, 5–30.
Lee, R. (1980), 'Age Structure, Intergenerational Transfers and Economic Growth: An Overview', *Revue économique*, 31/6 (Nov.; special issue ed. G. Tapinos).
—— (1988), 'Declining Fertility and Aging Populations: Consequences for Intergenerational Transfers Within and Between Households', manuscript of the Graduate Group in Demography, University of California, Berkeley.
Lee, R. and Lapkoff, S. (1988), 'Intergenerational Flows of Time and Goods: Consequences of Slowing Population Growth', *Journal of Political Economy*, 96/31 (June), 618–51.

Lee, R. with Cohen, N. (1991), 'Evaluating Externalities to Childbearing in Developing Countries: The Case of India', in *Consequences of Rapid Population Growth in
Developing Countries* (New York: Taylor and Francis, for the United Nations),
297–344.

Lobitz, J. and Prihoda, R. (1984), 'The Use and Costs of Medicare Services in the Last
Two Years of Life', *Health Care Financing Review*, 5/3 (Spring), 117–31.

Mason, A. (1987), 'National Saving Rates and Population Growth: A New Model and
New Evidence', in D. G. Johnson and R. Lee (eds.), *Population Growth and
Economic Development: Issues and Evidence*, Madison, Wis.: University of Wis-
consin Press, 523–60.

Mueller, E. (1976), 'The Economic Value of Children in Peasant Agriculture', in
R. Ridker (ed.), *Population and Development: The Search for Selective Interventions*
(Baltimore: The Johns Hopkins Press, for Resources for the Future), 98–153.

Nerlove, M., Razin, A., and Sadka, E. (1987), *Household and Economy: Welfare
Economics of Endogenous Fertility*, New York: Academic Press.

Preston, S. H. (1982), 'Relations Between Individual Life Cycles and Population
Characteristics', *American Sociological Review*, 47 (Apr.), 253–64.

Samuelson, P. (1958) 'An Exact Consumption-Loan Model of Interest with or without
the Social Contrivance of Money', *Journal of Political Economy*, 66/6 (Dec.), 467–
82.

Tobin, J. (1967), 'Life Cycle Saving and Balanced Economic Growth', in W. Fellner
(ed.), *Ten Economic Studies in the Tradition of Irving Fisher*, New York: Wiley Press,
231–56.

United Nations, Department of International Economic and Social Affairs (1984),
Concise Report on the World Population Situation in 1983, Population Studies, no.
85, New York: UN.

Willis, R. (1980), 'The Old Age Security Hypothesis and Population Growth', in T. K.
Burch (ed.), *Demographic Behavior: Interdisciplinary Perspectives on Decision
Making* (Boulder, Colo.: Westview Press).

—— (1987), 'Externalities and Population', in D. G. Johnson and R. D. Lee (eds.),
Population Growth and Economic Development: Issues and Evidence (Madison, Wis.:
University of Wisconsin Press), 661–702.

—— (1988), 'Life Cycles, Institutions and Population Growth: A Theory of the Equilibrium Interest Rate in an Overlapping-Generations Model', in R. Lee, W. B.
Arthur, and G. Rodgers (eds.), *Economics of Changing Age Distributions in Developed Countries* (Oxford: Oxford University Press), 106–38.

7 The Intergenerational Distribution of Resources and Income in Japan

ANDREW MASON, YOKE-YUN TEH, NAOHIRO OGAWA, AND TAKEHIRO FUKUI

There are two distinct ways in which the term intergenerational distribution of income is applied. In some instances it is used to describe the relative lifetime economic status of successive generations. In a country such as Japan, rapid economic growth ensures that the material standard of living of current generations substantially exceeds that of previous generations. And, if rapid growth continues, future generations will be considerably better off than those living today.

The term is also applied in a more static sense to compare standards of living among members of different generations, the old and the young, for example. The issue is of particular concern in a society ageing as rapidly as is Japan's, because the burdens on the younger generation, either through public provision of social security or through familial support, may be substantial if the elderly are an economically disadvantaged class.

The rapid growth in the number of elderly over the next few decades may itself lead to deterioration in their relative economic well-being. As the number of older workers grows, suitable jobs may be increasingly scarce and wages may decline relative to those paid to young workers. Because saving rates among the elderly in Japan are so high by international standards, they have been less dependent on labour income to maintain higher household income. However, the returns to capital relative to labour may well decline in the coming decades as changes in the age-composition of the population increase the abundance of capital relative to labour.

Demographic trends may also undermine the traditional system of familial support for the elderly. The multi-generation extended family, still common in Japan today, should come under increased pressure as Japan's low childbearing cohorts reach old age. A decline in the availability of surviving offspring, along with improved standards of living, will almost assuredly lead

This paper was prepared as part of a collaborative project undertaken by the Statistic Bureau of Japan, Nihon University Population Research Institute, and the East–West Center's Program on Population. The authors would like to express their appreciation to Yuki Miura, of the Japanese Statistical Association, and Takinosuke Dateki, of the Statistics Bureau for their support and encouragement. We would also like to thank David Ho and Wai-Man Wu for their research assistance.

more elderly to live independently of their children than is the case today. Thus, more elderly in the future may be relying on their own economic resources and less on the resources of other, younger household members.

Of course, the role of the state in the provision of old-age support is pervasive in most ageing societies, and no analysis of intergenerational inequality can be complete without a discussion of the impact of ageing on social insurance schemes and other government programmes. The government of Japan today actively provides services and funds to the elderly, and the combined tax-and-transfer system effects a significant redistribution of income across generations. What will be the needs of the future and how will economic realities be compromised with political necessities in the years to come?

The research results reported below attempt to shed some light on these issues. The first part of the paper presents a macroeconomic model used to determine the distribution of national income among households. The model distinguishes four sources of income: labour income; property income, including returns to domestically invested capital and assets held abroad; intergenerational transfers in the form of bequests; and net government payments, i.e. transfers less taxes. The income attributed to households is different from the traditional notion of disposable income in one important respect. Essentially, we lift the corporate veil by attributing all corporate earnings, retained or not, to households on the basis of ownership of assets.

The second part of the paper implements the theoretical model relying on data from Japan drawn from a variety of sources. This sort of undertaking is possible only with a considerable number of simplifying assumptions. Frequently we must rely on data that was collected or analysed for another purpose and is not ideally suited to our needs. Fortunately, vast amounts of high-quality economic and demographic data are available for Japan. Even so, the findings reported should be considered quite tentative in nature and merely suggestive of what the next four decades of ageing are likely to bring. One would be well advised to view the results here as representing a hypothetical country sharing many of Japan's particular features.

The third part of the paper reports the results of a simulation starting in 1980 and running to 2025 based on: (1) continued growth in national product equal to that observed from 1980 to 1985; (2) additional improvements in mortality conditions and a continuation of below-replacement fertility; (3) an absence of fundamental changes in the family system; and (4) no change in the redistributive role of the public sector. The discussion of the results highlights three features of the simulation—changes in the distribution of household income, changes in the distribution and level of bequests, and the rapid increase in foreign investment.

The Model

The purpose of the model is to examine changes in the intergenerational distribution of income likely to accompany the dramatic ageing of Japan's population. The accompanying flow-chart, Fig. 7.1, provides a schematic view of the model. The level and distribution of economic resources controlled by households lies at the core of the model. The factor income accruing to each household cohort is determined by the human and physical resources of the cohort and the relative returns to those resources.

Over time the resources of households change. Labour resources respond to changes in household composition, labour-force participation, and the household's labour productivity relative to that of other households. Physical resources are determined by the saving behaviour of households and the transfers of wealth between cohorts in the form of bequests. In addition, government redistributive policies influence the distribution of household income by imposing taxes and providing benefits that vary with the age-group to which the household belongs.

Household Disposable Income

Household disposable income consists of four components: labour income (Y^L), returns on assets (Y^A), net government payments, i.e. transfers less taxes (G), and private transfers (T^P).

$$Y_{xt}^D = Y_{xt}^L + Y_{xt}^A + T_{xt}^P + G_{xt} \tag{1}$$

Factor income is distributed in proportion to the real resources, human and physical, owned by each cohort of households. The share of aggregate labour income earned by age x households is equal to the share of total labour resources, measured in productivity units (L_{xt}/L_t), of members of age x households.[1]

$$Y_{xt}^L = Y_t^L L_{xt}/L_t \tag{2}$$

In like fashion, the share of asset income is determined by the share of national assets owned by age x households. Asset income includes returns to assets held abroad (Y_t^F) as well as returns to domestically invested assets or capital.

$$Y_{xt}^A = (Y_t^K + Y_t^F)A_{xt}/A_t \tag{3}$$

Domestic Factor Income

Net national product is determined by an exogenously given rate of growth, but the factor distribution of income is modelled using an aggregate production function with two factors of production, capital and effective labour, and Hicks-neutral technological growth:

$$Y_t = \Gamma_t F(K_t, L_t) \tag{4}$$

---

[1] Age x households are those in which the household head is aged x.

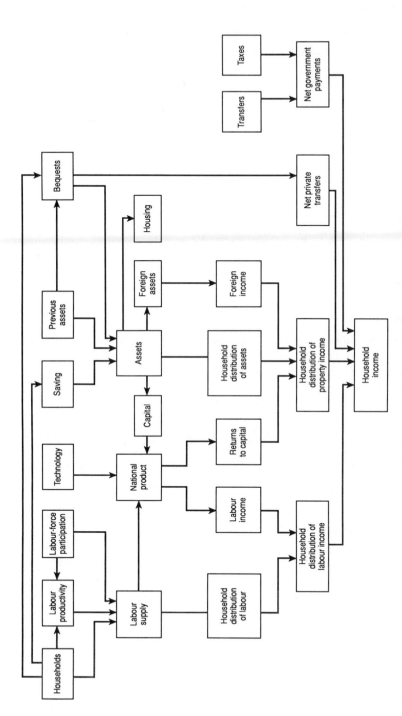

Fig. 7.1 Flowchart of the Model to Examine Changes in the Intergenerational Distribution of Income in Japan

and assuming constant returns to scale, total product is exhaustively divided between workers and owners of capital:

$$Y_t^L = \Pi_t^L Y_t \tag{5}$$

$$Y_t^K = \Pi_t^K Y_t \tag{6}$$

Assuming further that the production function, F, is translog, factor shares are linear in the natural logs of the ratio of capital to effective labor, k_t:

$$\Pi_t^L = \beta_0 + \beta_1 \ln k_t \tag{7}$$

$$\Pi_t^K = 1 - \Pi_t^L \tag{8}$$

Foreign Factor Income

Aggregate income from foreign assets, Y_t^F, is determined as the product of assets held abroad, A_t^F, and an exogenously given rate of return, i_t:

$$Y_t^F = i_t A_t^F \tag{9}$$

Labour Supply

The national labour supply, L_t, and the labour resources of each household cohort, L_{xt}, are measured in productivity units that account for variation in labour productivity associated with the age and sex of workers. Productivity differentials are captured by weights for male and female workers, w_{at}^m and w_{at}^f.

$$L_t + \sum_a w_{at}^m L_{at}^m + \sum_a w_{at}^f L_{at}^f \tag{10}$$

The relative productivity of different age-groups rises, in general, with age (experience) but is also influenced by cohort size.

$$w_{at}^i = f_a(L_{at}^i / L_{0t}^i) \tag{11}$$

where L_{at}^i is the number of workers aged a and sex i.

The labour resources of households aged x are determined by the number of workers belonging to each household cohort and their productivity relative to other workers. The number of workers is determined by the number of household members in each age-sex group, N_{axt}^i, and by exogenously given forecasts of age-sex specific labour-force participation rates, l_{at}^i.

$$L_{xt} + \sum_a w_{at}^m l_{at}^m N_{axt}^m + \sum_a w_{at}^f l_{at}^f N_{axt}^f \tag{12}$$

Saving and the Accumulation of Wealth

The assets of households aged x, A_{xt}, are determined by three factors: assets five years earlier, total saving over the preceding five years, and net private transfers (bequests) during the preceding five years.

$$A_{xt} = A_{x-5,t-5} + S_{x-5,t-5} + 5T^P_{x-5,t-5} \tag{13}$$

Household saving by each cohort is calculated as a fraction of its annual factor income plus net government payments.

$$S_{xt} = \beta s_{xt}(Y^L_{xt} + Y^A_{xt} + G_{xt}) \tag{14}$$

Annual saving is inflated to quinquennial saving using the factor, β.[2] Based on research by Ando, 1985 to be described in more detail below, the saving ratio, s_{xt}, depends on household age, the asset–income ratio, and demographic characteristics of the household.

$$s_{xt} = f(A_{xt}/Y^D_{xt}, x, N_{axt}) \tag{15}$$

Household assets are allocated among three end-uses: domestic investment in fixed capital and inventories, foreign investment, and housing. The capital stock in each year, K_t, and foreign assets, A^F_t, are calculated as:

$$K_t = \kappa_t \sum_x A_{xt} \tag{16}$$

$$A^F_t = \gamma_t \sum_x A_{xt} \tag{17}$$

whereas the remainder gives the value of housing.

Net Private Transfers

Net private transfers consist entirely of 'bequests', B_{xt}, associated with the 'death' of households belonging to each cohort. The percentage of cohort assets bequeathed in any period is equal to the percentage decline in the number of households aged x, H_{xt}.[3] Cohorts which do not decline during the preceding five-year interval do not generate bequests. Of course, the number of households may decline because the household head dies or because the headship mantle is passed on to the next generation. Private transfers generated by either event are not distinguished.

$$\begin{aligned} B_{xt} &= A'_{x-5,t-5}(H_{x-5,t-5} - H_{xt})/H_{x-5,t-5} && \text{if } \Delta H_{xt} \leq 0 \tag{18}\\ &= 0 && \text{if } \Delta H_{xt} > 0 \end{aligned}$$

where A' measures pre-bequest assets.

All bequests are assumed to be made to the descendant generation, i.e. from the household of the head to the offspring of the head. Offspring are assumed to share inheritances equally without respect to their parity. The share of bequests from households aged x inherited by all individuals aged

[2] The factor, β, would equal 5 in the absence of growth in cohort income during the quinquennia in question. It will exceed 5 given positive growth, the more typical case.

[3] This approximation is based on the assumption that wealth and mortality are independent and will be violated to the extent that the demise of a household is affected by the depletion of its financial resources. This assumption no doubt imparts a downward bias to the age-distribution of bequests.

a in year t, h_{axt}, is calculated using procedures described below. Per capita inheritances is given by:

$$I_{at}^{pc} = \sum_x h_{axt} B_{xt}/N_{at} \tag{19}$$

and the inheritance of the age x household cohort is:

$$I_{xt} = \sum_a N_{axt} I_{at}^{pc}. \tag{20}$$

Finally, net private transfers received by each cohort are calculated as the difference between inheritances received and bequests made:

$$T_{xt}^P = I_{xt} - B_{xt} \tag{21}$$

Net Government Payments

Net government payments to households aged x are equal to transfer payments received, R, less taxes paid, T.

$$G_{xt} = R_{xt} - T_{xt} \tag{22}$$

Taxes paid by each household cohort, T_{xt}, are assumed to be generated by proportional income taxes applied to factor income. Government benefits received by each household cohort, R_{xt}, are modelled in like fashion by assuming that transfers paid to any household are a fixed proportion of factor income. Both tax and benefit rates vary with age of the household head, x.

$$T_{xt} = \tau_{xt}(Y_{xt}^L + Y_{xt}^A) \tag{23}$$

$$R_{xt} = r_{xt}(Y_{xt}^L + Y_{xt}^A) \tag{24}$$

Implementation of the Model

Factor Shares

Labour's share, shown in (7), is estimated after introducing a term to control for short-term fluctuations in the economy which are associated with variation in capacity utilization and unemployment and, hence, labour's share of domestic product. The basic model estimated, then, is:

$$\Pi_t^L = \beta_0 + \beta_1 \ln k_t + \beta_2 f_t + e_t \tag{25}$$

where f_t measures short-run fluctuations as explained below.

All of the independent variables are measured using readily available published data. Capital is measured as private capital in billions of yen deflated using the private capital deflator provided by the Economic Planning Agency. Labour is measured by the labour-force (tens of thousands of workers) reported by the Statistics Bureau. Short-run fluctuations in the economy are captured using the average annual unemployment rate measured as a percentage.

Estimates of the labour share are difficult to construct for Japan because a large, but declining, fraction of workers are self-employed or unpaid family workers. Thus, labour-share estimates require the imputation of wages for a large number of workers. Our estimate of labour share was constructed using the following data: (1) the denominator of the share variable is gross national product; (2) the numerator for wage and salaried workers consists of compensation including year-end bonuses and employers' contribution to social security, extracted from the Japan Statistical Yearbook; (3) the real compensation of self-employed and family workers is imputed based on the average compensation of employees and data on the number of self-employed and family workers as reported by the Japan Statistical Yearbook.

The final estimates are based on an imputed annual wage for self-employed and family workers that is one-half the annual average earnings of waged and salaried workers. Efforts to estimate relative wages of different types of workers statistically did not prove to be successful. However, sensitivity analysis revealed that the relationship between the labour share and the capital–labour ratio is not sensitive to the weight used. Obviously, the level of the labour share will depend on the assumption employed. In 1986 about 25 per cent of all workers were self-employed or family workers, so quite clearly any estimate of the labour share is subject to considerable uncertainty.

Two previous studies of the Japanese economy provide time-series data necessary to estimate the labour share equation for earlier periods that can be compared with the results obtained here. Ohkawa and Rosovsky (1973) provide annual estimates of capital, labour, and the factor shares of each for the private non-agricultural sector for two periods: 1908–38 and 1954–64. Denison and Chung (1976) provide annual estimates for the non-residential business sector for the 1952–71 period. Labour share equations using these series have been estimated with short-run fluctuations measured as the deviation in the annual rate of GNP growth from a five-year moving average. Statistical results, corrected for first-order autocorrelation using Cochrane–Orcutt procedures, are reported in Table 7.1.

The only important issue as far as the macro-model is concerned is the elasticity of the share with respect to the capital–labour ratio. For the three post-war periods the elasticity is estimated at −0.119 for 1955–62; at −0.045 for 1954–69; and at 0.104 for 1965–85. Taken at face value, these results say that additional increments in the capital stock relative to the labour-force during earlier periods did not depress the returns to capital relative to wages sufficiently to lead to a decline in capital's share. More recently, as the capital–labour ratio has reached new heights, additional increases depress the returns to capital relative to wages so much that capital's share is actually declining.

Table 7.1. Statistical Estimates for Labour-Share Equation

	Coef.	S.E.	Ohkawa/Rosovsky		Denison/Chung	
			Coef.	S.E.	Coef.	S.E.
Intercept	0.255	0.116	0.574	0.038	0.779	0.030
ln K/L	0.109	0.037	0.059	0.047	−0.045	0.028
f	−0.0101	0.0287	−0.000172	0.000173	0.000179	0.000771
D	—	—	0.146	0.040	—	—
$D * \ln K/L$	—	—	−0.178	0.085	—	—
$D * f$	—	—	−0.000470	0.000537	—	—
N	21		40		16	
$\bar{R}^2$	0.904		0.957		0.480	

Note: $D = 1$ for years after 1954.

For simulation purposes, we are not concerned about short-run fluctuations in the economy or the share of labour. Thus, we set the unemployment rate at its mean, and labour's share is calculated as:

$$\pi_L = 0.2327 + 0.1038 \ln K/L \qquad (26)$$

For the base year, total wages are calculated as the product of the calculated share and observed national product. Thereafter, national product is assumed to grow at the real rate observed between 1980 and 1985, 3.6 per cent per annum.

Labour Supply

Labour supply is calculated as the product of age- and sex-specific labour-force participation rates and the corresponding populations. The participation rates employed are based on forecasts from the Nihon University Population Research Institute's long-term macro-model, phase III (Ogawa *et al.*, 1988). The major factors determining participation in the NUPRI model are (1) rising school enrolment among young adults; (2) declining fertility among childbearing women; and (3) increased pension benefits among elderly men.[4] Equations for two age-groups of men, 15–24 and 60 and older, and four age-groups of women, 15–24, 25–44, 45–54, and 60 and older, were statistically fitted to annual time-series data for the 1965–84 period.

Two trends are noteworthy. The increased participation among women of childrearing age is a continuation of recent changes and a by-product of

---

[4] Participation rates are not endogenously determined in this paper, and labour-force participation rates are not affected by differences in the way pension benefits are modelled in this and the NUPRI model. In any case, the effects of pensions are small and not statistically significant (Ogawa *et al.*, 1988).

Table 7.2. Age- and Sex-Specific Labour-Force Participation Rates

Year	Age-Group							
	15–19	20–4	25–9	30–4	35–9	40–9	50–9	60+
Males								
1980	0.202	0.750	0.975	0.986	0.987	0.982	0.960	0.564
1985	0.172	0.703	0.957	0.974	0.966	0.974	0.928	0.478
1990	0.183	0.750	0.957	0.974	0.966	0.974	0.927	0.492
1995	0.207	0.847	0.957	0.974	0.966	0.973	0.928	0.463
2000	0.196	0.804	0.957	0.974	0.966	0.973	0.929	0.418
2005	0.181	0.740	0.957	0.974	0.966	0.973	0.924	0.385
2010	0.172	0.705	0.957	0.974	0.966	0.974	0.925	0.379
2015	0.178	0.730	0.957	0.974	0.966	0.974	0.927	0.317
2020	0.193	0.790	0.957	0.974	0.966	0.973	0.928	0.283
2025	0.194	0.793	0.957	0.974	0.966	0.973	0.928	0.278
Females								
1980	0.185	0.714	0.493	0.463	0.554	0.618	0.549	0.224
1985	0.164	0.716	0.542	0.509	0.593	0.682	0.561	0.220
1990	0.174	0.756	0.535	0.503	0.586	0.677	0.564	0.224
1995	0.168	0.733	0.565	0.531	0.618	0.700	0.564	0.215
2000	0.169	0.736	0.588	0.552	0.644	0.735	0.580	0.205
2005	0.158	0.689	0.587	0.552	0.643	0.746	0.577	0.205
2010	0.152	0.662	0.594	0.558	0.651	0.755	0.574	0.200
2015	0.156	0.678	0.607	0.571	0.665	0.773	0.591	0.189
2020	0.161	0.703	0.615	0.578	0.673	0.786	0.603	0.185
2025	0.159	0.692	0.626	0.589	0.686	0.802	0.614	0.188

reduced rates of childbearing. The decline in participation among elderly women and especially elderly men is primarily a consequence of changes in the age-distribution of those aged 60 and older. Participation among prime-age males, i.e. those aged 25–59, is subject to little systematic variation and is held constant at the sample mean. More detailed age-specific rates were obtained by holding relative rates within broad age-groups constant. The resulting age-specific rates are presented in Table 7.2.

Relative Wages and Labour Productivity

Labour productivity is critical to two aspects of the model presented here. First, the distribution of national income between capital and labour varies with the capital–labour ratio which, ideally, measures both factors with provision for improvements in quality. Although we have made no provision for improvements in the quality of capital other than those captured by price changes, we estimate changes in labour quality associated with changes in the age-distribution of the labour-force. Second, the share of labour income earned by labour-force cohorts depends on both their numbers and their productivity relative to members of other labour-force cohorts.

As is true in other countries, wages rise with the age of the worker and are higher for males than females. Are these differentials solely productivity-related or do they reflect institutional features of the Japanese labour-market? The seniority-based wage system, whereby salaries are closely related to age and duration of service, is a major feature of the male labour-market in Japan. Although productivity certainly rises with general and firm-specific experience, it is widely believed that young workers are paid less than the value of their marginal product and older workers are paid more. In recent years, however, the wage-system has been changing from a seniority-based system to a performance-based one that ties wages more closely to productivity. In 1984, for instance, only 5 per cent of all Japanese companies relied exclusively on the seniority-based system.

Sex differentials in wages also reflect 'institutional' factors as well as differences in productivity. Until recently, female participation was relatively low in Japan. Women typically withdrew from the labour-force upon marriage or the birth of their first child. Recent years have witnessed an impressive growth in female participation, but women generally have less experience than their male counterparts, work shorter hours, have slightly lower educational attainment and are in lower-paying occupations. But the available evidence indicates that wage differentials are greater than can be accounted for by productivity-related factors alone (Ogawa, 1987).

The divergence between wages and productivity is more critical to determining the rate of growth of Japan's effective labour-force and, hence, its share of total output, than in determining the distribution of labour's share among different labour-cohorts. Japan's labour-force has been undergoing two important demographic shifts: the ageing of the labour-force and the feminization of the labour-force. To the extent that wage differentials overstate the relationship between age (experience) and productivity, using wages as a proxy for productivity will overstate recent growth in Japan's effective labour-force. By contrast, to the extent that wage differentials understate the relative productivity of women, using wages will understate recent growth in Japan's effective labour-force. In the absence of any clear basis for adjusting wages for non-productivity-related components, we have assumed that the growth-rate of the effective labour-force is adequately measured using wages to capture age–sex productivity differentials.

The model employed here is also based on the assumption that the current sex differential in wages, in relative terms, will persist into the future. However, the age-earnings profile is expected to change in response to changes in the age composition of the labour-force. Several studies (Martin and Ogawa, 1988; Mosk and Nakaka, 1985) have analysed Japanese data to examine the well-known observation that if workers of different ages are not perfect substitutes in the production process, labour productivity and, hence, wages of any labour cohort will move inversely to its relative size.

The wage-earnings profiles estimated here are based on a replication of the Martin–Ogawa study using the Basic Survey on Wage Structure conducted annually by the Ministry of Labour. The survey is nationwide in its coverage and, in 1986, included about 70,000 firms with ten or more employees. The analysis here is based on data collected from 1962 to 1986. A very simple specification is employed. Wage equations are estimated separately for males and females in seven age-groups. The regression equation used is:

$$\ln w_{at}^i / w_{0t}^i = \beta_0 + \beta_1 \ln L_{at}^i / L_{0t}^i + \beta_2 \text{CYCLE}_t + \eta_t \qquad (27)$$

where w_{at}^i and L_{at}^i are the wage and labour-force figures for age-group a and gender group i and w_{0t}^i and L_{0t}^i are the wage and labour-force figures for male or female workers aged 20–4. CYCLE is included to capture short-run effects associated with the business cycle and is the residual obtained from regressing the natural logarithm of per capital GNP on year. Ordinary least-squares estimates exhibited first-order autocorrelation and Cochrane–Orcutt procedures were used to obtain the statistical estimates presented in Table 7.3.

Despite the simplicity of the model employed, a partially supportive picture of the cohort-size effect emerges. For most male age-groups, a 1 percentage point increase in the number of workers depresses wages by about 0.02 to 0.04 percentage points. Whereas for most female age-groups, wages are depressed by about 0.03 to 0.07 percentage points. Most coefficients are not estimated with sufficient precision to satisfy standard criteria for statistical significance. The estimated coefficients for women aged 60 and older is large and positive, contrary to our expectations.

The model is not intended to incorporate the estimated effects of short-run economic fluctuations so that CYCLE is set to its expected value of zero for forecasting.

Consumption Functions

The consumption functions employed in this model are based on extensive analysis of the 1974 and 1979 National Surveys of Family Income and Expenditure conducted by Ando (1985) in co-operation with the Economic Research Institute, Economic Planning Agency, the Government of Japan. Ando employed a life-cycle framework to investigate the high rate of personal saving, particularly among the elderly. Of course, saving among the elderly in Japan continues to be a puzzle to proponents of the simple life-cycle model, because Japanese households do not appear to be consuming a large portion of their wealth as they approach the 'end of their life'.

To summarize Ando's result quite briefly, he finds that among households aged under 62, the marginal propensity to consume out of assets ranges from

Table 7.3.   Statistical Estimates of Age–Earnings Profile

Age-group	INTERCEPT	L_{at}/L_{ot}	CYCLE$_t$	R^2
Males				
15–19	−0.29893	−0.01858	0.23374	0.94
	(0.08069)	(0.04660)	(0.12029)	
25–9	0.23845	0.01590	−0.01547	0.79
	(0.01814)	(0.03229)	(0.06247)	
30–4	0.43866	−0.03630	−0.15908	0.77
	(0.01147)	(0.03174)	(0.06662)	
35–9	0.54267	−0.02677	−0.24393	0.77
	(0.01101)	(0.02983)	(0.06612)	
40–9	0.63797	−0.02844	−0.36849	0.87
	(0.01944)	(0.02565)	(0.07324)	
50–9	0.57969	−0.04188	−0.39134	0.87
	(0.01291)	(0.02579)	(0.07628)	
60+	0.17960	−0.11204	−0.49531	0.91
	(0.01293)	(0.04474)	(0.08320)	
Females				
15–19	−0.23320	−0.06335	0.02236	0.88
	(0.01455)	0.01259	(0.03547)	
25–9	0.10205	−0.03014	−0.16601	0.79
	(0.00814)	(0.02487)	(0.04442)	
30–4	0.10060	−0.04570	−0.53359	0.93
	(0.00755)	(0.02168)	(0.04843)	
35–9	0.08215	−0.04035	−0.39324	0.84
	(0.01960)	(0.05135)	(0.11156)	
40–9	0.12376	−0.06810	−0.27263	0.80
	(0.02068)	(0.02733)	(0.07867)	
50–9	0.10497	−0.00905	−0.33947	0.68
	(0.01273)	(0.02680)	(0.08735)	
60+	0.02809	0.20729	−0.04917	0.82
	(0.02319)	(0.07449)	(0.13248)	

Note: Standard errors are in parentheses.

0.03 to 0.04 and varies little with the age of the household head. For households aged over 62, he estimates a marginal propensity to consume out of assets of only 0.016. Ando also analyses the impact of demographic and other variables which we have been able to incorporate into our model in a limited way. For households under 62, he finds that the consumption ratio increases with additional members and that the effect depends upon the age of the member. Those over 56 have the greatest impact and those under 18 have the smallest impact on the consumption ratio.[5] For households with heads aged 62 and older, Ando found no evidence of demographic effects.

It is not possible to incorporate the full detail of Ando's estimated consumption functions into our model. A number of variables have been excluded or collapsed into broader categories with compensating adjustments in the intercept. Nor did Ando employ standard five-year age-of-head categories available from our household projections. There are also important definitional differences between variables measured at the aggregate level, on which we rely, and conceptually similar variables measured at the household level. Although we have tried to maintain as much consistency as possible there are some important slippages. For example, for older households consumption is measured as a fraction of disposable household income which would not include retained earnings, whereas our measure of disposable income does include all corporate earnings whether distributed or not. To maintain consistency at the aggregate level to the extent possible, the consumption ratio has been adjusted by a constant fraction to the observed 1980 consumption ratio.

For households with a head under the age of 60, the unadjusted consumption function used is:

$$C_{xt}/Y_{xt}^{dL} = 0.336 + 57.051/Y_{xt}^{dL} \tag{28}$$
$$+ (0.034DA_1 + 0.032DA_2 + 0.036DA_3 + 0.035DA_4)A_{xt}/Y_{xt}^{dL}$$
$$+ 0.055N_{xt}^{<19} + 0.06N_{xt}^{19-55} + 0.07N_{xt}^{56+}$$

where C_{xt} is consumption by age x households in year t, Y_{xt}^{dL} is disposable labour income, DA_i are age-of-head dummies used to distinguish households with heads under 30, 30–9, 40–9, and 50–9, and N^i are the number of household members in the indicated age-groups. All monetary variables are measured in ten-thousands of yen.

For households with a head aged 60 or older, the consumption function used is:

$$C_{xt}/Y_{xt}' = .310DA_1 + 0.299DA_2 + 0.262DA_3 + 82.41/Y_{xt}' + 0.016A_{xt}/Y_{xt}' \tag{29}$$

where Y_{xt}' is household disposable income net of private transfers and DA_i are dummy variables that distinguish households with heads aged 60–9, 70–4, and 75 and older.

The Accumulation and Distribution of Wealth

Saving by each household cohort x in year t is calculated as the difference between consumption and disposable income net of private transfers. Because

---

[5] Ando's specification allows for non-linear relationships between consumption and household membership, but it is not possible to incorporate these into the macro-level forecasts since the size-distribution of household membership is not projected.

Table 7.4. Estimated Age–Wealth Profile, 1980

Age	Number of Households	Per-HH Wealth	Cohort Wealth	Adjusted
15–19	639,299	60.5	386.9	493.2
20–24	2,532,778	227.0	5,749.9	7,329.5
25–9	3,957,034	605.1	23,943.6	30,521.4
30–4	4,945,355	993.7	49,141.0	62,641.1
35–9	4,422,225	1,266.3	55,999.9	71,384.4
40–4	4,095,544	1,456.3	59,642.2	76,027.2
45–9	4,052,603	1,633.5	66,198.9	84,385.1
50–4	3,606,936	1,786.1	64,424.6	82,123.4
55–9	2,853,402	1,890.5	53,942.4	68,761.6
60–4	2,004,401	1,866.6	37,413.7	47,692.1
65–9	1,444,539	1,785.5	25,792.7	32,878.5
70–4	833,324	1,740.7	14,505.5	18,490.5
75–9	392,739	1,691.1	6,641.7	8,466.2
80–4	154,447	1,572.0	2,427.9	3,094.9
85+	52,545	2,022.7	1,062.8	1,354.8
TOTAL			467,273.6	595,643.8

forecast values are calculated at five-year intervals, saving between t and $t +$ 5 is approximated. We assume that during the interval total saving grows at the same rate as NNP, and that, for any cohort, saving per household grows at the same rate as NNP per household.

Estates are settled at the end of each five-year interval. Pre-bequest wealth of each household cohort is calculated as the sum of assets at the beginning of the period and saving during the five-year interval. Cohort wealth is reduced in response to 'mortality' among households and distributed to beneficiaries using procedures described below, to arrive at cohort wealth at the end of the five-year interval (or the beginning of the next interval).

Cohort wealth in the base year, 1980, is calculated as the product of the number of households age x and mean assets of age-x households calculated on the basis of the age-profile reported in Ando (1985). Ando reports values separately for one-person and multi-person households in five-year age categories, less than, 21, 21–5, etc. We calculated weighted mean assets for all households based on our estimates of the relative size of one- and multi-person households. We adjusted the resulting profile to conform to standard age-categories, i.e. less than 20, 20–4, 25–9, etc., using geometric interpolation. The resulting values are reported in Table 7.4. A final adjustment was undertaken by calculating total national wealth, comparing the results to independent estimates of total national wealth in 1980, and adjusting the age-profile proportionately so as to maintain the Ando profile, but reproduce reported total wealth. Among other reasons, the Ando estimates understate

Table 7.5. Real Wealth Estimates

Year	Private Capital	Total Capital	Housing	Foreign Capital	Total Wealth
1969	132,780	161,177	16,054	5,642	182,872
1970	453,460	545,789	20,678	7,278	573,745
1971	172,630	208,188	24,873	10,088	243,149
1972	193,520	230,412	36,476	13,427	280,315
1973	212,950	254,762	51,392	14,646	320,799
1974	231,630	282,948	61,367	17,230	361,545
1975	248,150	304,998	68,800	17,967	391,766
1976	264,470	328,157	82,487	20,941	431,585
1977	280,570	351,113	90,873	24,659	466,644
1978	297,100	373,367	101,808	27,781	502,956
1979	317,640	398,034	122,919	27,885	548,838
1980	339,940	423,341	133,684	38,618	595,644
1981	363,210	451,714	140,349	43,944	636,007
1982	385,750	479,835	146,478	53,051	679,364
1983	410,866	511,918	149,179	64,454	725,551
1984	439,580	548,392	154,831	78,819	782,042
1985	497,480	611,993	159,136	111,176	882,305

Source: Prime Minister's Office, various.

total wealth because certain categories are excluded, e.g. family-owned businesses. To the extent that excluded categories have age-profiles differing from included categories, the age-profile employed will deviate from the actual.

Estimates of the distribution of wealth among capital, housing, and foreign assets are reported in Table 7.5 for 1969 to 1986. Capital includes both private and government capital. Government capital has been deflated using the deflator for private capital because no deflator for government capital is currently available. The labour share equation is a function of private capital which is assumed to remain a fixed proportion of total capital (0.8).

As is apparent from the table, Japan is exporting capital at a remarkable pace. The percentage of assets held abroad increased from 3 per cent in 1970 to reach 13 per cent by 1985. In the simulations presented here, the ratio of foreign to domestic assets is held constant at the 1985 level so long as the return to capital exceeds the interest rate for foreign assets, assumed to be 3 per cent per annum. Otherwise, the foreign sector absorbs sufficient assets to maintain equal rates of return to foreign and domestic assets.

Net Private Transfers

All private transfers are generated by bequests which are assumed to be distributed equally among all surviving offspring. The number of surviving

Table 7.6.   Results of Government Redistribution Survey

Age of Head	Income	Taxes	Benefits	Net Government Transfers	Disposable Income
<30	255.7	32.0	15.8	−16.2	239.5
30–9	402.2	61.4	34.8	−26.6	375.5
40–9	479.3	83.2	43.5	−39.7	439.5
50–9	544.0	104.9	65.3	−39.6	594.4
60–9	343.7	68.5	150.5	82.0	425.7
70+	276.6	57.4	159.8	102.4	379.0
All	424.1	75.3	69.5	−5.8	418.3

Source: Income Redistribution Survey.

offspring aged a belonging to women aged x in year t is designated as O_{axt} and is calculated as the product of the population aged a in year t, N_{at} and intergenerational weights, ω_{axt}, which are based on the distribution of births by age of mother in year $t - a$ (for details see Mason and Martin, 1982). The share of bequests by households aged x transferred to individuals aged a is given by h_{axt}, where:

$$h_{axt} = \frac{\omega_{axt} N_{at}}{\sum_a \omega_{axt} N_{at}}. \tag{30}$$

The Government Sector

The tax- and benefit-rates employed are based on a survey by the Ministry of Health and Welfare querying 7,165 households about their income, taxes, and public-sector benefits for the calendar year 1983 (Ministry of Health and Welfare, 1984). The results of that survey are reported in Table 7.6. Income includes wages, salaries, rent, interest, dividends, private-pension benefits, gifts, and other private transfers. Taxes include social insurance contributions by the employer. Benefits include social security payments, other cash transfers, and in-kind benefits, e.g. publicly provided health care.

Tax-rates, benefits-rates, and net government-transfer rates are calculated by dividing taxes, benefits, and net government transfers, respectively, by income. The average tax-rate, thus calculated, is 17.8 per cent of household income. This compares with a household tax-rate based on calendar year 1983 national-income account statistics, calculated as the ratio of direct taxes plus social security contributions (including the employer's contribution) divided by total household receipts, of 15.7 per cent.

Taxes levied directly on households comprise only a portion of all taxes collected. In 1983, for example, roughly 56 per cent of all taxes were paid by

Table 7.7. Tax- and Benefit-Rates for Government Sector

Age of Head	Tax-Rate	Adjusted Tax-Rate	Benefit-Rate	Net-Rate
<30	0.125	0.246	0.087	−0.159
30–9	0.153	0.274	0.112	−0.162
40–9	0.174	0.295	0.116	−0.179
50–9	0.193	0.314	0.145	−0.169
60–9	0.199	0.320	0.463	+0.143
70+	0.208	0.329	0.603	+0.274
All	0.178	0.292	0.164	

households (including social security contributions by employers) whereas the remaining 44 per cent was comprised of indirect taxes and direct taxes on corporations. The impact of these taxes on the intergenerational distribution of disposable income is a complex issue beyond the scope of this study. We will assume that taxes not paid directly by households are neutral with respect to the intergenerational distribution of income, i.e. that disposable income is reduced proportionately without respect to age of head.

Age-specific household tax-rates and the non-household tax-rate are held constant. Of course, both the overall tax-rate and benefit-rate will vary with the intergenerational distribution of pre-tax income. The tax-rates, reported in Table 7.7, have been calculated by adjusting the unadjusted rates (adding a constant fraction to each age-specific rate) so as to achieve a total tax-rate of 0.292 in the base year—the calculated tax-rate for the calendar year 1980.

The simple approach employed will no doubt fail to capture important changes in Japan's tax and transfer programmes, many of which may be adaptations to the rapid increase in the number of elderly and changes in their relative economic well-being. Indeed, a number of important changes have been instituted since the survey on which our model is based.

In 1986, for example, a major pension reform was carried out, integrating fragmented, occupation-based programmes, and establishing a base pension level for all beneficiaries. The pension rights of spouses of employees were also broadened substantially. In this and in subsequent action, the government is attempting to achieve a uniform and older pensionable age. Major reform has also been undertaken in the health-care area in recent years. Between 1965 and 1979, medical care expenditure grew by nearly 20 per cent per annum, but the rate of growth slowed considerably in the 1980s as the government began controlling price increases and, in 1983, abolished free health care for those aged 70 and older by requiring a nominal payment. Beginning in 1984, co-payment ranging from 10 to 30 per cent of all costs is required of those covered by medical care insurance. Finally, a major change

Table 7.8. Key Demographic Variables

Year	TFR	e_o^m	e_o^f	Population (millions)	Percentage aged 65+	Percentage aged 75+
1985	1.76	74.9	80.4	121.1	10.3	3.9
1990	1.70	75.8	81.4	124.0	11.9	4.7
1995	1.72	76.8	82.4	126.8	14.2	5.4
2000	1.75	77.6	83.2	129.9	16.5	6.3
2005	1.74	77.9	83.4	132.1	18.5	7.7
2010	1.76	78.0	83.5	132.7	20.6	9.2
2015	1.80	78.1	83.6	131.8	23.4	10.2
2020	1.80	78.1	83.6	130.1	24.6	11.3
2025	1.82	78.1	83.6	128.2	24.5	13.0

Source: Ogawa et al., 1986.

in the government tax system was implemented on 1 April 1989 with the adoption of a nationwide 3 per cent consumption tax.

The simple treatment of the government sector also affects results because we do not explicitly model taxes on bequests. In Japan transfers in excess of 600,000 yen per year are subject to a progressive tax, although there are means, e.g. trust funds, by which inheritance taxes are frequently avoided. An additional complication is that a significant fraction of private transfers as defined in this paper would not be subject to tax in any case. Inheritance taxes are included in the income redistribution survey used as the basis for our treatment of the government sector. Thus, inheritance taxes are implicitly included but they are not affected by changes in the relative magnitude of bequests or by changes in the distribution of bequests described below.

Household and Population Projections

Projections of households and household membership require as input projections of the population in five-year age-groups separately for males and females and underlying age-specific fertility rates. The projections are drawn from Ogawa et al., 1986. Forecast trends in fertility are based on a fertility specification based on the Butz–Ward model applied to Japanese time-series data (Ogawa and Mason, 1986). Continued improvements in mortality are factored into the projection. The projected values of key demographic data are reported in Table 7.8.

The number and demographic composition of households are projected using a macro-simulation model called HOMES (Mason, 1987). The model uses a headship method whereby age- and sex-specific headship rates are multiplied by projected population data to obtain the number of household heads

Table 7.9. Headship Rates Using Data from the 1984 FIES and 1985 Census

Age	Males		Females	
	FIES	Census	FIES	Census
15–19	0.052	0.047	0.026	0.025
20–4	0.311	0.301	0.118	0.188
25–9	0.534	0.494	0.063	0.074
30–4	0.726	0.681	0.057	0.064
35–9	0.854	0.798	0.069	0.079
40–4	0.903	0.892	0.091	0.103
45–9	0.939	0.932	0.118	0.122
50–4	0.966	0.960	0.141	0.139
55–9	0.972	0.971	0.170	0.158
60–4	0.936	0.941	0.198	0.187
65–9	0.878	0.893	0.200	0.217
70–4	0.769	0.819	0.188	0.217
75–9	0.623	0.703	0.162	0.200
80–4	0.489	0.565	0.135	0.155
85+	0.366	0.413	0.095	0.110

and, hence, the number of households. Households with male and female heads are projected separately and four types of households are further distinguished: (1) intact households, those with head and spouse both present; (2) single-headed households, households in which the head's spouse is absent; (3) primary individual households, i.e. households consisting of unrelated individuals; and (4) one-person households. The total number of households by age of head, the required input for the model presented here, is obtained by aggregating across sex of head and type of household.[6]

Headship rates are based on special tabulations from the 1984 Family Income and Expenditure Survey (FIES) prepared by the Statistics Bureau. The FIES is used to maintain consistency between the household projections and the consumption functions, which are also based on FIES data. The most important difference between the FIES and alternative sources of data, e.g. the population census, is the way in which the household head is determined. The FIES employs a breadwinner concept that essentially designates the principal earner as the head. In the population censuses, on the other hand, the household head is designated by the household.

The practical implications of the definitional difference is apparent in Table 7.9, which compares FIES sex- and age-specific headship rates with those

---

[6] To be more precise calculations are all oriented around the household marker, who is the female householder, if present, or the male head, if his spouse is absent.

based on the 1985 population census (calculated from special tabulations prepared by the Statistics Bureau). FIES definitions imply the transfer of headship at a much younger age and, hence, a much younger age-distribution of heads at any point in time.

Less apparent in the comparison of headship rates is a substantially lower incidence of one-person headship in the FIES, which is primarily a consequence of the procedures used to select the sample. In order to improve the representativeness of the projections, one person headship rates based on the 1985 census have been substituted for FIES rates.

For each age of head, sex of head, and household-type group, the number of male and female members in five-year age-groups is projected using a kinship or relationship-to-head basis. Five relationships are distinguished: spouse, child, grandchild, parent, and other household members. Because household structure in Japan is predominantly lineal, children, grandchildren, and parents, along with spouse and head, make up the great majority of household members. In 1980, for example, 98.7 per cent of the members of ordinary households fell into one of the five relationship to head categories.

For details of the procedures employed to project household membership, the reader is referred to Mason (1987). The basic idea, however, is as follows. For each household group, the number of candidates for household membership as a child of head, parent of head, or grandchild of head, are calculated for the base year, 1984 in this case. The number of candidates is compared with the number of co-residents to calculate age- and sex-specific rates that quantify the likelihood that members of the population will reside in each household group. Using population projections and underlying age-specific fertility rates, the number of candidates for household members are then projected taking trends in mortality and the level and timing of fertility into consideration. The rates calculated for the base year are then applied to the projected number of candidates to distribute members of the population among households. Any undistributed members of the population are allocated to the other household member category and distributed among households in proportion to the age- and sex-specific distribution observed in the base year.

The resulting projections of household membership provide the age- and sex-distribution of the household membership for all households classified by the age of the marker (female householder, if present; male householder, otherwise), sex of the head, and type of household. Projections of the number of households and household membership assume no changes in the underlying rules that govern household formation and co-residence. To the extent that Japan experiences such changes, the household projections used here will prove to be inaccurate. Recent experience in Japan does indicate important changes in household formation, e.g. an increase in the prevalence of one-person households, a delay in the age at which young adults marry and establish family households, and increased headship among Japanese elderly (Mason et al., 1992).

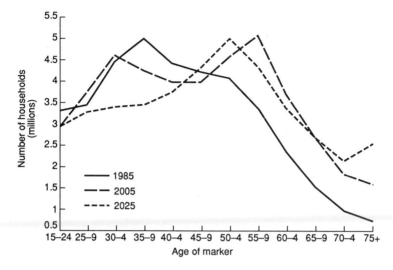

Fig. 7.2   Number of Households by Age of Household Marker

Results

Ageing in Japan

The broad outlines of future ageing in Japan are captured in Table 7.8, presented on p. 176. The table shows that, whereas 1 in 10 Japanese is over 65 today, nearly 1 in 4 will be over 65 by the year 2025. Moreover, the group of very old people is growing even more rapidly than the elderly as a whole. By 2025 over half of all elderly will be 75 or older.

The ageing of Japan's population is reflected in projected characteristics of Japanese households as well. Trends in the number of households by age of head, pictured in Fig. 7.2, are dominated by two factors: the passing of the post-war baby-boom generation and by population ageing. The baby-boom translates into a peak at ages 35–9 in 1985, a peak at ages 55–9 and its echo at ages 30–4 in 2005, and the remnants of the echo at ages 50–4 in 2025. Because of population ageing, the number of households headed by those aged 65 and older is expected to increase quite rapidly over the next four decades, and during the later part of the projection, the increase in the number of households headed by those aged 75 and older is particularly noteworthy.

The response of average household size to population ageing varies with the age of the household head. Among older households, average size is expected to decline markedly as reduced levels of childbearing affect the size and prevalence of three-generation families. Among middle-aged households, i.e. those aged 40–54, average household size is projected to rise. This occurs as adults assume increased responsibility for their parents because their parents are living longer and because they have fewer siblings with whom to share the responsibility. The three panels of Fig. 7.3 show the changes in average household size and the particularly large increases in the number of elderly per household among the offspring generation.

An Overview of Economic Forecasts

Table 7.10 provides basic national income account statistics for the simulation. Net national product, by assumption, grows at 3.6 per cent per annum over the 45-year simulation. National income, which includes returns on assets invested abroad, grows somewhat faster than NNP, particularly towards the end of the simulation, because the difference in returns to domestic and foreign assets narrows with time and a larger fraction of assets are invested abroad starting in 2005. Disposable income grows slightly faster than national income as the tax-rate drops modestly between 1980 and 2010. Consumption as a fraction of disposable income increases steadily from 75.4 per cent in 1980, peaking at 81.4 per cent in 2005, and declining to reach 78.3 per cent in 2025. Saving, as consumption's complement, grows somewhat more slowly than disposable income between 1980 and 2005 and somewhat more rapidly after 2005.

The dramatic changes in factor proportions and shares presented in Table 7.11 are quite a contrast to the gradual changes characteristic of the national income aggregates. Two distinct periods are evident. Between 1980 and 2005, the private capital stock is forecast to grow quite rapidly—at an average rate of 4.9 per cent per annum. During the same period, growth of the effective labour-force slows to a halt and, over the entire 25-year period, averages an annual increase of only 0.4 per cent. As a result, the capital–labour ratio increases threefold. As labour becomes increasingly dear, the growth of real wages, at 4.0 per cent per annum, outpaces the general economy. At the same time, the returns to capital decline from an annual rate of 15.8 per cent in 1980 to only 3.1 per cent in 2005.

The last twenty years of the simulation are greatly influenced by the low rate of return to capital associated with the extraordinarily high capital–labour ratio. Private capital is actually forecast to decline in pace with the effective labour-force as investors look abroad for satisfactory rates of return. The rate of return is forecast to increase gradually because technological innovation is increasing output at a relatively fast rate even though factors of production are forecast to decline. For the same reason, the real wage continues to grow at 4 per cent per annum even though labour's share of national product increases only marginally over the two decades tracked. The shift in the contribution of labour, capital, and foreign investment to national income is summarized in Table 7.12.

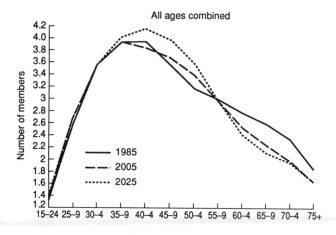

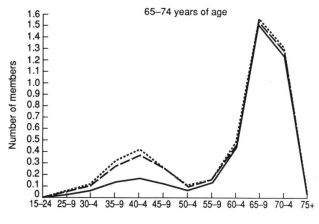

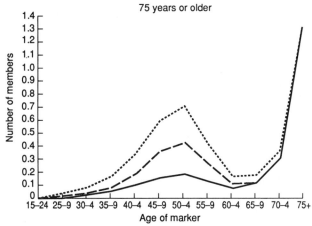

Fig. 7.3 Members of Households in Various Age-Groups

Table 7.10. National Income Aggregates, 1985–2025

Year	Net National Product	National Income	Disposable Income	Consumption	Saving	Taxes Net of Transfers
1980	206,860	209,183	182,495	137,516	44,979	26,687
1985	247,656	250,875	218,970	171,241	47,729	31,905
1990	296,499	300,669	263,209	209,302	53,907	37,460
1995	354,973	360,220	315,981	253,580	60,401	44,239
2000	424,980	431,483	378,738	306,504	72,234	52,745
2005	508,793	517,068	455,362	370,516	84,845	61,707
2010	609,136	629,470	557,884	444,396	113,488	71,587
2015	729,269	764,939	677,547	534,842	142,705	87,392
2020	873,093	927,074	818,099	643,587	174,512	108,976
2025	1,045,282	1,122,134	989,666	774,891	214,775	132,467

Note: All values in billions of yen, in 1980 prices.

Table 7.11. Factors of Production and their Share

Year	Private Capital	Effective Labour	Capital per Labour	Labour Share	Rate of Return	Wage
1980	328,795	7,150	46.0	0.749	0.158	2.17
1985	455,577	7,434	61.3	0.801	0.108	2.67
1990	590,268	7,790	75.8	0.838	0.082	3.19
1995	742,672	8,124	112.8	0.869	0.063	3.79
2000	920,406	8,157	140.0	0.901	0.046	4.69
2005	1,119,435	7,993	140.0	0.933	0.031	5.93
2010	1,088,002	7,771	140.0	0.935	0.036	7.33
2015	1,065,971	7,614	140.0	0.941	0.041	9.01
2020	1,063,722	7,598	140.0	0.947	0.044	10.88
2025	1,049,200	7,494	140.0	0.953	0.047	13.29

Note: Private capital is measured in billions of yen; effective labour in tens of thousands of workers; and wage in millions of yen per year.
All values are deflated to 1980 prices.

The Distribution of Economic Resources

The distribution of national income is the product of three factors: the distribution of human resources; the distribution of wealth; and the economic return to human resources *vis-à-vis* wealth. Fig. 7.4 shows the per-household distribution of effective labour in 1985, 2005, and 2025.[7] Labour resources are

---

[7] The values graphed in this and subsequent figures are the per-household values for each age-group divided by the simple average for all age-groups.

Table 7.12.   National Income by Source

Year	Labour	Capital	Foreign Investment
1980	74.1	24.8	1.1
2005	91.8	6.6	1.6
2025	88.8	4.4	6.8

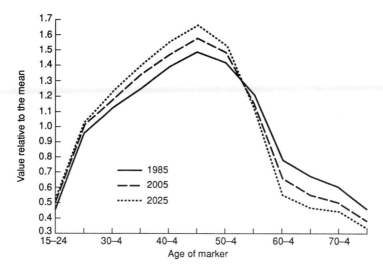

Fig. 7.4   Effective Labour per Household

concentrated among young and middle-aged households because their membership includes more adults of prime working age. Moreover, because productivity among men increases substantially with age, peaking during the forties, households with middle-aged men are particularly advantaged with respect to labour resources.

Over the 40 years pictured, the distribution of labour resources shifts even more in favour of young households. Several factors account for this change. First, labour-force participation declines steadily among older adults as they choose to retire at a younger age. Second, the average number of adults of prime working age living in elderly households declines significantly during the period. For example, the average number of adults 15–64 years of age living in a household aged 65–9 declines by over 50 per cent from 0.7 to 0.3 between 1985 and 2025. During the same period, the number of adults 15–64 living in households aged 50–4 declines by much less, from 2.8 to 2.7 members per household in 2025. Third, the age–productivity profile shifts in an unfavourable way for the elderly. In 1985 men aged 60 and older received a wage averaging 17 per cent more than that received by men aged 20–4.

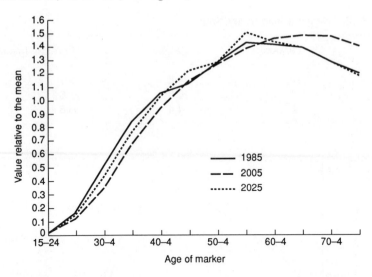

Fig. 7.5 Wealth per Household

By 2025 the premium will have dropped to 14 per cent in response to the increased supply of older workers. But of the three factors contributing to the changing distribution of labour resources, changes in the age–productivity profile were projected to have a relatively minor impact. In fact, the relative wage of women will actually have risen somewhat, offsetting the forecast decline among men.

Per-household wealth in Japan is concentrated among older households. The 1985 profile, shown in Fig. 7.5, rises rapidly with age, peaking among households aged 55–9 and declining gradually thereafter. The cross-section reflects both the distinct saving behaviour and the earnings history of each household cohort about which there is only limited information. From the evidence that is available, however, the lower per-household wealth of older households no doubt reflects their lower lifetime earnings rather than any tendency to dis-save during the retirement years.

During the first two decades of the simulation there is a very clear shift in the distribution of per-household wealth towards older households. And during the final two decades of the simulation, the distribution returns very nearly to the pattern 'observed' in 1985.

Because of the complexity of the wealth simulation, it is difficult to un-tangle the reasons for these changes, but two factors stand out. First, older households, who did not participate fully in Japan's post-war economic mira-cle, are being replaced by households whose members were just entering the labour-force at the end of World War II and have fully enjoyed the benefits of economic growth. A second factor is the change in the pattern of bequests. We will have more to say about this below, but there is a significant change in the distribution of inheritances between 1985 and 2005. In both 2005 and

2025, per-household inheritances are much more heavily concentrated among households with a head aged 35–49 and much less heavily among those under age 30 or over age 60. The changing pattern of inheritance leads to a somewhat slower accumulation of wealth among young households and a catching-up during middle age, followed by slower accumulation among the elderly.

The changes in the distribution of per-household wealth between 1985 and 2005 are not a product of changes in saving behaviour. In fact, the saving ratio of young households (those under 35 years of age) increases throughout the simulation in response to a decline in their wealth–income ratio. But the change in the wealth distribution after 2005 reflects a significant increase in saving among the young and a substantial decline in saving among middle-aged households.

Beyond these elements there are several features of the model that may affect the reliability of our results, particularly estimates of the wealth of young households. First, for young households labour-force participation is undoubtedly underestimated because no account is taken of the statistical dependence between participation and headship. A higher percentage of young household heads are undoubtedly employed than we are forecasting. Second, there is no provision for private transfers other than bequests. To the extent that parents provide their offspring with 'start-up' capital, we will underestimate the wealth of young households and overestimate the wealth of the parents of young household heads. Third, the initial distribution of wealth is based on incomplete data and subject to error that may be systematically related to age. But, all in all, the age-distribution of wealth shows a surprising stability and a plausible trend despite the simplifying assumptions employed in the model and errors in the data.

The Distribution of Household Income

Between 1985 and 2005 shifts in both the distribution of wealth and the distribution of the effective labour-force contributed to an increased concentration of income per household among young households. Moreover, throughout the simulation, labour's share of income is increasing. Because labour resources are much more concentrated among young households than wealth, the increase in labour income relative to capital income contributed substantially to the shift in national income towards young households. Thus, all three factors contributed to the shift in per-household income pictured in Fig. 7.6.

For the remaining two decades of the simulation, national income is increasingly concentrated among young households. Although labour's share increases only marginally after 2005 and the distribution of wealth shifts towards older households, such a substantial percentage of national income accrues to labour, that the continued increase in effective labour among young households dominates the trend in the distribution of national income.

Transfers have an important impact on the distribution of income.

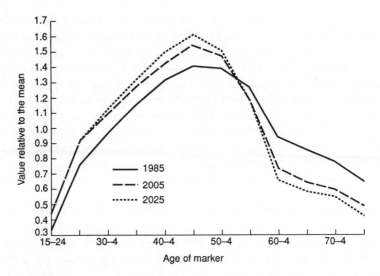

Fig. 7.6 National Income per Household

Government payments, combining taxes and transfers, raise the disposable income of households with a head aged 60 or older by a substantial amount: more than 20 per cent in the case of households with a head aged 60–9 and by more than 40 per cent in the case of households with a head aged 70 or older. Moreover, very young households are taxed at a somewhat lower rate than middle-aged households. The shift in disposable income is apparent in Fig. 7.7, which shows substantially higher relative income among older households. The impact of private transfers, or bequests, on the income distribution is somewhat mixed. In 1985 the greatest beneficiaries, in terms of the percentage increase in their disposable income, are households in their late twenties and early thirties, which had below average pre-transfer incomes. On the other hand, older households benefited the least from transfers so that in relative terms they are generally worse off.[8] Since 1985 private transfers have been increasingly concentrated among middle-aged households and quite clearly contribute to a less equal distribution of household income.

The trend in intergenerational inequality in per-household income and the impact of transfers are summarized by Table 7.13, which presents the variance of the natural log of per-household income. Two sets of values are provided—one that includes all age categories and a second that excludes households with a head aged under 25 years.[9] Several conclusions stand out.

---

[8] This finding is true by construction because all transfers are assumed to be intergenerational in nature and no account is made of intragenerational transfers or reverse intergenerational transfers.

[9] These households are excluded because they have such a large impact on summary measures and because values for them are less reliably estimated.

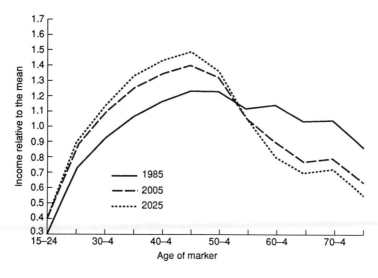

Fig. 7.7 Disposable Income per Household

Table 7.13. Variance in Log of Per-Household Income

	All Households		People Aged 15–24 Excluded	
Year	National Income	Disposable Income	National Income	Disposable Income
1985	0.151	0.131	0.062	0.023
2005	0.175	0.120	0.138	0.060
2025	0.217	0.155	0.187	0.099

First, the impact of government transfers on the intergenerational distribution of income is quite significant. In 1985 the log-variance is reduced from 0.062 to 0.023 for households over the age of 25. Equally large effects of government taxes and transfers occur in the other two years presented, 2005 and 2025. Second, intergenerational inequality in income increases quite substantially throughout the simulation. Again, confining our attention to households over 25, the variance of the log of per-household disposable income increases from 0.023 in 1985 to 0.060 in 2005 and to 0.099 in 2025.

However, a widely used alternative approach to measuring income inequality leads to a quite different conclusion. Following Kuznets (1976) and Schultz (1982), we have calculated household income per capita by dividing per-household income by the number of members. Table 7.14 presents new values of the log-variance based on per capita income. The differences are

Table 7.14.   Variance in Log of Per Capita Income

	All Households		People Aged 15–24 Excluded	
Year	National Income	Disposable Income	National Income	Disposable Income
1985	0.026	0.048	0.022	0.039
2005	0.019	0.010	0.020	0.007
2025	0.022	0.006	0.024	0.003

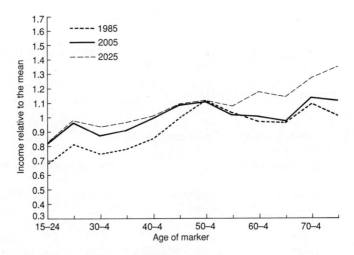

Fig. 7.8   Disposable Income per Capita

remarkable. First, the extent of intergenerational inequality is generally much lower using per capita income as an index of well-being rather than per-household income. Second, once we control for variation in household size, intergenerational inequality in disposable income declines throughout the simulation and particularly between 1985 and 2005. Finally, the net impact of government payments is to increase rather than to reduce the extent of intergenerational inequality in 1985. On the other hand, the current tax and benefit policies very effectively equalize disposable per capita income in the future, reducing the log-variance to 0.007 in 2005 and to 0.003 in 2025.

The results as summarized in Fig. 7.8 are equally clear in the detailed plot of per capita household disposable income. In 1985 per capita household income increases almost monotonically and linearly with age. By 2005 and 2025, however, the age-distribution of per capita household disposable income is very nearly uniform.

Table 7.15. Trends in Bequests and Wealth (trillion of yen)

| Year | Wealth | Bequests | | |
		total	as a %age of total wealth	as a %age of total saving
1980	596	—	—	—
1985	825	69	9.7	30.0
1990	1,069	103	10.9	42.2
1995	1,345	143	11.8	51.8
2000	1,667	192	12.7	59.6
2005	2,043	258	13.9	68.6
2010	2,485	324	14.3	73.3
2015	3,075	403	14.5	68.3
2020	3,816	496	14.4	66.9
2025	4,723	648	15.2	71.4

Bequests and Inheritance

Bequests arise in this model as a direct result of a net decline in any five-year period in the number of households headed by individuals in a given five-year cohort. Thus, we do not distinguish the transfer of assets associated with the death of the head from a transfer associated with the merger of an old household into a young household or even the redesignation of the head within a household that in other respects experiences no changes in its demographic character. The relevant issue is control over wealth and the timing of the transfer of control from one generation to the next. Of course, in many instances no single point in time can mark the transfer of control, but there is no obvious measure of control preferable to the household headship designation.

An important shortcoming of the approach taken here is that the probability of 'dying' and wealth are assumed to be independent. Individual mortality may be influenced by financial well-being and, perhaps more importantly, the continued existence of older households may be critically related to wealth. By failing to account for the statistical dependence we overestimate bequests by younger households and underestimate bequests by older households. Likewise, our estimates of the distribution of wealth and income described above are affected.

Setting these shortcomings aside, several clear trends in bequests and wealth stand out. First, total bequests are expected to grow quite rapidly. Figures reported in Table 7.15 show total bequests per quinquennia increasing from 69 trillion yen during the 1980–5 period to 648 trillion yen in the 2020–5 period. This amounts to an annual rate of growth of 5.0 per cent as compared

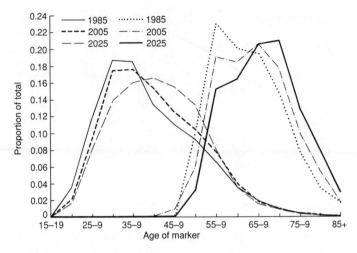

Fig. 7.9 Bequests and Inheritances by Age of Head of Household

with a 3.6 per cent rate of growth for NNP and a 4.6 per cent rate of growth for total wealth. As a result, bequests per five-year period increase from about 10 per cent of wealth in 1980–5 to just over 15 per cent of total wealth in 2025. For the economy as a whole, bequests generate no increase in real wealth. But for households that continue to exist, inheritances constitute an important means by which they increase their real wealth. Between 1980 and 1985, inheritances are estimated to equal 30 per cent of total saving. But the percentages increase remarkably fast, peaking at 73 per cent during 2005–10.

There are also important changes in the age-distribution of bequests and inheritances. Fig. 7.9 shows the age-of-head distribution of bequests and inheritances for the five-year periods preceding 1985, 2005, and 2025. The distributions of bequests are systematically shifting towards older households. The mean yen-weighted age of bequests increased from 65.1 years in 1985, to 66.6 years in 2005, and to 68.8 years in 2025. Although part of the shift between 1985 and 2005 in a consequence of a similar shift in the age-distribution of wealth described above, the driving force is the ageing of the population, because the average age of those dying also increases. The age-distribution of inheritances shifts in response to the ageing of the bequest distribution. The average age of inheritance increases by about 2.4 years over the four decades tracked, increasing from 41.2 years of age in 1985 to 43.6 years of age in 2025. The mean age of inheritance increased by less than that of bequests because of an increase in the mean generation length, measured in this unusual way, from 23.8 years to 25.2 years between 1985 and 2025.

The economic impact of inheritance from the household's perspective is clarified by Fig. 7.10. The contribution of inheritance to household disposable

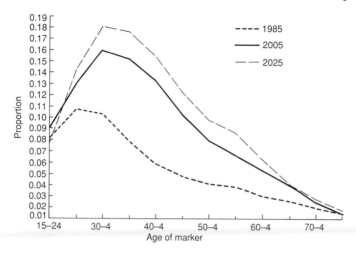

Fig. 7.10 Inheritances as a Proportion of Disposable Income

income declines steadily with household age. In 1985 the average annual inheritance exceeded 10 per cent of disposable income for households aged 20–4 and 25–9, but declined steadily, contributing less than 5 per cent of disposable income for households aged 40–4. For nearly all household ages, the importance of inheritance will increase remarkably over the next four decades, contributing nearly 20 per cent of disposable income for households aged 30–4 in 2025. For households aged 35–64, the percentage contribution of inheritance will more than double. What explains this remarkable increase? Two factors are primarily responsible. First, as indicated above, total bequests are growing more rapidly than national income. Second, the reduced level of fertility among successive cohorts of those who bequeath means that those who inherit must share their estates among fewer siblings.

Foreign Investment

One of the most startling results of the simulation is the decline in the returns to capital associated with a rapidly rising capital–labour ratio. Capital's share is projected to decline from one-quarter of net national product in 1980 to only 10 per cent in the year 2000. The importance of changes in the relative returns to human and physical capital is highlighted above. The impact on foreign investment and economic relations between Japan and the rest of the world may be even more important.

The simulation model provides a relatively crude rendering of the likely course of foreign investment. During the first 20 years of the simulation, 1980–2000, the percentage allocations of investment between the private sector (excluding housing), the public sector, housing, and the foreign sector are held constant at their 1985 levels. During that period, the rate of return to domestically invested capital has declined to 3 per cent as the capital–labour ratio reached 140. Thereafter, additional investment, except that necessary to maintain a domestic rate of return of 3 per cent, flows abroad. Were this scenario to hold true, the percentage of Japanese wealth held abroad would be relatively constant at around 13 per cent through 2005, but would increase to 33 per cent in 2015 and 46 per cent in 2025. From approximately 100 trillion yen (1980 prices) in 1985, assets held abroad would reach 1,000 trillion yen in 2015 and 2,100 trillion yen in 2025.

One can easily imagine variants to this broad phenomenon. First, the private sector may absorb a smaller share of total investment during the first two decades of the simulation. In recent years the share of investment going to the foreign sector has increased and one could well expect this to continue. During the period 1986–8, dollar-denominated long-term capital transfers averaged twice the amount observed in 1985 (World Bank, 1990). However, a great deal of the increase could be traced to appreciation of the yen; yen-denominated long-term capital transfers in 1988 were no greater than those observed in 1985.

Second, the simulation assumes that the share of investment going to housing and the public sector will remain constant, but one can easily imagine a substantial increase in both components. Indeed, the government is already increasing spending on public infrastructure and the need for additional investment in housing has been widely noted. Finally, the simulation assumes that changes in the rate of interest will have no impact on the saving rate. A decline in the return to capital should have some adverse impact on the rate of saving, reducing the amount of investable funds available. Despite all of these qualifications, slower labour-force growth and high rates of saving will no doubt guarantee rapid growth in the export of capital to the rest of the world.

Concluding Remarks

The results from an exercise as ambitious as this one must be subject to considerable scrutiny before reaching any firm conclusions. Any of the findings reported above should be viewed as tentative and subject to further research and revision. But accepting the tentative nature of our findings, what conclusions stand out?

A surprising conclusion is the lack of intergenerational inequality in per capita income in 1985. Even more surprising is the finding that per capita income of households headed by the elderly are quite satisfactory as compared with other households. Several factors contribute to this conclusion. First, the elderly have maintained high rates of saving, achieved relatively high levels of personal wealth, and have enjoyed interest income nearly sufficient to offset the decline in labour earnings associated with retirement. Second, the continued prevalence of extended households in Japan means that many elderly households have members of prime working age. Thus, effective labour per capita among elderly households is not that much less than in younger households. Third, government taxes and transfers have a very significant impact on the intergenerational distribution of disposable income—increasing income of those 60–9 by over 20 per cent and of those 70 and older by over 40 per cent.

In the same vein, the forecasts described above do imply a deterioration in per capita household income of elderly households relative to younger households, but current public policy seems sufficient to maintain a remarkably equitable intergenerational distribution of income.

The second important finding in this paper is the conclusion that inheritance will become an increasingly important component of disposable income. In general, we know very little about the impact of inheritance on household behaviour. But in the model employed here, increased bequests have for many household age-groups reduced the wealth–income ratio and depressed the average rate of saving. In Japan, it is obviously important to have direct evidence about the impact on household saving or, alternatively, labour-force participation of a rise in inherited wealth.

As we have repeatedly warned, however, the findings must be qualified to the extent that important processes that are underway in Japan are not captured by our model. Most importantly the roles of both the government and the family are in transition. The simple tax and transfer model employed does not begin to capture the complexity of the issues that public policy-makers will face in an increasingly aged society. The approach employed here implies a relatively slow growth in transfer payments even though the numbers of elderly are increasing rapidly. This is because transfer payments are a fixed percentage of income received by each age-group and the pre-tax and transfer income of the elderly grows much more slowly than their numbers. In 1980, for example, households headed by the elderly were 8.0 per cent of all households and earned 6.6 per cent of total factor income. Thus, they earned about 20 per cent below their pro rata share. But by 2000 we forecast an increase in the proportion of elderly households to 12.8 per cent of the total while their share of factor income rises to only 7.4 per cent. It may be unrealistic to expect a relative deterioration in transfer payments in step with the relative economic status of the elderly. On the other hand, it is also unrealistic to expect public-sector action sufficient to overcome the relative decline in the income of the elderly. Recent steps in Japan have signalled rather clearly the intent of the government to reduce the potential public-sector burden of a rapidly ageing population.

Important changes in the Japanese family may prove to be as important as changes in public policy. In the traditional Japanese family, elderly relatives continued to live with their children, and were apparently able to count on their economic and emotional support. In modern Japan elderly people are increasingly likely to live independently of their children and, often, by themselves. In 1985, for example, elderly women were nearly twice as likely to live alone as they were in 1970 (Mason *et al.*, 1992). With fewer children, increasing rates of divorce, and high rates of widowhood among the very old, the percentage of elderly men and women living alone may continue to rise rapidly in Japan in the foreseeable future. It would be simplistic to equate separate living with isolation, however, because many Japanese children continue to be involved in their elderly parents' lives even when they are living separately (Martin, 1989; Martin and Tsuya, 1989). None the less, the economic problems faced by the elderly may be more serious than is outlined here.

The macroeconomic implications of this model also merit further attention. The results presented here are based on the assumption that net national product will continue to grow at the same rate as during the first part of the 1980s. At the same time, returns to domestically invested capital are forecast to decline rapidly in the face of increased capital per worker. It seems questionable that technological innovation will be sufficient to sustain the rate of growth assumed in the face of a stagnant labour-force and rapidly diminishing returns to capital. A slowdown in the rate of growth of the Japanese economy would generally twist the intergenerational distribution of income against younger generations and in favour of older generations. Of course, all generations, young and old alike, will be worse off in absolute terms with a slowdown in economic growth.

References

Ando, A. (1985), *The Savings of Japanese Households: A Micro Study Based on Data from the National Survey of Family Income and Expenditure, 1974 and 1979*, Tokyo.

Denison, E. F. and Chung, W. K. (1976), *How Japan's Economy Grew So Fast: The Sources of Postwar Expansion*, Washington, DC: Brookings Institute.

Kuznets, S. (1976), 'Demographic Aspects of the Size Distribution of Income: An Exploratory Essay', *Economic Development and Cultural Change*, 25 (Oct.), 1–94.

Martin, L. G. (1989), 'The Graying of Japan', *Population Bulletin*, 44 (June).

—— and Ogawa, N. (1988), 'The Effect of Cohort Size on Relative Wages in Japan', in R. D. Lee, W. B. Arthur, and G. Rodgers (eds.), *Economics of Changing Age Distributions in Developed Countries*, New York: Oxford University Press, 59–75.

—— and Tsuya, N. O. (1989), 'Interactions of Middle-Aged Japanese with their Parents', paper presented at the Population Association of America annual meetings, Baltimore, Md., 29 March–1 April.

Mason, A. (1987), *HOMES: A Household Model for Economic and Social Studies*, Papers of the East-West Population Institute no. 106, Honolulu: East-West Center.

—— and Martin, L. G. (1982), 'Intergenerational Differences in Income: An Analysis of Japan', in Y. Ben-Porath (ed.), *Income Distribution and the Family, Population and Development Review*, Supp. to vol. 8, 179–92.

—— Ogawa, N., and Fukui, T. (1992), *Household Projections for Japan 1985–2025: A Transition Model of Headship Rates*, Tokyo: Japan Statistical Association, Nihon University Population Research Institute, and Program on Population, East-West Center.

Ministry of Health and Welfare, *Results from the Income Redistribution Survey*, 1984, Tokyo.

Mosk, C. and Nakata, Y.-F. (1985), 'The Age–Wage Profile and Structural Change in the Japanese Labor Market for Males, 1961–1982', *Journal of Human Resources*, 20/1, 100–16.

Ogawa, N. (1987), 'Sex Differentials in Labour Force Participation and Earnings in Japan', in *Women's Economic Participation in Asia and the Pacific*, Bangkok: UN ESCAP, 305–32.

—— et al. (1986), *Jinko Keizai Iryo Moderu Ni Motozuku Choki Tenbo: Feisu II* ('Long-term Prospects Based upon a Demographic, Economic, and Medical Model: Phase II'), Tokyo: Nihon University Population Research Institute.

—— et al. (1988), *Jinko Keizai Iryo Moderu Ni Motozuku Choki Tenbo: Feisu III* ('Long-term Prospects Based upon a Demographic, Economic, and Medical Model: Phase III'), Tokyo: Nihon University Population Research Institute.

—— and Mason, A. (1986), 'An Economic Analysis of Recent Fertility in Japan: An Application of the Butz–Ward Model', *Jinkogoku Kenkyu* ('The Journal of Population Studies'), 9 (May), 5–14.

Ohkawa, K. and Rosovsky, H. (1973), *Japanese Economic Growth*, Stanford, Calif.: Stanford University Press.

Prime Minister's Office, Statistics Bureau (various dates), *Japan Statistical Yearbook*, Tokyo.

Schultz, T. P. (1982), 'Family Composition and Income Inequality', in Y. Ben-Porath (ed.), *Income Distribution and the Family, Population and Development Review*, Supp. to vol. 8, 137–50.

World Bank (1990), *World Development Report*, Oxford: Oxford University Press.

Appendix

Equation List

$$Y_{xt}^D = Y_{xt}^L + Y_{xt}^A + T_{xt}^P + G_{xt} \tag{1}$$

$$Y_{xt}^L = Y_t^L L_{xt}/L_t \tag{2}$$

$$Y_{xt}^A = (Y_t^K + Y_t^F)A_{xt}/A_t \tag{3}$$

$$Y_t = \Gamma_t F(K_t, L_t) \tag{4}$$

$$Y_t^L = \Pi_t^L Y_t \tag{5}$$

$$Y_t^K = \Pi_t^K Y_t \tag{6}$$

$$\Pi_t^L = \beta_0 + \beta_1 \ln k_t \tag{7}$$

$$\Pi_t^K = 1 - \Pi_t^L \tag{8}$$

$$Y_t^F = i_t A_t^F \tag{9}$$

$$L_t = \sum_a \omega_{at}^m L_{at}^m + \sum_a \omega_{at}^f L_{at}^f \tag{10}$$

$$\omega_{at}^i = f_a(L_{at}^i/L_{0t}^i) \tag{11}$$

$$L_{xt} = \sum_a \omega_{at}^m l_{at}^m N_{axt}^m + \sum_a \omega_{at}^f l_{at}^f N_{axt}^f \tag{12}$$

$$A_{xt} = A_{x-5,t-5} + S_{x-5,t-5} + 5T_{x-5,t-5}^P \tag{13}$$

$$S_{xt} = \beta s_{xt}(Y_{xt}^L + Y_{xt}^A + G_{xt}) \tag{14}$$

$$s_{xt} = f(A_{xt}/Y_{xt}^D, x, N_{axt}) \tag{15}$$

$$K_t = \kappa_t \sum_x A_{xt} \tag{16}$$

$$A_t^F = \gamma_t \sum_x A_{xt} \tag{17}$$

$$B_{xt} = A'_{x-5,t-5}(H_{x-5,t-5} - H_{xt})/H_{x-5,t-5} \quad \text{if } \Delta H_{xt} \le 0 \tag{18}$$
$$= 0 \quad \text{if } \Delta H_{xt} > 0$$

$$I_{at}^{pc} = \sum_x h_{axt} B_{xt}/N_{at} \tag{19}$$

$$I_{xt} = \sum_a N_{axt} I_{at}^{pc} \tag{20}$$

$$T_{xt}^P = I_{xt} - B_{xt} \tag{21}$$

$$G_{xt} = R_{xt} - T_{xt} \tag{22}$$

$$T_{xt} = \tau_{xt}(Y_{xt}^L + Y_{xt}^A) \tag{23}$$

$$R_{xt} = r_{xt}(Y_{xt}^L + Y_{xt}^A) \tag{24}$$

Variable Names and Definitions

Y_{xt}^D — disposable income of households aged x in year t.

Y_{xt}^L — labour income of households aged x in year t.

Y_{xt}^A — asset income of households aged x in year t.

G_{xt} — net government transfers including taxes to households aged x in year t.

T_{xt}^P — net private transfers to households aged x in year t.

Y_t^L — total labour income in year t.

Y_t^K — total capital income in year t.

Y_t — total national product in year t.

Π_t^K — capital's share of output in year t.

Π_t^L — labour's share of output in year t.

Γ_t — index of technology in year t.

K_t — capital stock in year t.

k_t — ratio of capital to effective labour in year t.

L_t — effective labour supply in year t.

L_{xt} — effective labour supply of households aged x.

A_{xt} — assets of households aged x.

A_t — total assets.

A_t^F — assets invested abroad.

Y_t^F — income on assets held abroad.

L_{at}^i — number of male (m) or female (f) workers in age-group a.

ω_{at}^i — relative productivity of male (m) or female (f) workers in age-group a.

l_{at}^i — labour-force participation rate of males (m) or females (f) aged a.

N_{axt}^i — number of males (m) or females (f) aged a in year t living in households with a head aged x.

S_{xt} — saving by households aged x in year t.

$s_{x,t}$ — ratio of saving to disposable income net of private transfers.

κ_t — fraction of total wealth invested in domestic enterprise excluding housing.

γ_t — fraction of total wealth invested abroad.

i_t — real interest rate (international).

R_{xt} — government transfers to households aged x.

r_{xt} — benefit rate for households aged x.

T_{xt} — taxes paid by households aged x.

τ_{xt} — tax rate for households aged x.

B_{xt} — 'bequests' by households aged x during the interval t-5 to t.

h_{axt} — proportion of bequests made by households aged x received by individuals aged a.

I_{at}^{pc} — per capita inheritances received by individuals aged a in year τ.

I_{xt} — inheritances received by households aged x in year τ.

8 Public Intergenerational Transfers as an Old-Age Pension System: A Historical Interlude?

TOMMY BENGTSSON AND GUNNAR FRIDLIZIUS

One of the major benefits modern industrial society offers the individual is a relatively long period of active life following retirement from full-time work. This provides an opportunity for inner reflection, travel, the pursuit of hobbies, and a number of other activities. However, financial security is necessary to assure a fulfilling life for the individual after retirement. Without adequate financial resources these possibilities instead pose increasing risks for the retired. Without adequate financial resources, instead of satisfaction, they find themselves unable to maintain meaningful social functions and are estranged from society at large. Today, persons above 65 years of age are guaranteed a certain standard of living through the Swedish national pension system, which is a public intergenerational transfer system. Only 10–15 per cent of the income of retired people comes from sources other than this public pension system. With 18 per cent of the population retired in Sweden, public pensions consume a substantial part of the GDP (11–12 per cent to be exact). The many elderly people also demand other resources, especially in the form of health care. However, the vast majority are very healthy at the age of retirement. As a group, they are also rather wealthy, although disparities within the group are great: 48 per cent of bank savings belong to the retired. Since the 1940s, Swedish people have been able to retire from work at a fixed age, irrespective of working capacity, and participate in the benefit system.

This chapter gives a historical overview of the rise of the Swedish national pension system, and provides some projections regarding its probable future. Our thesis is that public intergenerational transfers, in the form of a national pension system as it is today, will soon be seen as a historical interlude.

When people plan their future, they are aware of the different stages they are going to pass through during their lives. The individual person would like such basic needs as food, clothing, and shelter met and to have these allocations as equitably distributed over his or her lifetime as possible, regardless of life-span. Adjustments must be made for the fact that income during childhood and old age do not match demand at these times. Consumption needs

We are grateful to Denis Kessler, Agneta Kruse, and Rolf Ohlsson for their comments.

must therefore be satisfied through savings and by private or public inter-generational transfers.

Most people in pre-industrial Sweden continued to work as long as they could, irrespective of occupation. Thus, most did not retire at all, in the modern sense of the word. But at the age when their consumption exceeded their production and they became dependent on private or public inter-generational transfers, they adjusted to the new situation by a change in their work status: they became semi-retired. The change in work status could be in terms of intensity, working hours, and content. The productivity of this semi-retired period varies to a great extent, depending on the amount of personal savings a person has at his or her disposal during this time, and whether these savings are bound or unbound.

People with liquid personal savings such as bank savings could, in theory, as long as they had them, continue to work and pursue the same occupation even if their consumption exceeded their personal production. They would manage by spending some of their savings concurrently with their earnings, making necessary adjustments as they aged. However, the fact is that few people's savings are limited to the form of liquid personal savings. This is true of farmers as well as of those from higher strata of society. Furthermore, liquid savings are often in the form of working capital. Persons with illiquid personal savings, such as farms, were able to make private contracts even at the time their consumption exceeded their production. These contracts could either be with a relative, a son or a daughter, with a private person outside the family, or with an institution. Such contracts existed as early as the eighteenth century, but were only evident among farmers and the upper classes (Odén, 1989).

During the nineteenth century in Sweden, people without savings, such as farm labourers or industrial workers, were taken care of by their employers. When their working capacity decreased, they either worked less intensively or they changed to an easier job. Farm labourers were sometimes given a small cottage where they were able to support themselves, perhaps with some help from their former employer. If a person was unable to work, had no savings, and was granted no help from his or her former employer, he or she was dependent on his or her children. If all other measures failed and the children were unable to provide support, in the last resort the individual was dependent on public means, and was, in plain language, sent to the poorhouse. Thus, for almost everybody, and in particular for labourers, there was a constant downward mobility as their working capacity declined and their consumption exceeded their income. Private intergenerational transfers failed within the family, with private persons outside the family, or with the employer, and during the twentieth century were replaced by public intergenerational transfers.

In the present chapter, we start with an overview of private intergenerational transfers in pre-industrial Sweden, and then analyse factors behind the historical failure of private transfers. Next, the birth and maturation of the public intergenerational transfer system is described. In the final section, we discuss the future of public intergenerational transfers; will future changes in the population structure, with a growing proportion retired, demolish the public pension system and make it a historical interlude?

The Age of Private Intergenerational Transfers

Highest in the early nineteenth-century Swedish social hierarchy stood the estate-owner; he was followed by the peasant owner, the peasant tenant, the crofter, the farm-hand, the *statare* (married, non-landholding farm labourers), and at the bottom the groups of cottagers and lodgers.[1] Among the peasant owners, there were great differences according to economic and social position. These differences increased as the commercialization of Swedish agriculture proceeded during the nineteenth century. Some regions were characterized by a large-scale process of land parcelling, which led to the emergence of a group of semi-peasants who were unable to live off their small holdings. At the same time there was an expanding group of large farmers producing for the market.

The tenant group was more homogeneous from an economic and social point of view. The average size of their holdings was also smaller. In some ways they had more in common with the crofters than with the peasant owners. Most tenants lived on the great plains in southern and eastern Sweden, where the land belonged to large estate owners. During the mid-nineteenth century, about 20 per cent of all peasants belonged to the tenant group. Like the tenants, the crofters occupied land by contract, although their holdings were smaller and the rent was paid by day-work on the main farm. The farm-hands and the *statare* were contracted for one year. The farm-hands ate at the farmer's table and were unmarried. The *statare* in the estate regions were married and their families lodged together in a common house located close to the manor house. They had a little garden of their own for the cultivation of potatoes and they were often allowed to raise a pig.

The class of cottagers and lodgers was a more peculiar phenomenon from a social point of view. Like the crofters, the cottagers occupied land but they had no day-work obligations to the owner. Their allotments were, however, very small and limited to the cultivation of potatoes and the breeding of poultry and pigs. For their maintenance they often had to work as farm labourers for the peasants. It is often difficult to distinguish between cottagers and lodgers. The latter sometimes lived in the house of a peasant or a crofter and sometimes in a separate little cabin, i.e. in reality as a cottager. Swedish

---

[1] This survey of the class structure relies on Fridlizius and Ohlsson (1985) and Fridlizius (1979).

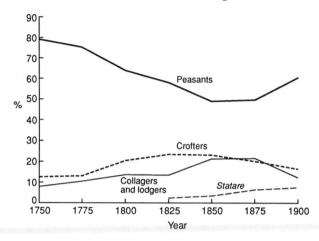

Note: Male family heads are given in per cent; farm-hands and sons over 15 years are not included.
Source: Wohlin (1909).

Fig. 8.1 Main Groups of Workers in the Agricultural Sector in Sweden, 1751–1870

occupational statistics do not differentiate between these two categories. Both could pay for the allotment or housing as day labourers.

At the end of the eighteenth century the peasants were the totally dominant group. However, as we can see from Fig. 8.1, the rapid population growth in the first half of the nineteenth century radically changed this occupational structure, and by 1870 the combined size of the lower classes was as large as the size of the class of peasants.

We know little about what happened to the elderly of these different categories, but in short the following pattern stands out.[2] Among the peasant owners, the elderly could be set on *undantag*. This meant that at the time of sale or takeover of his holdings, the old peasant made a contract with the new owner, often his own son, which gave him certain privileges: to eat at the owner's table or receive a certain amount of grain and potatoes or a certain amount of money; possibly to stay on in a room of his former house; he might also get a dwelling or rights to a plot of land with a little cabin. The new situation did not mean full retirement. Often the contract demanded that the older man help the new owner in his work as long as physically able. What this meant in reality is difficult to say; it also depended on the willingness of the older man to provide assistance to the new owner.

Thus, it was not physical weakness which in the first place determined the time of retirement, which was to a large extent connected with the demand from the younger generation to take over the family holdings. The earlier

[2] This problem has been analysed in a number of studies. The main sources for this survey are Odén (1983) and Gaunt (1983). A more detailed analysis of the demographic pattern of ageing is undertaken in Bengtsson and Fridlizius, 1989.

they married, the sooner this claim rose as an issue in the family, and this was often a cause of conflict between generations. Another problem was the increased burden for the new owner, especially if the holding was small, when the amount of time the elderly ex-owner was able to devote to work fell off. The difficulties increased with a rise in fertility and a fall in infant and child mortality in the early nineteenth century. The oldest son often bought parts of the farm that were to be inherited by his brothers and sisters. A growing number of siblings could seriously increase the economic burden for the new owner even if he paid a price below its market value.

The common view is that the *undantag* practice dominated pre-industrial peasant society in Sweden. However, recent investigations tend to diminish its importance.[3] The prevailing mortality and marriage pattern (in terms of age) gives support to this conclusion.

For the elderly of the tenant class, the situation was more difficult since they did not own their holdings. Besides, the holdings were smaller than those of the peasant owners. It seems, however, that the tenant often had a contract with the landowner, which allowed him to live as a semi-retired person in one form or another as a lodger or a cottager. If his son took over the contract, his situation was similar to that of a retired peasant.

Life as a cottager during one's retirement period must, however, have been common among the crofters. In many cases the crofter's holding was too small to support two families. A considerable number of the cottagers were elderly retired crofters. This also meant that the way to the poorhouse must have been shorter for the crofters than for the categories of farm-worker desccribed above.

For old farm-hands and farm labourers, the situation was different, at least theoretically: in these cases, the employer had certain obligations to take care of the elderly. In practice, however, this varied from employer to employer. In many cases it is likely that the old farm-hands and farm labourers had to go the same way as many of the old crofters: to a cabin and then perhaps to the poorhouse. As regards the group of cottagers, however, it must be made clear that it did not consist solely of old retired people; as a result of the rapid population growth, many young people became cottagers and lived and died as such.

So what happened to the elderly in pre-industrial Swedish towns? First, we have noticed that only a very small part of the population lived in town—in 1800 about 10 per cent. On the whole this proportion was constant up until about 1850. From this time on, the urban population increased more rapidly than the rural population and in 1870 13 per cent of the total population lived in towns. Of the urban population one-third lived in Stockholm, the only town in Sweden with a metropolitan character (Bengtsson and Fridlizius, 1989).

---

[3] An investigation of inheritance practices in three parishes in south-western Sweden shows that only a small fraction of the parents transferred their farm to the next generation during their lifetime (see Winberg, 1981).

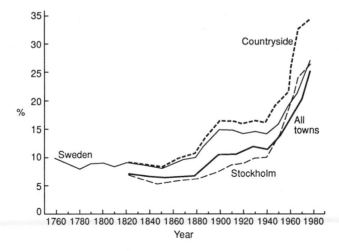

Note: The figure is based on the ratio of the population aged 65 years and over to the population aged 15 to 64 years.
Sources: Tabellverkev, SCB; Bisos A and SOS, Befolkning.

Fig. 8.2 Ageing in the Countryside and Towns of Sweden and in Stockholm, 1760–1980

As seen in Fig. 8.2, the percentage of the elderly aged 15–64 was considerably lower in the towns than in the countryside. On the whole, however, the trend is the same, except for the period 1850 to 1870, when the towns show a lag and do not demonstrate the rapid increase in the elderly observed for the countryside.

Our knowledge of the situation of the elderly in the towns is also incomplete. However, for the large group occupied in handicrafts and trade, an old-fashioned patriarchal system as maintained by many employers seems to have functioned as a social safety-net for retired old people.[4] Possibly, the increasing number of elderly day labourers was included in this category. However, in the towns, as in the countryside, an increasing number of proletarians must have been an urgent problem for the local government, which led to calls for modernization of the poor relief system.

Although only a minor part of the Swedish population during the pre-industrial period was reliant on local government, this development undoubtedly worsened the situation for a relatively large number of elderly people. It is interesting to note in this context that mortality at ages over 65 years gradually declined from about 1860. This seemingly paradoxical observation is, however, beyond the scope of this paper (Fridlizius, 1988). Regarding the influence that later changes in the age-structure could have on the

---

[4] Concerning the situation of the elderly in towns, see Edgren (1987).

performance of the retirement system we can note that during the period under discussion we had quite a constant age-distribution—despite a complicated demographic pattern (Bengtsson and Fridlizius, 1989). Thus, there was no demographic pressure on the old-age transfer system during this period.

The Failure of Private Intergenerational Transfers

The period from 1870 to 1914 is often taken to be the period of industrial breakthrough in Sweden's economic development. The percentage engaged in industry increased from 9 to 26, in trade and communication from 2 to 10. At the same time the percentage engaged in agriculture declined from 72 to 47 and the share of the total population living in towns increased from 13 to 26 per cent.

These profound changes in Sweden's economic and social structure led to fundamentally new conditions for the elderly. The debate on how to provide for the elderly, which had begun at the end of the pre-industrial stage, was further accentuated. In a gradually commercialized economy the old *undantag* contracts exerted considerable pressure on the peasants.[5] The credit institutions, for instance, were unwilling to give credit to farmers burdened with different kinds of contracts. An increasing number of heirs also put pressure on the system. As a result, peasants began to hand over the farm on strictly commercial terms when they retired, i.e. they would sell in accordance with the current market value. Then they could retire and live on the interest of the capital, sometimes in a neighbouring town, which meant that the old semi-retirement system was abandoned. This was particularly noticeable in the case of farmers with large holdings. However, for many holdings the *undantag* contract still existed at the end of the period.

For the elderly among the crofters, cottagers, and farm-hands the increasing commercialization also led to changes in a negative direction. In modern efficient agriculture, it was more difficult to engage a large group of old workers whose productivity was low. This problem was even more serious for the growing group of elderly industrial workers, who had even fewer opportunities after retirement. The patriarchal conditions still prevailing in the old mining industry or among the craftsmen in the towns, giving a certain amount of protection to the elderly, did not exist in such new industries as sawmills, textiles, engineering, etc. As a result, the number who were forced to take refuge in the poorhouses tended to increase.

The problem of the elderly living in these new conditions began to influence the social debate to an even larger extent than before and several attempts were made by parliament to bring about a general old-age insurance plan. The problem was undoubtedly aggravated by the demographic development

[5] See fn. 3, above.

which meant that the ratio of the elderly to the whole population aged 15–64 more than doubled in the countryside and almost doubled in the towns. The dominant factor behind this change was the large-scale overseas emigration. Between 1870 and 1900 the net emigration from Sweden was about 670,000 persons, most of them in their twenties, which meant that about 10 per cent of the active population had left the country. To some extent the increase in the numerical share of the elderly was an effect of the decline in mortality for this group.

However, it was not until 1913 that Sweden's first universal pension system was implemented. The new pension system was safer from an economic point of view, and from a social point of view it was more encompassing than the old relief system for the poor. Modern research is, however, not convinced that this aspect actually dominated when the new law was planned. The new system is regarded as a result of the government's efforts to make possible an intensification of the industrial sector, without making the system of local government poor relief responsible for the newly retired workers (Olsson, 1983).

Thus, in a long-term perspective, the new pension system was an unavoidable result of the industrialization process. In the new sectors which had evolved, the elderly could not be taken care of by private intergenerational transfers. At the same time, as a result of commercialization, private intergenerational transfers lost their importance in the agricultural sector. A growing number of the elderly as a proportion of the labour-force as a whole added to the problem.

The Rise and Maturation of Public Intergenerational Transfers

The pension system of 1913 meant only minor, if any, improvements in the living conditions of old people: taking a married couple in 1914 each received about 11 per cent of the earnings of a factory worker (Elmér, 1960: 256, Table v: 4). This means that the old-age pension would have been about one-third of the subsistence minimum (Elmer, 1960: 261, table v: 6). The pension was low not only in comparison to industrial wages and a minimum standard of living but also relative to pensions in other countries, such as Germany, Denmark, Great Britain, Australia, and New Zealand. But Sweden was the only country with a national pension system covering the entire population; in other countries, the pension systems applied to industrial workers only.

What then were the effects of the new system? One essential point is that employers were no longer responsible for old workers. Another important effect was that a retirement age was set for the entire labour-force. This mandatory retirement age was no longer a question of the working capacity of the individual, as it had been on the farm. This had a special implication which we will discuss later.

Normally, rapid changes in fertility do not greatly influence the size of the labour-force, nor the number of persons married, nor the size of the retired population. This is because all members of a birth cohort do not start to work, or marry, or retire at the same age. The effect of a fast increase in fertility is sometimes described as what happens when throwing a stone into a pond. The waves grow smaller and smaller away from the centre, to vanish before reaching the shore. This was certainly also the case for fertility waves up until 1913. A shock rise in fertility is smoothed somewhat due to the different ages of those entering the labour-force and marrying, but if all persons retire at the same age, say 67, the shock simply reappears 67 years later.

The national pension system was, and still is, a transfer system, i.e. a system which transfers resources from the labour-force to the retired through annual taxes without substantial reserved funds. This method of financing was discussed very little in parliament at the time when the system was introduced. Its advocates meant that the costs should be compensated for by a decrease in the demand for public assistance (poor relief, poorhouse, etc.). The costs were to be covered by the state, the communes, and the county councils, and a special tax on individuals financed the system.

During the 1920s, the pension declined in relation to the wages of industrial workers even after a change in the rules in 1921 (Elmér, 1960: 247). By new laws of 1935 and 1943, the situation for the retired was somewhat improved but they were still unable to live on their pensions, particularly if they lived in towns. The public assistance they needed took various forms. After 1919 local authorities were allowed to pay extra pensions, but it was not until after the Second World War that a regular supplement for housing costs was introduced. However, the standard of living for the poorest had not changed very much during this period. It was only the channels through which they received their support that had changed (Elmér, 1960: 247).

Up until the 1940s the number of people above the age of 65 years in the entire population was stable (Fig. 8.2, above), so there were no demographic pressures on the system. There was, however, some pressure, but for other reasons. As employment in industry increased, so did the need for an improved pension system (Fig. 8.3). This is because it is more difficult to continue working after retirement in a white- or blue-collar job than in agriculture: the percentage continuing to work after the age of 67 went down from 60 per cent in 1910 to 40 per cent in 1950.

At the same time, a large number of young people left rural areas to work in towns: while in 1900 20 per cent had lived in towns, the figure for 1950 was 50 per cent. As a result, it became more difficult for children to look after their parents. But this process also had positive effects for the elderly: they were under less pressure to leave their houses to provide room for the next generation.

By a new pension law passed in 1946, which came into effect in 1948, the old-age security system was considerably improved. As before, the entire

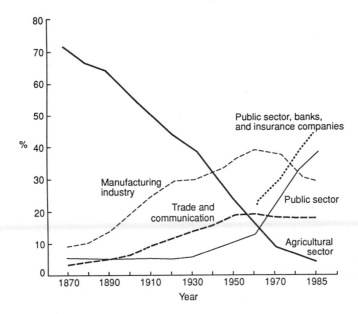

Note: The figure is based on the percentage of the total number employed.
Sources: Carlsson (1968) and Bengtsson (1988).
Fig. 8.3 Employment in Different Economic Sectors in Sweden, 1870–1985

population was covered, and the old-age pension was supplemented with housing allowances from the local government. This part of the pension was, unlike the national one, dependent on income. For the first time, it was possible for almost all retired people to live on their pensions without other financial support. Consequently, laws were no longer required to oblige children to look after their parents. It also became less common for elderly people to continue to work. This is an international phenomenon related to industrialization, but there are 'strong reasons for assuming that the increase in pensions from 1948 onwards have accelerated this course of events' (Elmér, 1960: 597). The general pension as well as the housing supplement were improved further during the 1950s.

As shown in Fig. 8.2 (above), the ratio of the elderly to the whole labour-force increased considerably from 1940 to 1950, after a long period of stability. It has been increasing continuously from then onwards, although not at the same rate. These changes are not a result of variations in the size of the labour-force but of variations in the number of the retired, as the number of persons aged 15 to 64 years increased continuously during the eighteenth and nineteenth centuries. The only exceptions are in the 1880s, when the demographic base of the labour-force was constant due to emigration, and in the 1970s, when it was stable as a result of past variations in fertility.

A new general supplementary pension system was introduced in 1960 after a referendum, and payments began in 1963. This pension is based on the principle that a certain part of the loss of income after retirement should be compensated for. Unlike the base pension, this pension is thus related to income prior to retirement, although within certain limits. Those who will receive no pension, or a low general supplementary one only, due to low income prior to pension, are entitled to a special pension supplement and compensation for housing costs (Kruse, 1988). The pension system includes disability pensions and income compensation for widows (based on husbands earnings), in addition to the old-age pension. The level of replacement for loss of income after retirement is about 72–75 per cent after tax for normal and high incomes (up to a certain income) and more (even over 100 per cent) fox those on low incomes (Kruse, 1988). These figures do not include health services, which are almost free of charge.

In addition to these national pension systems, there are pensions regulated by agreements between the labour-market organizations as well as private pension systems. The national old-age pension system, i.e. the base system from 1913, is a pure transfer system while the supplementary system from 1960 is basically the same. However, a special fund has been developed as a buffer to short-term variations in in- and out-payments. The idea was also that it would compensate for an expected decrease in private savings after the new system had been introduced and that it should be used for the financing of industrial investments.

The demographic pressure on the pension system has been strong since 1960 (see Fig. 8.2), but it has functioned effectively, mainly due to very rapid economic growth. As a consequence, the standard of living for retired people improved as the pension system developed. Pensions were directly related to the cost of living index, so that, in the 1970s, when the real wages of workers fell, the real income for the retired remained unchanged. The fact that 48 per cent of bank savings today are owned by people over 65 years of age is one indication of the improvements in the pension system.[6]

Will the Public Intergenerational Transfer System also Fail?

With 18 per cent of its population at or above 65 years of age, Sweden has the highest proportion of elderly in the world today; it also has the highest proportion of people of 80 years and above (4 per cent). Life expectancy, 80 years for women and 75 years for men in 1990, is one of the highest in the world; only people in Japan and in Iceland live longer. Another important characteristic is that many of the elderly live without a husband or a wife: in

---

[6] Snickars and Axelsson (1985): 74. The figure refers only to bank savings; if additional savings, such as e.g. houses, are included, the figure would probably be lower. In any case, the figure shows that the retired are a group with high saving capacity.

1986 more than 60 per cent of all retired women lived alone or with their children. This is mainly a consequence of differences in life expectancy between men and women. The figure for women was 80 years in 1986 as opposed to only 74 years for men, and as a result Sweden has more than twice as many women as men aged 80 years and above.

The marked difference in life expectancy between men and women is quite a new phenomenon in Sweden, as in many other countries. Until the 1960s the difference was only a couple of years, but in the following years, mortality decreased faster for women than for men. This difference will probably not disappear in the next 30–40 years. One factor that may close the gap is the declining frequency of smoking observed among young males at the same time as it is increasing among females. In addition, the fact that most men marry younger women adds to the number of women living without husbands at the end of their lives. Moreover, the proportion of elderly people without spouses will increase further in the future as divorce has become more frequent in the last 20 years.

The increase in the proportion of the elderly is to a considerable extent a result of a fall in mortality rates (although the change in the shape of the age-composition from a pyramid to an onion is caused by the fertility decline). The mortality decline has changed the whole structure of society. A very high proportion of all children born (more than 90 per cent) serve their entire working life in the labour-force. Following retirement, they are expected to live another 14 years. It is important to note that life expectancy at age 65 has changed little during the past 200 years (Bengtsson and Fridlizius, 1989: Fig. 5). It is only a recent phenomenon that so many reach the age of 65 years: 100 years ago less than half the population reached the age of 65 years. The mortality decline also means that a natural order of death is established: parents nowadays seldom see their children die, and grandparents live long enough even to see their grandchildren grow up. This was rare in the agricultural society.

The future of the pension system has been a focus of debate in Sweden during the last few years. The reason is that it has not functioned as well during periods of slow economic growth after the oil crises as during the 1960s. Whether the system is sensitive to demographic changes or not has also been a matter of some controversy. This issue is very important as Sweden is going to face further changes in age-composition in the near future. Even if Sweden does not have the highest proportion of the elderly in the future (for example, Japan and West Germany will have a higher proportion of old people, as displayed in Fig. 8.4), there will be a substantial increase. Today, we have 31 retired people per 100 persons aged 20–64. This figure is expected to increase in the future, particularly when the baby-boom generation of the 1940s reaches retirement age. Table 8.1 shows figures for the year 2025, based on official projections. According to the main alternative case, there will be 38 people aged 65 years and above per 100 people aged 20–64

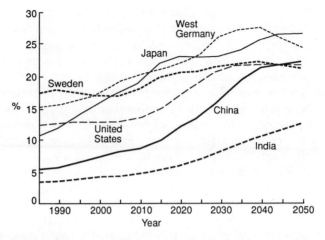

Source: Banister (1990), fig. 2.
Fig. 8.4 Percentage of the Population Aged 65 and over in Selected Countries, 1987–2050

in 2025. About 10 per cent of people aged 20–64 do not belong to the labour-force for various reasons.[7] Thus, there will be 42 people aged 65 years and above per 100 workers, according to the main alternative case. Various alternative estimates have also been made, by changing one assumption at a time. The result and the assumptions are shown in Table 8.1, from which it follows that a further mortality decline, increasing life expectancy by 2 years, would increase the number of persons aged 65 and above per 100 in relation to the age-group 20–64 by about 2.

The long-term decline in fertility has recently been broken by an increase. This has been taken as an indication of a stabilization of fertility at a TFR (total fertility rate) of about 1.9 in the last official estimate. However, the increase is very small and cannot be taken as a guarantee of change in the longer term. Thus, there is reason to expect fertility rates to fall in the future as well. A fall in fertility to a TFR of 1.8 would increase the number of retired people by about 1 per 100 aged 20–64 in the year 2025. A TFR of 1.8 is still higher than that of 1.4 over the last few years in Denmark and Germany.

It is, of course, very difficult to predict the future migration in and out of Sweden. In the latest estimate, future net migration was adjusted upwards as a response to the increase in recent immigration. As a result of the adjustment in the fertility and migration assumptions upwards, the new estimates are very different from the ones made in 1986. In those estimates, it was

---

[7] The figure for 1989 is 12 per cent; i.e. 88 per cent of people have jobs or are actively looking for jobs, which is a very high figure compared with other industrialized countries.

Table 8.1. People Aged 65 Years and Above Relative to Persons in the Labour-Force Aged 20–64 in the Year 2025, Based on the 1989 Official Population Estimate (%)

	High	Main	Low
Mortality	39	42	44
Life-expectancy			
Men	74	76	78
Women	80	82	84
Fertility	40	42	43
Total fertility rate	2.0	1.9	1.8
Migration	40	42	44
Net migration	20,000	10,000	0

Note: High = high mortality and fertility projection;
 Low = low mortality and fertility projection;
 Main = main alternative projection.
Source: Sveriges framtida befolkning, Statistics, Sweden, 1989; adjusted for people outside the labour-force.

shown that Sweden would experience population decline from around the year 2025, when 8.5 million people would be living in Sweden. In the new estimate, the population will continue to increase, reaching 9 million by the year 2020.

The combined effect of different fertility, mortality, and migration assumptions has not been published. It is evident that even a somewhat lower mortality than assumed in the main alternative, which, in our opinion, is too high, and a moderate fall in mortality, which may take place in the next century, when the first non-smoking generation reaches old age, will increase the number of retired people per one hundred workers to about 45–50. Will we be able to support the elderly under such circumstances?

One problem is that our pension system is based on transfers between generations, i.e. it is not a premium system in which individual funds are being built up. Thus, changes in the age-composition directly affect the system. But it has been shown that a transfer system is more dependent on economic growth than on demographic changes (Keyfitz, 1981; Ståhlberg, 1984). As long as the economy grows steadily, there is no problem. The experience from the 1960s seems to provide evidence in that direction. Table 8.2 shows how different changes in the age-composition and labour supply will affect the costs of pensions.

One alternative is a growth of the labour-force, which would necessitate a substantial increase in fertility or in net migration. However, the effects of a 'baby-boom' on the size of the labour-force in the year 2010 would be small as very few will have entered the labour-force by then. Thus, a fertility increase will reduce the demographic pressure on the pension system but will

Table 8.2. Percentage of Workers' Income Transferred to the Retired, According to Different Assumptions, under the Same Pension Rules as Today

Assumption	% transferred
33 retired per 100 workers (today)	20
50 retired per 100 workers	30
6 hours' work per day	27
Increase in e_0 with 5 years	27

Source: Kruse (1988).

take time, and meanwhile the pressure will remain unchanged. Could migration solve the problem? If it were to do so, Sweden would need a tremendous gross immigration in order to make up for the decline in the labour-force. (Ohlsson and Brohmé, 1988). As the situation with respect to age-composition is similar all over Europe, such a migration is unlikely to take place.

It is likely that the 'baby-boom' generation born after the Second World War will be found to be very healthy. Thus, on average, there will be no need for full retirement when this cohort reaches 65 years of age. In order to stimulate them to work, there will probably be gradual changes in the tax system resulting in decreasing pensions in relation to wages for the labour-force. And as the number of people employed in industry will be quite low, there will be employment opportunities for many elderly people. This does not mean that they have to keep the same occupation as before. Today, discussions are being conducted about raising the retirement age for engine-drivers from 60 to 65 years of age, meanwhile making it possible for them to get an easier job at the end of their working life. The fact that the share of the labour-force working in the industrial sector has been decreasing since the 1960s also makes it easier to make the age at retirement more flexible. For countries like China, where the proportion of the elderly is increasing (Fig. 8.4) at the same time as employment in industry is increasing, the problem is much greater. The service sector has also been aware of the fact that vital retired persons could solve some of their recruitment problems. As a result, the slight decline in average age at retirement during the last decade will be altered. Thus, one very likely outcome of the pressure on the pension system is that ages at retirement are going to vary and that many old people will go on working although neither at the same intensity nor with the same hours—they will become semi-retired.

Another very likely outcome is that private pensions will become more important. Personal savings in the form of private pensions have increased rapidly in the last few years. The contributions to a private pension are exempt from tax and it is not until benefits begin to be paid (at an age over 55), that tax is payable. Given the high marginal taxes in Sweden, and the high returns to the accumulated funds, the private pension system gives one good value for one's savings. Changes in the inheritance laws are working in the same direction: children do not inherit their parents' property until they both have died. Thus, private intergenerational saving has become a common complement to the public pension system.

To sum up, the system of private intergenerational transfers failed with the growth of the industrial sector and the commercialization of agriculture. It was replaced by a national pension system which matured as Sweden became an industrial nation. Today, the service sector is increasing rapidly. At the same time, we have slightly more than 30 retired people per 100 workers, which puts the pension system under pressure. As a result, a discussion about age at retirement has started and private pension funds have increased. Future demographic developments will put even more pressure on the public intergenerational transfer system. However, in answer to our main question, whether public intergenerational transfers as an old-age pension system will give the retired a high and steadily increasing standard of living, we not only have to consider the demographic pressure of the system but also the growth of the economy. With steady economic growth at 2–3 per cent per year, the system will have a good chance of survival. The experience of the 1960s was that the pension system could even be extended during a period when numbers of retired people were increasing, given rapid economic growth. But will we experience such growth in the next 20–40 years? Since this is inevitably uncertain, we have to develop a system that could operate even given slower economic growth.

Thus, the answer to our main question is that it is very likely that the situation where Sweden's public intergenerational transfer system is alone able to provide a good standard of living for the retired will be seen as a historical interlude. We believe that we will return to a system of both private and public transfers based on a flexible retirement age and semi-retirement. However, there will be one major difference in relation to the past: transfers will not only be between generations but over an entire generation's lifetime as well. Intergenerational transfers will be turned to intragenerational transfers. This means that we have to create substantial pension funds. These funds could be run by public organizations, trade unions, or private companies, such as insurance companies. But it will take time. The movement towards private intragenerational transfers will be a gradual one.

References

Banister, J. (1990), 'Implications of the Ageing of China's Population,' in Z. Yi, Z. Chunyuan, and P. Songjian (eds.), *Changing Family Structure and Population Ageing in China*, Beijing: Peking University Press.

Bengtsson, T. (1988), 'Industrins tjänstemän och den tekniska utvecklingen' (Blue-collar workers and technological development), Lund University: mimeographed.

—— and Fridlizius, G. (1989), 'Population Ageing in Sweden—Past, Present and Future', paper presented at the conference Changing Family Structure and Population Ageing in China and the West, Beijing University (Oct.).

Carlsson, S. (1968) *Yrken och samhällsgrupper* [Occupations and social groups], Uppsala: Almquist and Wiksell.

Edgren, L. (1987), *Lärling—Gesäll—Mästare* (Apprentice—Journey-man—Master), Lund: Universitets Förlag Dialogos.

Elmèr, Å. (1960), *Folkpensioneringen i Sverige* (Old-age pensions in Sweden), Malmö: Gleerups.

Fridlizius, G. (1979), 'Population, Enclosure and Property Rights,' *Economy and History*, 22/1, 3–37.

—— (1988), 'Sex Differential Mortality and Socioeconomic Change, Sweden 1750–1910', in A. Brändström, and L.-G. Tedebrand (eds.), *Society, Health and Population During the Demographic Transition*, Umeå: Almquist and Wiksell.

—— and Ohlsson, R. (1985), 'Folket: tabellerna' (The people in the tables), University of Lund: mimeograph.

Gaunt, D. (1983), 'Den pensionerade jordbrukaren: Dennes egendom och familjerförhållanden sedan medeltiden: Norra och centrala Europa' (The retired farmer since the middle ages: north and central Europe), in B. Odén, A. Svanborg, and L. Tornstam (eds.), *Äldre i samhället, Del 1–2: Probleminventering* (The elderly in society, part 1–2, problem inventory), Stockholm: Liber.

Keyfitz, N. (1981), 'The Limits of Population Forecasting', *Population and Development Review*, 7/4, 579–93.

Kruse, A. (1988), 'Pensionssystemets stabilitet,' *Swedish Official Investigations (SOU)*, 57.

Odén, B. (1983), 'Åldrandet och arbetslivet: En introduktion' (Ageing and work: an introduction), in B. Odén, A. Svanborg, and L. Tornstam (eds.), *Äldre i samhället, Del 1–2: Probleminventering*, Stockholm: Liber.

—— (1989), 'Planering inför ålderdomen i senmedeltidens Stockhom' (Planning for becoming elderly in the late middle ages in Stockholm), in B. Sawyers, and A. Göransson (eds.), *En bok till Gunhild Kyle* (A book for Gunhild Kyle), *Meddelande från historiska institutionen i Göteborg*, Göteborg: Department of History, Göteborg University.

Ohlsson, R. and Brohmé, P. (1988), *Ålderschocken* (The age shock), Stockholm: SNS Förlag.

Olsson, L. (1983), 'Industrialiseringen, de äldre och pensioneringen' (Industrialization, the elderly, and retirement), in B. Odén, A. Svanborg, and L. Tornstam (eds.), *Äldre i samhället, Del 1–2: Probleminventering*, Stockholm: Liber.

Snickars, F. and Axelsson, S. (1985), *Om hundra år* (In 100 years' time), Stockholm: DsSB 1984: 2 (Official publication).

Ståhlberg, A. C. (1984), 'Överföringar från förvärvsarbetande till den äldre generationen' (Transfers from the working to the elderly generation), *Meddelande*, Stockholm: Institutet för social forskning (Institute for Social Research).

Sveriges framtida befolkning (1989), 'Prognos för åren 1989–2025' (Forecasts for 1989–2025), *Demografiska rapporter* (Demographic Reporter), Stockholm: Statistics Sweden.

Winberg, C. (1981), 'Familj och jord i tre västgötasocknar' (Family and land in three parishes in the middle west of Sweden), *Historisk tidskrift*, 3, 278–310.

Wohlin, N. (1909), 'Den jordbruksidkande befolkningen in Sverige' (The agricultural population in Sweden), *Emigrationsutredningen*, 9.

9 Public and Private Intergenerational Transfers: Evidence and a Simple Model

HELMUTH CREMER, DENIS KESSLER, AND PIERRE PESTIEAU

When observing the structure of intergenerational transfers, one cannot help being struck by their variety. A list of a few of the more important ones will illustrate the point: parents' attention to their children, public education, mandatory public pensions, private annuities, bequests and donations in cash and kind, and filial attention to ageing parents. A taxonomy of these transfers could be established on the basis of three criteria: the direction of the transfers (upwards or downwards); the content of the transfer; and the sector through which the transfer is effected (private or public, i.e. through the family or the state). There are many unanswered questions concerning the structure of upward and downward transfers within families. Among them, the main motivation for such transfers is not understood: do they merely reflect altruism or could they be explained by market interactions or strategic considerations?

This chapter is divided into three main sections: the first provides some evidence of the variety and details of the relative size of intergenerational transfers in France, although good data on these areas are scarce. The second section briefly addresses some of the main questions raised by intergenerational transfers. The third is more theoretical and indicates the kind of private intergenerational transfers one can expect to find in a family with three co-existing generations where there is no altruism and where exchanges are based on strategic considerations. In such a situation every individual has three phases in his life: as a dependent child, as a productive worker, and as a retired dependant. In this third section the analysis is confined to a small range of transfers: bequests, children's attention to parents, and public education and social security. We first describe the various transfers taking place given various allocation mechanisms, and we then try to assess the need for government intervention through public education or social security to increase social welfare.

Intergenerational Public and Private Transfers: Some French Evidence

This section presents a tentative accounting framework for intergenerational transfers and some corresponding data in the French case. We then check whether or not the relative importance of intergenerational transfers varies over time.

A Tentative Accounting Framework for Intergenerational Transfers

Even though there is no precise and widely accepted definition of an intergenerational transfer, we draw up a list of the transfers most commonly considered to take place between successive cohorts:

—financing of human capital investment, i.e. educational expenditure;
—public transfers such as family allowances;
—transfers by social security and pensions schemes;
—transfers implemented through national health services;
—bequests (inheritances and *inter vivos* gifts);
—private income transfers benefiting the elderly;
—private income transfers made by the elderly benefiting younger adults;
—transfers operated through public-debt;
—parental attention to the children;
—filial attention devoted by children to their parents or grandparents.

Some of these transfers are directed up the generation scale (in other words they are ascending), others are directed downwards (and are descending); some transfers are compulsory, others are voluntary; some are minor, others are important; some transfers concern an entire cohort, others concern only a limited fraction of an age-group; some are in cash, others are in kind, and others are in time; some transfers are taxed, others are tax-free; some transfers are planned or intentional, others are unplanned; some transfers are made within the family, others are made through the market, and others are monitored by the government.

It is an interesting challenge to draw up an accounting framework which is able to capture the pattern of some of these intergenerational transfers, from the old to the young and from the young to the old. Such an accounting framework would indeed help us to measure the relative importance of intergenerational transfers and better assess their efficiency and equity implications. A correct accounting of intergenerational transfers would help us to determine the in- and out-flows for each generation and see whether the succeeding generations are net givers or net receivers. In tracking most of the intergenerational flows we wish to avoid treating a given transfer—such as social security for instance—in isolation and without taking into account the existence of counterbalancing private bequests. If the various flows are not considered together, it is difficult to assess the redistributive nature—equalizing or disequalizing—of a given intergenerational transfer.

But the size and direction of the net transfer (positive, negative, or neutral) occurring between generations may be misleading. A balanced situation with no net transfer across generations (where upward and downward transfers fully compensate each other), should not be equated with a situation where

Table 9.1.   An Illustration of the Various Intergenerational Transfers

Giving generations	Receiving generations		
	Children	Parents	Grandparents
Children			
Private		attention to children	attention to children
Public		public debt	
Parents			
Private	child support, education, and attention		care and attention
Public	education, health insurance, and family allowances		social security, pensions, health insurance, and public debt
Grandparents			
Private	attention, inheritance, and gifts	attention, inheritance, and gifts	
Public			

Note: Public debt appears as a transfer from children to parents (or from parents to grandparents), since the latter benefit from less taxes and the former will pay the tax without benefiting from the corresponding public expenditure.

no transfers take place at all. Each transfer may indeed have incentive or disincentive effects on the parties involved, and a zero net transfer does not imply that these effects cancel out. To tackle the effects on efficiency and equity of intergenerational transfers, it therefore seems necessary to know the magnitude of each transfer as well as the net resulting transfer. This is one of the reasons why it seems necessary to go as far as possible in the estimation of all the transfers. But this is not an easy task.

To present these various transfers, we consider three generations: the parents, the children, and the grandparents. Most existing models consider only two overlapping generations, either the children and their parents, or the parents and the grandparents. While the two-generation approach can sometimes be justified, it can hardly be denied that we live in a world of three (or even four) co-existing generations.

The two criteria used to classify these transfers are their upward or downward orientation and their public or private nature. Table 9.1 presents the transfers we are considering in brief. This table is of course still incomplete, as all intertemporal phenomena are likely to induce an intergenerational transfer one way or another. For instance, we could consider, as Lazear (1979) did, that seniority rules, leading to a gap between the productivity-profile and the wage-profile, entail a *de facto* intergenerational transfer from younger workers to older workers. Following the same line of reasoning, the tax system and the public expenditure structure can also lead to some important inter-generational transfers—even in the case of a balanced budget.

This is a rather static approach and there are good reasons to prefer a more dynamic one, where a particular generation is followed over its whole lifespan. Everything this generation receives from and gives to previous and next generations would be recorded. The balance between what this generation receives, gives, and leaves could be calculated at each age. Such a dynamic longitudinal approach would allow us to determine whether this generation is a gainer or a loser, but the scarcity of data prevents us from using this approach.

Some Estimates of the Size of Intergenerational Flows in France

It is tempting to estimate at a given point in time the various transfers occur-ring between generations. Such an exercise is of course subject to criticism, but the idea here is to give only rough estimates of the size of some upward and downward transfers. As we shown below, work-in-progress tries to es-timate the historical development of these transfers.

We try to estimate some of the intergenerational flows: bequests, social security and pensions, family allowances, public health expenditures, public and private education, and public debt. As far as bequests are concerned, the value of assets transferred through inheritances amounted to FF. 155 bn. in 1984 and taxed *inter vivos* gifts amounted to FF. 62 bn. in the same year. The calculation of these estimates uses standard information about taxes collected and data from a study carried out in 1984 for the ratio of taxes to taxable assets transferred.[1] As far as social security and pensions operating under the pay-as-you-go principle are concerned, the amount of benefits (that is about equal to the amount of contributions) reached FF. 647 bn. in 1988; only FF. 8 bn. of these are in kind. Under French legislation family allowances are based on the level of income and number of children. In 1988 family allow-ances amounted to FF. 93 bn. For the same year, the total amount of health insurance expenditure represented FF. 383 bn. It is estimated that at least 50 per cent of this expenditure benefited the elderly aged 60 and over. Thus, more than FF. 190 bn. are transferred from younger adults to people aged 60 and over.

The total expenditure on public education was FF. 335 bn. in 1989. It is estimated that central and local governments finance 84 per cent of all edu-

---

[1] There are however rather large tax exemptions for certain assets in France. Most small inheritances (amounting to less than FF. 250 000 per heir) are tax exempt. The figure of FF. 217 bn. is therefore likely to be an underestimate.

cational expenditure, while firms finance 4 per cent and households 12 per cent. The total increase in public debt should also be taken into account as the deficit through the issuing of public debt may shift the burden of tax to future generations. In most cases, the public debt is redeemed by the same generation. But some people benefit from lower taxes when the debt is created and escape higher taxes later because they have already died (or emigrated). In France the total amount of public debt financing—roughly equal to the amount of the budget deficit—amounted to FF. 87 bn. in 1987. Only a fraction of this amount should be considered as an intergenerational transfer. We have no reliable data on the size of private income flows between generations. As far as parental attention is concerned, it is obvious that valuation is not an easy task: there are almost no data on the amount of time adults spend with their elderly parents, or parents spend with their children.[2]

It seems impossible to draw any definitive conclusion from these incomplete data, in particular because the attention devoted by parents to their children or to their own parents has not been valued. Only public transfers can be valued easily, while most private transfers can only be estimated. However, three comments can be made on the available figures on intergenerational transfers in France. First, social security seems to be by far the most important intergenerational transfer, but public health insurance benefiting the elderly, public educational expenditures, and private bequests also appear to be far from negligible. Second, the source of most intergenerational transfers is, of course, the parents' generation (the economically productive segment of population). They appear to be in a tricky position since they face a trade-off between transferring resources to their children or to their own parents, and devoting attention to their children or to their parents. It is worthwhile noting that downward transfers appear to be dominant, as if the judgement of the parents' generation leans more in favour of the children. This is not surprising: children are penniless and defenceless whereas retired people can rely on their own savings and at times on market and non-market work. Third, most of the 'large transfers' are mandatory; discretionary transfers appear to be of less importance. Even in the case of bequests, let us recall that a fraction of inheritances are unintentional. Estimates of the value of 'attention' could, however, lead us to a different conclusion.

Are Intergenerational Transfers Stable through History?

To consider only a given year—or a given period—may be misleading. It is interesting to check whether or not the magnitude of the different transfers has changed over time. Has the hierarchy of transfers changed? Did some

---

[2] A survey carried out in France gives some figures on the use of time by different age-groups and by making assumptions on the value of the time, it would be then possible to estimate the size of the intergenerational transfers taking place this way. Such an estimation is being undertaken but is not yet completed.

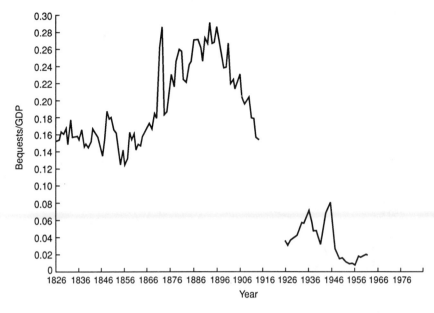

Fig. 9.1 Bequests as a Proportion of GDP in France, 1826–1976

transfers decline and others increase? Has the direction of the net transfer changed? Rather than looking only at the last quarter of a century, we are building up a database to check the change in transfers for the last 180 years. We present here some preliminary results on bequests, public debt, educational expenditure, and social security.

Fig. 9.1 represents the change in the ratio of inheritances to GDP since the beginning of the nineteenth century. It is striking to see that in each year of that century the amount of inheritances represented between 12 and 30 per cent of GDP, whereas today it has dropped to less than 2 per cent. This dramatic change could be linked to the change in life expectancy, but is mainly related to the highly inflationary pressures following World War I, and the resulting diverging trend between the consumer price index and the assets price index. It is well known that many savers who held financial assets were ruined during the twentieth century (their assets being eroded by price increases) and were not able to transfer their accumulated wealth to their descendants during their lifetime. To summarize, while bequests played a crucial role in the nineteenth century, their importance has declined dramatically since then.

Fig. 9.2 represents the change in the ratio of public debt to GDP. As can be seen, the outstanding public debt reached 2.6 times the French national income just after World War II. This ratio moved upwards during the nineteenth century, and has fluctuated wildly during the twentieth century, mainly

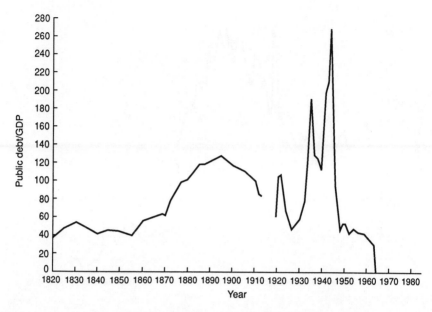

Fig. 9.2   Public Debt as a Proportion of GDP in France, 1820–1980

because of wars.[3] It is worth noting that the public debt seems very limited today in France, since it represents less than four months' GDP. However in France, as in most industrialized countries, the level of public debt has been increasing again since the mid-1970s.

Fig. 9.3 represents the ratio of public educational expenditure to GDP since 1870. Public educational expenditure was considered to be nil before 1870, the date which roughly corresponds to the introduction of mandatory schooling in France. It is worth noting that the increase in public educational expenditure is quite a recent phenomenon, dating back to the 1950s. We do not have reliable estimates of the historical value of private educational expenditure, but it seems to be small.

These preliminary results on the evolution of intergenerational transfers over time show clearly that their relative importance has changed quite dramatically. Social security, which was introduced on a large scale in France only in the 1940s, seems to have replaced public debt in terms of shifting resources through time. Public educational expenditure increased, as private bequests decreased. When we have completed the database, we will be in a

---

[3] The evolution of public debt in France in the nineteenth century is quite different from its evolution in the UK during the same period. Whereas the French public debt increased throughout that century, the UK public debt appears to have declined sharply. According to available data the evolution of public debt during the twentieth century seems to be quite similar in the UK, France, and the United States (see Barro, 1978).

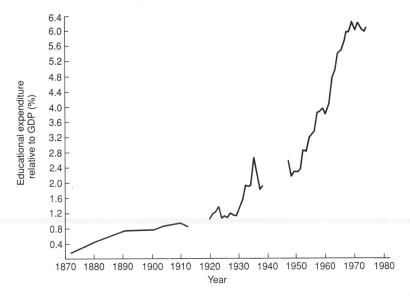

Fig. 9.3 Public Expenditure on Education as a Proportion of GDP in France, 1870–1980

better position to give some answers to the questions surrounding the subject of intergenerational transfers. The remaining sections of this chapter examine five of those questions in greater depth.

Intergenerational Transfers: Questions and Puzzles

Why are Some Transfers Public (and Compulsory) and Others Private (and Discretionary)?

The direction and purpose of a given transfer does not explain *per se* why it should be public or private. Expenditure on higher education is almost entirely public in France, but is mostly private in the United States. Moreover, in most cases, there is a 'transfer mix', where public (or private) transfers supplement private (or public) transfers. The same kind of argument can be applied to transfers benefiting the elderly. We can assume that, at least in the nineteenth century, the aged benefited from private income transfers from their children (even if saving and then dis-saving represented alternative ways to finance retirement). There is no obvious a priori reason why income flows to the elderly should be public. Naturally, in some instances, the public nature of transfers can be explained by factors related to merit goods, externalities, or distributive considerations.

Are given Public and Private Transfers Substitutable or Complementary?

The question here is whether or not given public or private transfers with specific and well-identified goals are fully, partially, or not at all substitutable. This question has been raised for instance by Barro (1978), arguing that public social security transfers were offsetting private intergenerational transfers in favour of the elderly. Barro (1974) previously argued that potential intergenerational transfers due to public-debt financing of government expenditures were neutralized through an increase of private wealth transfers in the opposite direction. Others have argued that public intergenerational transfers were necessary because of the absence or inadequacy of private transfers. Private short-termism or selfishness would be the prime rationale for public transfers. In that case, public transfers would be largely independent of private transfers, which would have little effect. But one needs to keep in mind the classic problem of the crowding-out of private transfers by public transfers.

Can Different Kinds of Transfer be Substituted for Each Other?

The question is somewhat different from the previous one. Let us consider the transfers associated with public debt. Barro (1974) argues, for instance, that transfers linked to public debt may be offset by bequests going in the opposite direction and Drazen (1978) has added that private human capital investment by parents benefiting their children may offset the burden imposed by parents on children by public debt. It is clear in these examples that intergenerational transfers could be fully substitutable, no matter their direction, their nature, or their purpose. If transfers are based on market exchanges or on strategic considerations, one is forced to consider that income and wealth transfers are related to non-monetary transfers, such as attention and care. It does not really need repeating that it is difficult to value empirically the time parents devote to their children or children to their parents. The value of attention and care is not the easiest phenomenon to compute and assess. Can we pretend, for instance, that a child receiving parental attention but no bequest is in the same situation as a child receiving little parental attention but a large bequest?

Is there a Relationship between Intergenerational Transfers and Intragenerational Transfers?

Can the deficiency of market allocation mechanisms in some given generation—the ruin of some savers due to an economic or financial crisis for instance—be the main cause of the appearance of an intergenerational transfer mechanism, such as social security? It seems paradoxical that the sources of public intergenerational transfer schemes often lie in the intra-cohort allocative inefficiencies and distributive problems.

Are Transfers Rooted in Altruism, in Market Exchanges, or in Rational Strategy?

Altruism would mean that each generation would desire to transmit human or non-human resources to the preceding or succeeding generations without expecting anything in exchange. Individuals would increase their utility simply by giving to others. In a market exchange, one generation might exchange attention for a bequest from the other generation. These market exchanges are considered as equivalent; in other words, transfers would balance each other at a given price. Assuming a rational strategy would mean that relations between generations could be modelled in a game-theoretical framework. This central question needs to be explored in detail, as it is in the next section.

A Three-Generation Model with Different Allocation Mechanisms

In this section we provide a non-technical presentation of a model describing different types of allocation mechanism between generations.[4] We also address the rationale for government-administered transfers. The basic idea underlying this presentation is that many settings concerning the nature of relationships and exchanges within families can prevail, ranging from a world of perfect harmony to one of complete suspicion. We want to show the type of transfers which emerge from each setting and what kind of public intervention each requires.

A Model of Intergenerational Private Transfers in an Non-Altruistic Setting

After a presentation of the features of the model, we will study the equilibria corresponding to different allocation procedures.

The Basic Features of the Three-Generation Model. Let us sketch a model to explore some of the intergenerational transfers. This model has five main characteristics:

(1)   it is a three-generation model (children, working adults, retirees);
(2)   dependent children do not make any decisions;
(3)   there is no altruism;

---

[4] For a complete version of this model, see Cremer *et al.* (1992).

(4)   there are three types of transfers: educational spending, attention to the elderly from the working population, and bequests from the retired to the working population. There is no 'generation skipping';

(5)   exchanges are not simultaneous: on one side parents give attention to the elderly from whom they expect bequests, on the other side, parents give education to their children from whom they hope to get attention in the future.

There are three overlapping generations. Each generation t consists of N^t identical individuals who live for three periods. Each indvidual has n children so that the population grows at the constant rate $n - 1$. The lifetime utility of a member of generation t is:

$$U^t = u_2(C_2^t, R_2^t) + u_3(C_3^t, n\, A_3^{t+1}) \tag{1}$$

In words, lifetime utility depends on the utility when adult, u_2—which is a function of consumption, C_2, and leisure, R_2—and the utility when old u_3—which is a function of consumption, C_3, and of the attention, A_3, the individual receives from his n children when retired. Note that the education that a child receives does not increase his utility when a child, but his earnings capacity when an adult. The three budget constraints defining both the levels of consumption and the allocation of time are the following:

$$C_2^t = w(C_1^{t-1}/n) + h^{t-1}/n - C_1^t - s^t \tag{2}$$

where w stands for the wage-rate (a function of educational costs previously incurred by the individual's parents); h^{t-1} is the bequest received from parents; C_1^t is overall educational spending, and s^t is saving.

$$C_3^t = rs^t - h^t \tag{3}$$

Consumption when retired is equal to the accumulated saving invested at a rate of interest r minus the bequest transferred to the next generation. The golden rule equality, $r = n$, is assumed to hold throughout the analysis.

$$L = R_2^t + A_3^t + 1 \tag{4}$$

The total amount of time of generation t is divided between leisure R_2, attention to the aged A_3, and work (set to unity).

Optimality Conditions.   Let us assume a steady state, in which the choices made by each generation are the same. In this case, the transfers given are equal to the transfers received for each generation. In such a harmonious society, attention received also equals attention given for each individual as well as for each generation. To determine the amount of attention parents devote respectively to their children and to their retired parents, and the amount of inheritance, we assume that individuals maximize their lifetime utility function subject to the three constraints given above. Under plausible assumptions concerning the utility and education functions, we can expect the three flows to be positive: we are here in a society with positive intergenerational transfers. This optimum can be compared with three alternative types of allocation: a market allocation, a Nash equilibrium and, finally, a strategic bequest equilibrium. The present setting can be interpreted in two ways. First, it could be the result of a benevolent and omnipotent planner maximizing steady-state utility. Alternatively, it can be seen as the result of perfect altruism; that is, when each generation is concerned with the welfare of both the next and the previous generation.

A Market Equilibrium. We assume that attention devoted by adults to their parents and bequests are exchanged in a market. We also assume that a child can borrow educational resources at the market interest rate. He pays off this debt one period later, when he works and his parents are retired. So there is a demand and a supply for attention and for education depending on the respective prices of education and attention. Assuming market clearing, we end up in a situation where there is a positive bequest and a positive amount of attention devoted by adults to children and parents. This situation is optimal in the sense used above. However, if there is no market for education because the child cannot borrow, the level of education will surely be sub-optimal.

A Nash Equilibrium. We now consider a game-theoretical setting in which individuals behave non-cooperatively (i.e. binding agreements between generations are not possible). We assume that each individual chooses his decision variables given the decisions by the other generations. For example, a member of generation t chooses the level of education, the level of attention devoted to the retired, and the size of bequests as a function of the decisions of the previous and next generations. It is obvious that Nash equilibrium implies that the amounts of bequest, education, and attention devoted to the retired are zero. The intuitive idea behind this is quite simple: an individual takes the transfers he receives as given. In the absence of altruism there is thus no point in giving any transfer to another generation. A Nash equilibrium, resulting from such selfish and non-interactive behavioural assumptions, leads to a situation which is clearly sub-optimal. In particular, educational transfers and attention to elderly parents converge to zero.

A Strategic Bequest Equilibrium. Following Bernheim *et al.* (1985), we assume that there is an 'exchange' between the retired parent and his working children: the parent will leave some bequest h_t in exchange for some attention. By threatening his children with disinheritance, the parent leaves them with a level of utility equal to that obtained with no attention and no bequest. Thus, bargaining from strength, the retired parent chooses the attention level and the amount of bequest which maximizes his utility. This leads to a situation where the bequest-for-attention exchanges are efficient with all the surplus being absorbed by the parents. However, there is still no incentive for parents to provide education for their children and the level of educational spending is generally equal to zero. It thus appears that in these non-altruistic settings, the intergenerational transfers may end up being far from optimal. In particular, educational expenditures are generally too low (or even zero). This calls for public intervention. Can public intergenerational transfers restore optimality by correcting inefficient allocation of time and resources between generations?

The Efficiency of Government Operated Intergenerational Transfers

It appears from the data presented in the first section that, among the different ways a government can affect the intergenerational allocation of resources, the two most widespread are public education and social security. Are these policy tools sufficient to restore optimality when decentralized decisions yield an inefficient outcome?

Government Intervention and Market Equilibrium.   When there is a well-functioning market for education, public education is not necessary, since private educational expenditure is optimal. But if the educational market is imperfect—namely because it is impossible to borrow money to finance all education with only human capital as guarantee—public education can restore optimality.[5] Social security is not necessary, since the level of savings is optimal.

Government Intervention and Nash Equilibrium.   Public education can improve the outcome. Optimality can, however, not be restored as neither of the two instruments can influence the exchange between retired parents and adult children.

Government Intervention and Strategic Equilibrium.   Strategic bequest motives have an adverse effect in the sense that private educational expenditure falls to a minimum. It can be shown that the government can restore optimality by combining the two instruments.

A Sketch of the Proof

A formal proof of these propositions is provided in Cremer *et al.* (1992). We will just provide a non-technical proof of the results. For simplicity we assume $n = 1$, i.e. each individual has one child. We thus assume that the strategic bequest model works even within this environment. Further, we introduce an *ad hoc* separation between the educational choice and the decision to

---

[5] Note that we assume inelastic labour supply such that a wage tax does not create any efficiency loss.

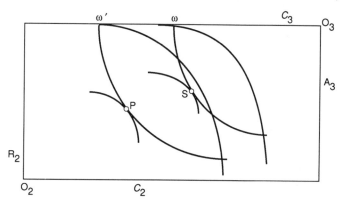

Fig. 9.4 Alternative Solutions to the Bequests-for-Attention Exchange

bequeath. To keep the notation simple, we drop the time index, which is legitimate in the steady state.

We first focus on the choice of bequests and attention where the aged parent consumes C_3 and A_3 and the working adult consumes C_2 and R_2. The problem is presented in Fig. 9.4. With no exchange and no social security, the solution ω prevails. At this point there is no attention ($A_3 = 0$), consumption by the elderly parents comes exclusively from savings. The working child uses all the available time for leisure and work which brings him some income y out of which C_2 is consumed and s is saved. We are in a stationary equilibrium where the child saves the same amount as his parent saved one period earlier.

We further assume that the optimum is given by P. That is, P is the allocation which maximizes the utility of an individual who would have full control of all variables with the sole constraint that what he receives from his parent will be given one period later to his child (see Fig. 9.4). One can show that without public intervention, the market mechanism leads to P, the Nash solution to ω, and the strategic bequest solution to S. Note that w depends on the wage-rate and hence, on the level of education. At w the level of education is zero while it is positive at ω'. One can also show that mandatory pensions cannot help in the Nash case but can achieve efficiency in the strategic bequest case. Basically, in the latter case, optimal social security imposes a forced increase in savings such that the initial solution becomes ω' and the strategic bequest becomes P.

Finally let us consider the determination of spending on education. Expression (2) obviously implies that the optimal level of education, C_1^*, is such that $w'(C_1^*) = n$, i.e. the marginal benefit of education is equal to its marginal cost. Assuming that children can borrow money for education at the market interest rate, they choose a level, C^E, such that $w'(C_1^E) = r$. Note that the individual pays for his education during the same period in which he receives its benefits (i.e. in period 2). Accordingly he maximizes the net return on education, hence the condition for C_1^E. Under the golden-rule assumption $r = n$, we obviously have $C_1^E = C_1^*$: a well-functioning market leads to an efficient level of education. As argued above, in the Nash and strategic-bequest solutions, providing education is costly but individuals perceive no pay-off, hence educational spending is reduced to a minimum.

As to the government, by an appropriate choice of public education, it can bring about optimality when there is no market for education or when the Nash solution prevails. Otherwise, there is no room for public education within the present setting. In that respect, we should recall that we have assumed away dynamic inefficiency, intragenerational inequalities, externalities, and bounded rationality. If all these features were introduced, the case for social security and public education would be even stronger.

Conclusion

Transfers and exchanges across generations are as old as society itself. Yet, for decades social scientists and particularly economists have only been concerned with this reality to a limited extent. The basic concepts and data that would provide a fair estimate of the size and direction of transfers are still missing. This chapter can be viewed as an attempt to deal with this matter. In an initial section, it presents a taxonomy of the major public and private intergenerational transfers. It then raises several questions as to the nature and the determinants of those transfers. It clearly appears that the traditional determinants, altruism for private transfers, merit goods, externalities, and equity for public transfers, cannot explain the complexity of and the interaction between those transfers. The third section sketches a simple model which shows within different settings that private transfers might occur even without altruism. It also shows that public transfers may be needed even though they are not necessarily able to restore optimality.

References

Barro, R. (1974), 'Are Government Bonds Net Wealth?', *Journal of Political Economy*, 82, 1095–117.
—— (1978), *The Impact of Social Security on Private Saving*, Washington, DC: American Enterprise Institute.
Bernheim, B. D., Schleifer, A., and Summers, L. H. (1984), 'Bequests as a Mean of Payment', discussion paper no. 1055, Harvard University.
—— —— —— (1985), 'The Strategic Bequest Motive', *Journal of Political Economy*, 93, 1045–76.

Cremer, H., Kessler, D., and Pestieau, P. (1992), 'Intergenerational Transfers within the Family', *European Economic Review*, 36, 1–16.

Drazen, A. (1978), 'Government Debt, Human Capital and Bequests in a Life Cycle Model', *Journal of Political Economy*, 86/3, 505–16.

Lazear, E. P. (1979), 'Why is there Mandatory Retirement?', *Journal of Political Economy*, 87, 1261–84.

Index of Names

Notes: Contributions to this publication are shown in bold type. Page numbers in italics indicate tables or figures.

Ando, A. 163, 169–71, 172–3
Arthur, W. B. 140, 141 n.
  and McNicoll, G. 137
Axelsson, S., *see* Snickars, F., and
  Axelsson, S.

Bachrach, C. A., and Horn, M. J. 12
Barmby, T., and Cigno, A. 75–6
Barro, R. 224
Becker, G. 46, 57, 65
Beckman, M., *see* Koopmans, T., and
  Beckman, M.
Bengtsson, T., and Fridlizius, G., **Public
  Intergenerational Transfers as an
  Old-Age Pension System** 198–215
Bennett, N. G., Blanc, A. K., and Bloom,
  D. E. 35
Bergstrom, T.:
  and Cornes, R. 57 n
  and Lam, D., **The Effects of Cohort Size
  and Marriage-Markets in Twentieth-
  Century Sweden** 46–63
Bernheim, B. D., Schleifer, A., and
  Summers, L. H. 227
Blanc, A. K., *see* Bennett, N. G., Blanc,
  A. K., and Bloom, D. E.
Blanchet, D. 138
  and Ekert-Jaffé, O., **The Demographic
  Impact of Family Benefits** 79–104
Bloom, D. E., *see* Bennett, N. G., Blanc,
  A. K., and Bloom, D. E.
Blundell, R., and Walker, I. 115
Butz, H. P., and Ward, W. P. 94, 107, 176

Caldwell, J. C. 140, 151
Calhoun, C. A., and Espenshade, T. J. 66,
  69
Chung, W. K., *see* Denison, E. F., and
  Chung, W. K.
Cigno, A.:
  **Economic Considerations in the Timing of
  Births** 64–78
  and Ermisch, J. F. 73–5, 76
  see also Barmby, T. and Cigno, A.
Clayton, R. R. and Voss, H. L. 30
Cornes, R., *see* Bergstrom, T. and Cornes, R.

Cremer, H., Kessler, D., and Pestieau, P.,
  **Public and Private Intergenerational
  Transfers** 216–31

Denison, E. F., and Chung, W. K. 165, *166*
Drazen, A. 224

Eckstein, Z., and Wolpin, K. 138
Ekert-Jaffé, O. (with Blanchet), **The
  Demographic Impact of Family
  Benefits** 79–104
Ermisch, J. F. 139, 152, 154
  see also Cigno, A., and Ermisch, J. F.
Espenshade, T. J., *see* Calhoun, C. A., and
  Espenshade, T. J.

Fridlizius, G. (with Bengtsson), **Public
  Intergenerational Transfers as an Old-
  Age Pension System** 198–215
Fukui, T. (with Mason, Teh, and Ogawa),
  **The Intergenerational Distribution of
  Resources and Income in Japan** 158–97

Gale, D. 138
Gaunt, D. 201 n.
Gwartney-Gibbs, P. A. 11, 30

Heckman, J. 110, 111, 113
Higuchi, Y., *see* Shimada, H., and Higuchi,
  Y.
Hill, M. A. 110, 118, 123
Hodge, R. W. (with Ogawa), **Patrilocality,
  Childbearing, and the Labour Supply
  and Earning Power of Married
  Japanese Women** 105–31
Hoem, B., and Hoem, J. 31, 40
Hoem, J., *see* Hoem, B., and Hoem, J.
Horn, M. J., *see* Bachrach, C. A., and Horn,
  M. J.
Hotz, V. J., and Miller, R. A. 72

Kessler, D. (with Cremer and Pestieau),
  **Public and Private Intergenerational
  Transfers** 216–31
Keyfitz, N. 155
Kiernan, K. E. 9

Koopmans, T., and Beckman, M. 46
Kuznets, S. 187

Lam, D. (with Bergstrom), **The Effects of Cohort Size and Marriage-Markets in Twentieth-Century Sweden** 46–63
Lapkoff, S., *see* Lee, R., and Lapkoff, S.
Lazear, E. P. 219
Lee, R., **Fertility, Mortality and Intergenerational Transfers** 135–57
and Lapkoff, S. 139
Lobitz, J., and Prihoda, R. 153

McNicoll, G., *see* Arthur, W. B., and McNicoll, G.
Martin, L. G., and Ogawa, N. 108–9, 168–9
Mason, A., Teh, Y.-Y., Ogawa, N., and Fukui, T., **The Intergenerational Distribution of Resources and Income in Japan** 158–97
Michael, R. T. (with Willis), **Innovation in Family Formation** 9–45
Miller, R. A., *see* Hotz, V. J., and Miller, R. A.
Mincer, J. 118
Moffitt, R. 70 n., 85 n.
Mueller, E. 139, 140, 150–1, 155

Nerlove, M., Razin, A., and Sadka, E. 138
Newman, J. 72

Odén, B. 201 n.
Ogawa, N.:
    and Hodge, R. W., **Patrilocality, Childbearing, and the Labour Supply and Earning Power of Married Japanese Women** 105–31
    (with Mason, Teh, and Fukui), **The Intergenerational Distribution of Resources and Income in Japan** 158–97
    see also Martin, L. G., and Ogawa, N.
Ohkawa, K., and Rosovsky, H. 165, *166*

Pestieau, P. (with Cremer and Kessler), **Public and Private Intergenerational Transfers** 216–31
Pollak, R. A. 56
Preston, S. H. 140
Prihoda, R., *see* Lobitz, J., and Prihoda, R.

Razin, A., *see* Nerlove, M., Razin, A., and Sadka, E.
Rosovsky, H., *see* Ohkawa, K., and Rosovsky, H.

Sadka, E., *see* Nerlove, M., Razin, A., and Sadka, E.
Samuelson, P. 136, 142
Schleifer, A., *see* Bernheim, B. D., Schleifer, A., and Summers, L. H.
Schultz, T. P. 187
Shimada, H., and Higuchi, Y. 106
Snickars, F., and Axelsson, S. 208 n.
Summers, L. H., *see* Bernheim, B. D., Schleifer, A., and Summers, L. H.

Teh, Y.-Y. (with Mason, Ogawa, and Fukui), **The Intergenerational Distribution of Resources and Income in Japan** 158–97
Thornton, A. 23
Tobin, J. 153

Voss, H. L., *see* Clayton, R. R., and Voss, H. L.

Walker, I., *see* Blundell, R., and Walker, I.
Ward, W. P., *see* Butz, H. P., and Ward, W. P.
Weiss, Y., *see* Willis, R. J., and Weiss, Y.
Willis, R. J. 138, 139 n.
    and Michael, R. T., **Innovation in Family Formation** 9–45
    and Weiss, Y. 27
Wolpin, K., *see* Eckstein, Z., and Wolpin, K.

Index of Subjects

Note: Page references with only tables and figures relevant to the subject and no text are shown in italics.

age:
  at entry to marriage 2, 48–50, 56; and
    timing of births 67, 71, 72, 75
  at entry to partnership 18–20; and
    decision to cohabit 25, 27, *29*, 30–1,
    33–4, 40
  mean age: of consumption 137–8, 139,
    151; of inheritance 190; of labour
    137–8, 139; of marriage 48–50, 51
  relative to partner: and cohort size 2,
    46–53, 59–62; and decision to cohabit
    25, 27–8, *29*, 31, *33*
  of wife, and employment status 114, 116,
    121
age distribution:
  ageing population 152–3; in Japan 158,
    179–80, 194, 208; in Sweden 198, 204–5,
    207, 208–11
  of bequests 184–5, 186, 189–91, 193
  of consumption 169, 171–2
  and effects of the timing of births
    64–5
  and fertility changes 136
  future 209–11
  in Germany 209
  and intergenerational transfers 135–6, 147,
    203–4, 209–12
  in Japan 159–79, 184–5, 187, 189–91, 193,
    209
  and mortality changes 136, 141, 147,
    148–50, 209
  of national income 159–79
  of productivity 167–9
  of retirement 209–10
  of savings 169, 171–2
  in Sweden 203–4, 209–12
  of wealth 171–3, 184–5, 193
altruism:
  in fertility utility functions 138
  in intergenerational transfer utility
    functions 225
Australia 91, 205
Austria 91

baby boom 1, 5, 77, 209, 211–12
Belgium 88, 91, *95*, *98*, *100*

benefits, *see* family benefits; housing
    supplements; intergenerational transfers;
    pensions; social security; transfers
bequests 140, 159, 163–4, 191, 227–30
  in France 219, 220, 221
  in Japan 159, 163–4, 184–5, 186, 189–91,
    193
  see also inheritance
birth matrix 56
Bulgaria 91

Canada 91
capital dilution effect 139, 144, 147, 154–5
capital, human 65, 68–9, 71, 75, 77
capital/labour ratio 165–6, 167, 182
care:
  as component of intergenerational
    transfers 206, 207, 220, 224, 227–30
  see also child care; health care
child benefits, *see* family benefits
child care 65–6, 85, 117
childbearing:
  levels of 79–101; micro-model 80–1, 101
  timing of 64–78; and human capital 65,
    68–9, 71, 75, 77; models of 3, 65–72,
    73–6; and opportunity cost 65–7, 68–70,
    71
  see also fertility
children:
  costs of raising 65–71 *passim*, 80–1, 84,
    140
  dependency 149, 152
  number/age of: and employment status
    111–12, 114–18, *120*, 122–3, 127; and
    family benefits 80, 86–92; and the
    timing of births 65–6, 76
  opportunity cost of 65–7, 68–70, 71
  positive asset value of 151
China 212
cohabitation 9–41
  before marriage 10, 12, 13–18, 22–4, 40
  determinants of 24–41
  duration 22–3
  incidence 1, 2, 9, 13–18, 31, 39–40
  see also partnerships
cohort size 46–8, 50–5, 61–2

consumption:
  age distribution of 169, 171–2, 180, *182*, 198–9
  life cycle 4, 135–7, 139–45, 146–51, 152, 153, 155
  mean age of 137–8, 139, 151
contraception 72
costs, of raising children 65–71 *passim*, 80–1, 84, 140
Cyprus 88
Czechoslovakia 91

Denmark 205, 210
  family benefits in 91, *95*, *98*, *100*
dependency:
  child 149, 152
  old age 136, 139, 152, 199
discrimination, sexual:
  in Japan 107, 127
  and the timing of births 2, 72, 75, 78
duration:
  of cohabitation 22–3
  of marriage: and fertility 73–5; and the timing of births 69
  of partnerships 10–12, 22, 23, 39–40

earnings:
  joint 107–9, 126
  life cycle 135, 141, 142, 147–8
  see also income; wages
economic factors:
  and ageing population 158, 194
  and intergenerational transfers 194, 208, 209, 211, 213
  and labour force participation of women 1–2, 106
  and the timing of births 3, 64–78
education:
  as component of intergenerational transfer 219–20, 222–3
  of husband, and women's employment status 111, 114, 116, 119, 122, 123
  of mother, and fertility 72, 73–5, 77–8, 97
  of parents, as cohabitation factor 24, *25*, 26, 28, *29*, 30, *33*, 40
  of partners, as cohabitation factor *25*, 27, *29*, 31, *34*, 40
  of wife, in wage equation 111–14, 127
employers, care of the elderly 199, 202–3, 205
employment:
  as cohabitation factor *25*, 27, *29*, 32, *34*, 35, 40–1
  of mother, and the timing of births 65, 73, 75
  in retirement 212
  type of 106–28
  undantag 201, 202, 204

  see also labour force participation; occupation; work experience
Equal Employment Opportunity Law (1986), Japan 107, 127
expenditure, and the timing of births 65–71 *passim*, 76–7

families, *see* households
family benefits 72, 75–8, 79–101, 219
  cross-national differentials 88–101
  distribution of 85–8
  in France 88–91 *passim*, *95*, *98*, 99–101, 219
  natalist *v.* children's rights 88–92
family policy 3, 84–92, 93–9
fertility:
  and altruistic utility functions 138
  changes and fluctuations 64–5, 77–8, 136, 137–40; in Sweden 46–8, 50–5, 61–2, 206–7, 210–12
  decline 1, 82–3, 105, 107, 127
  developed countries 82–3, 105, 139, 140
  developing countries 139–40
  and education 97
  and family benefits 79–101
  and labour force participation of women 77–8, 92–3, 94, 98–9; in France 82–8; in Japan 107, 166–7; in model 81, 82, 85–6, 88
  Pollak's birth matrix 56
  timing of births 64–78
  and women's wages 79, 82–4, 92, 93–4, 95–7, *98*
  see also childbearing
Finland 91, *95*, *98*, *100*
France:
  family benefits in 88–91 *passim*, *95*, *98*, 99–101, 219
  fertility 82–8
  intergenerational transfers 216–30

Germany 91, *96*, 205, 209, 210
Greece 91, *96*, *98*, *100*
growth, economic, and intergenerational transfers 194, 208, 209, 211, 213

health care 152–3, 175–6, 208, 219, 220
hours, working:
  in Japan 108–9
  and the timing of births 66
households:
  as accounting unit for intergenerational transfers 138
  age distribution of head 176–9
  composition of 176–7, 178, 179–80, *181*
  distribution of labour resources 183–4, 185, 193

extended 105–6, 111–23 *passim*, 127, 158–9, 179–80, 193–4
  in Japan 3, 5, 158–9, 176–85, 193–4; patrilocal 105–6, 111, 114–23 *passim*, 127
  one person 177, 178, 194, 209
  see also partnerships
housing supplements 89, 206, 207, 208
Hungary 91

Iceland 208
income:
  family, and the timing of births 65–6, 68, 71
  of husband, and women's employment status 111, 114, 116–17, 119, 122–3, 127
  of parents, as cohabitation factor 24–6, 28, *29, 33*, 40
  of partners, as cohabitation factor *25*, 27, *29*, 31–2, *33–4*, 40
income, national, Japan 158–94
  factor 160, 162, 164–6, 180
  household disposable 160, 180, *182*, 185–8, 190–1, 192–3
  inequality of distribution 4, 187–8, 192–4
  intergenerational distribution 158–94
inheritance:
  and fertility levels 191, 202
  in Japan 176, 190–1
  in Sweden 213
  see also bequests
interest rates, and the timing of births 66, 68–9
intergenerational transfers:
  and age distribution changes 135–6, 147, 203–4, 209–12
  capital dilution effect 139, 144, 147, 154–5
  and economic growth 194, 208, 209, 211, 213
  and fertility changes 136, 137–40
  in France 216–30
  in Japan 158–94
  life-cycle effect 143, 146–51, 155–6
  market 135, 140, 225, 227, 228–30
  and mortality changes 136, 140–55
  nature of 217–19
  private 5, 199, 200–5, 213, 225–30
  private or public 223–4
  public 159, 164, 174–6, 186–7, 193–4, 199, 205–8
  rate of return effect 136, 151–2
  as rational strategy 225, 227–30
  in Sweden 5, 198–213
  see also bequests; inheritance; transfers
Ireland 91
Italy 64, 91, *96, 98, 100*

Japan:
  ageing population 158, 179–80, 194, 208
  benefits 89, 91, 164, 174–6, 193
  bequests and inheritance 159, 163–4, 184–5, 187, 189–91, 193
  Equal Employment Opportunity Law 107, 127
  fertility decline 1, 105, 107, 127
  foreign investment 173, *183*, 191–2
  intergenerational distribution of resources and income 158–94
  labour force participation of women 105–28, 166–7, 168
  labour supply 162, 166–7, 180, 182–4, 192
  life expectancy 105
  mean ages of consumption and labour 139, 152
  patrilocality 105–6, 111, 114–18, 119–23, 127
  productivity 162, 167–9, 183–4
  saving 162–3, 169, 171–2, 180, *182*, 184–5, 192–3
  taxation 164, 174–6, 193
  wages 106–7, 109, 127, 164, 168, 180, *182*
  wealth 171–3, 184–5, 193

labour force participation of women 80, 105, 106
  and fertility 77–8, 92–3, 94, 98–9; in France 82–8; in Japan 107, 166–7; in model 81, 82, 85–6, 88
  in Japan 105–28, 166–7, 168
  see also employment; labour supply; occupation; work experience
labour supply:
  in Japan 162, 166–7, 180, 182–4, 192
  mean age of 137–8, 139
  in Sweden 211–12
life cycle:
  consumption 4, 135–7, 139–45, 146–51, 152, 153, 155
  earnings 135, 141, 142, 147–8
  effect 143, 146–51, 155–6
  family 105, 109, 115
life expectancy 136, 144, 148–50, 151–2, 155
  in France 221
  in Japan 105
  sex differentials 209
  in Sweden 208–9
  see also mortality
location, urban/rural:
  as cohabitation factor *25, 29*, 30, *33*, 200–4, 206
  as women's employment factor 111, 116, 122, 127
Luxemburg 91, *96–7, 98, 100*

marriage:
  and cohort size 2, 46–62, 206
  determinants of choice 24–41
  following cohabitation 10, 12, 13–18,
    22–4, 40
  incidence *49*, 50–2, 53–5, 61
  models 46–7, 55–62
  parents', as cohabitation factor 24, *25*, 28,
    29, 30, *33*, 40
  in Sweden 46–63
  USA 13–41
  utility functions 57–8
  see also partnerships
migration and demographic change 205, 207,
  210–11
models:
  age distribution of national income
    159–79
  cohort size and marriage 46–7, 55–8
  family benefits and fertility behaviour
    79–88
  intergenerational private transfers 225–30
  labour force participation of married
    women 110–23
  levels of childbearing 80–1, 101
  mortality change 145–6
  of the timing of births 3, 65–76
mortality changes 136–56
  and age distribution 136, 141, 147, 148–50,
    209
  decline 153, 155–6, 203, 205
  developed countries 151
  developing countries 150–1
  interaction with fertility changes 154–5
  and intergenerational transfers 136,
    140–55
  and life-cycle consumption 4, 140–5,
    146–51, 153, 155
  neutral 141, 154–5
  and population growth 136, 141–3, 144,
    146–7, 151, 154, 155
  see also life expectancy

National Child Development Study, UK 9
National Longitudinal Study, USA
  High School class of (1972) 13–41
  Labour Market Experience 66
National Survey of Households and Families
  40
Netherlands 91, *97*, *98*, *100*
New Zealand 91, 205
Norway 9, 91, *97*, *98*, *100*

occupation:
  of husband, as women's employment
    factor 111, 114, 116, *121*, 122, 127
  of mother, and the timing of births 73, *74*,
    75

  see also employment; labour force
    participation
old-age dependency 136, 139, 152
one-sex models of marriage 56
opportunity cost of children 65–7, 68–70,
  71, 82

parity of children and family benefits 80,
  86–92
partnerships:
  age at entry 18–20, *25*, 27–31 *passim*,
    33–4, 40
  determinants 24–41
  duration 2, 10–12, 22, 23, 39–40
  econometric analysis 13–41
  ending 13–18, 22–3
  incidence 13–18
  second 13–18, 21–2
  stability 14–18, 20–2
  uncertainty in 10–12
  see also cohabitation; households; marriage
patrilocality 105–6, 111, 114–18, 119–23,
  127
  see also households, extended
pay-off matrix in marriage 58–9
pensions:
  financed by funds 208, 211, 213
  in France 219
  and housing supplements 206, 207, 208
  income related 207, 208
  as intergenerational transfers 5, 199,
    200–8, 213, 219
  in Japan 127, 175
  private 5, 199, 200–5, 212–13
  public 127, 144, 175, 199, 204–8, 219
  and spouses 175, 208
  in Sweden 198–213
  see also intergenerational transfers;
    retirement
Poland 91
population growth:
  and fertility changes 136, 139
  and mortality changes 136, 141–3, 144,
    146–7, 151, 154, 155
  and rate of return effect 139, 142, 143,
    144
Portugal 91
productivity, Japan 162, 167–9, 183–4
public debt, and intergenerational transfers
  219, 220, 221–2
public sector, intergenerational transfers 140
  in Japan 159, 164, 174–6, 186–7, 193–4
  in Sweden 198, 199, 205–13

rate of return effect 136, 139, 142, 143–4,
  151–2
religion, as cohabitation factor *25*, 26, *29*, 30,
  33

retirement:
   age of 175, 183, 201, 205–6, 209–10, 212,
      213
   earnings 193
   employment 212
   in Japan 175, 183, 184
   and mortality changes 143, 144, 154–5
   savings 184, 198–9, 208
   in Sweden 198–213
   and *undantag* 201, 202, 204
   see also pensions

savings:
   age distribution 169, 171–2
   in Japan 162–3, 169, 171–2, 180, *182*,
      184–5, 192–3
   and private pensions 212–13
   in Sweden 198–9, 208, 212–13
social security, in intergenerational transfers
   219, 220, 222
Spain 91
Sweden:
   ageing population 198, 204–5, 207, 208–11
   cohabitation 9, 31
   cohort size and marriage 46–62
   family benefits in 91
   fluctuations in fertility 46–8, 50–5, 61–2,
      206, 207, 210, 211–12
   intergenerational transfers 198–213

taxation:
   and demographic change 136–7, 144,
      155–6
   and fertility 72, 75–6, 78, 89
   inheritance 176
   in Japan 126, 127, 164, 174–6, 186–8, 193
   and private pensions 212–13
   and women's employment 126, 127
   see also intergenerational transfers;
      transfers
transfers:
   intergenerational or intragenerational
      224–5
   see also bequests; inheritance;
      intergenerational transfers; taxation
two-sex models of marriage 56

uncertainty:
   of partnerships 2, 10–12, 40
   and the timing of births 72, 75, 77

unemployment, as cohabitation factor 25, 27,
   34, 40–1
United Kingdom:
   family benefits in 91, *97*, *98*, 99–101, *100*
   incidence of cohabitation 9
   mean ages of consumption and labour
      139, 152
   National Child Development Study 9
   pensions 205
   Women and Employment Survey 73–6
United States:
   education 223
   family workers 106
   incidence of cohabitation 9, 13–18,
      39–40
   lack of family benefits in 88
   mean ages of consumption and labour
      139, 152
   National Longitudinal Study: High School
      class of (1972) 13–41; Labour Market
      Experience 66
   opportunity cost of children 69
USSR 91
utility functions:
   in fertility 67–70, 71, 138, 141
   in marriage 57–8
   mortality 141

wages:
   in Japan 106–7, 109, 127, 164, 168, 180,
      182
   performance-based 168
   seniority-based system 168
   sex differentials 106–7, 109, 127, 168
   women's 106–7, 109, 110–14, 127, 168; as
      employment factor 111–14, *116*, 118,
      119, *121*, 123, 127; and fertility 79,
      82–4, 92, 93–4, *95–7*, *98*; reservation 3,
      83–4, 94, 111; and the timing of births
      65–6, 68–9, 71, 75–6
wealth, age distribution:
   in Japan 171–3, 184–5, 193
   in Sweden 198
Women and Employment Survey, UK 73–6
work experience:
   as cohabitation factor 27, 32, *34*
   as women's employment factor 111–13,
      116, 119, *121*, *123*, 127
   see also employment; labour force
      participation